STRATEGIC CHALLENGES

STRATEGIC CHALLENGES

INDIA IN 2030

EDITED BY JAYADEVA RANADE

HarperCollins *Publishers* India

First published in India by HarperCollins *Publishers* 2022
Building 10, Tower A, 4th Floor, DLF Cyber City, Phase II,
Gurugram, Haryana – 122002, India
www.harpercollins.co.in

2 4 6 8 10 9 7 5 3 1

Copyright © Jayadeva Ranade 2022

P-ISBN: 978-93-5629-195-9
E-ISBN: 978-93-5629-196-6

The views and opinions expressed in this book are the contributors' own and the facts are as reported by them and the publishers are not in any way liable for the same.

Jayadeva Ranade asserts the moral right
to be identified as the editor of this work.

All rights reserved. No part of this publication may be reproduced, stored in a retrieval system, or transmitted, in any form or by any means, electronic, mechanical, photocopying, recording or otherwise, without the prior permission of the publishers.

Typeset in 11.5/15.2 Adobe Garamond at
Manipal Technologies Limited, Manipal

Printed and bound at
Thomson Press (India) Ltd.

To the people of India

Contents

Foreword		ix
Editor's Note		xi
Introduction		ix
VIJAY GOKHALE		
1.	China's Major Strategic Threats to India till 2035	1
	JAYADEVA RANADE	
2.	Pakistan: The Inevitability of Enmity	31
	VIKRAM SOOD	
3.	Security Challenges: India–US Relations	54
	ARUN SINGH	
4.	Russia and Eurasia in India's Calculus	86
	P.S. RAGHAVAN	
5.	Old Wars, New Wars: Strategizing for Future Land Warfare	123
	RAKESH SHARMA	

CONTENTS

6. Aerospace: A Security Perspective — 153
RAGHUNATH NAMBIAR

7. Trajectory of India's Maritime Security Challenges — 170
SHEKHAR SINHA

8. Emerging and Disruptive Technologies — 198
PRABHAT RANJAN

9. China–India Riparian Relations: Upstream–Downstream Dynamics — 241
UTTAM KUMAR SINHA

10. The Sky Above and the Air Around New Domains of Contention: In Cyber and Outer Space — 265
KIRAN KARNIK

About the Contributors — 303

About the Editor — 307

Foreword

With this compendium, *Strategic Challenges: India in 2030*, a piece of literature has been crafted that exposes the various eminent as well as imminent threats India could face during the present and the next pivotal decades. The book, however, differs greatly from other publications in that it not only describes such challenges, but also provides potential responses and solutions that will help India plan to tackle such threats head-on. Such problem-solving approaches not only serve to elevate the book to a great read but, more importantly, make it a crucial guide to current and future policies as well as actions to be taken by India's political elite.

Indian experts from a wide range of fields and with centuries of cumulative on-the-ground operational knowledge were involved in this endeavour focused on a comprehensive overview of security threats arising from a variety of different spheres, such as the aerospace, marine and land-based security domains. In this way, the book undoubtedly achieves the rare feat of providing a 360-degree perspective on India's current and future strategic security realities.

Moreover, the present book comes at a critical juncture for India in a rapidly changing geopolitical scenario in which the subcontinent is increasingly becoming a key player on the international security arena. In my long career, I have found that it takes a great deal of intuition, tact and sensitivity to come up with the right idea and initiative at the right time. That this has been achieved so flawlessly in the case of the present publication is self-evident and deserves all the plaudits.

I am particularly honoured to have had the opportunity, in my capacity as the resident representative to India of the Konrad-Adenauer-Foundation (Konrad-Adenauer-Stiftung [KAS]), to closely accompany the genesis of the book, for it expresses accurately the message that the Konrad-Adenauer-Foundation has been exhorting for decades: namely, that it is only through the diverse forms of multilateral cooperation and partnerships that cohesion between our like-minded democracies can strengthen the institutions of multilateralism to jointly promote security, prosperity and stability in the Indo-Pacific and the rest of our planet.

In this sense, we can view this publication as a tribute to the cooperative spirit of deeply devoted and concerned individuals whose profound analytical insights will serve as a valuable tool to support visionary policymaking aimed at India playing an increasingly global and multilateral role in the decades to come.

Peter Rimmele
India Office of KAS

Editor's Note

As global alliances shift in attempts to alter the existing world order, India finds itself in a difficult position, calling for dexterous, nimble and, at times, bold policies. It also presents an opportunity for India to influence the unfolding changes and place itself in an advantageous geopolitical position. Articles in newspapers and magazines have sought to touch on aspects of these changes, but the challenges ahead require a deeper understanding. This book, in which India's leading experts identify the challenges in their respective domains, brings together the various pieces in this shifting kaleidoscope to form a fuller picture.

While the nature of the ongoing changes and the large uncertainties that accompany them make it difficult, if not impossible, to anticipate the shape of the coming world order, it is useful to identify the challenges that India is likely to confront in the near term. As such, a realistic time frame of a decade, or 2030, which has been set by many countries as the target date for achieving major goals was considered apt. Already, major powers like China and Russia are adopting muscular policies with the intent of changing the global order and advancing their civilizational values. This includes attempts to take territories—claimed by them on the basis of, at times, imagined history—through the use of military force. At the same time, the US and the West are struggling to retain their pre-eminence, while emerging powers in the Indo-Pacific are demanding representation at the global high table. Each one is seeking to shape events to their advantage.

The arrangement of the chapters suggests the immediacy of the challenges that confront us. Since identifying the challenges itself implies the remedial measures needed to address them, the articles largely refrain from offering prescriptive solutions, except where necessary. I am grateful to each of the experts, who have contributed their analysis, for responding positively to the idea when I approached them and writing their chapters within a tight time frame on their areas of expertise.

The other authors and I are also grateful to Swati Chopra, executive editor at HarperCollins, who willingly took on the task of bringing out this book and agreeing to publish it before China's 20th Party Congress in October, Antony Thomas for playing a key role in the entire process and dragooning us all into complying with the deadlines, and all others at HarperCollins for designing the cover and ensuring the publication of the book.

Finally, I hope this book helps India's policymakers and the readers get a clearer idea of the immense challenges that India faces and the need to revamp systems and procedures, and tap into India's immense latent talent to spark indigenous solutions to these challenges.

Jayadeva Ranade
New Delhi, August 2022

Introduction

BY VIJAY GOKHALE

At the turn of the millennium, Western civilization was triumphant and there was no challenger in sight. The United States was enjoying its unipolar moment and the world looked set to experience another American century. After the Treaty of Maastricht (1992), Europe had embarked on an experiment that boded a significant change to the Westphalian system of state sovereignty. Russia appeared to be mortally wounded. The world was beginning to take notice of China and it was assumed that the country would segue into the US-led global order in the new millennium. India, too, was starting out on a new developmental journey and—after coping initially with the fundamental changes that had transformed the world since the Cold War ended—had begun to demonstrate strategic independence.

As barriers fell, free trade was set to become the norm. It became possible for businesses to invest across the world in order to leverage local advantages and supply chains became truly global. The internet revolution promised to do for the twenty-first century what Columbus, De Gama and Magellan had done at the turn of the fifteenth century: it created a barrier-free transit, albeit in virtual mode. Democracy had seemingly demonstrated its superior system of values, having defeated monarchy, fascism and communism in the last century. We entered the new millennium with a sense of optimism and hope.

However, two American wars (Afghanistan and Iraq) and a couple of global crises (the global financial crisis of 2008 and the COVID-19 pandemic) appear to have belied these expectations. American hegemony has been damaged and is being challenged by an ascendant China that has risen more swiftly than the world had anticipated, or was prepared for. Russia is back in the global arena. The European Union, which was aspiring to offer a credible alternative model, is racked by political uncertainties and beset by financial troubles. Iran and North Korea have demonstrated the limits of American power. New equations are forming between Russia, China, Turkey and Iran with geostrategic ramifications for the Eurasian landmass. And the political reordering in Afghanistan may portend a difficult and different future for the Central Asian heartland.

The possibility of a return to a bipolar world based on a Sino–US rivalry cannot be ruled out. Protectionism is on the rise. Technology is a mixed blessing because of its implications for climate change. The promise of global connectivity, both physical and virtual, is threatened by state or non-state actors, including cyber criminals. Moreover, the pandemic has shown that an interconnected world could fall apart, despite the impressive scientific gains of the previous century. And democracy—that idea holding such promise earlier—has a challenger in China, which is increasingly convinced that its model has shown the world that development is not synonymous with democracy.

In India's larger neighbourhood, from West Asia, where the Gulf states are being confronted with a possible Turkey–Qatar–Iran axis, to East Asia, where the union of Southeast Asian nations (ASEAN) looks weaker than it appeared at the beginning of this century, change appears to be the new normal. Nearer home, the situation in Afghanistan has complicated India's security dilemma to its west. The Indian Ocean is becoming a strategic playground for great powers. China is pushing into South Asia and the seas surrounding it, and is thus expanding its security perimeter. India is now set to confront two entirely new realities that it has never faced so far in its independent history. First, the existence of a superpower (China) at her own doorstep, and second, the possibility that India might become a frontline state in the twenty-first century rivalry between China and America, in a manner similar to what western Europe faced during the era of Soviet–American competition.

As a country, we have done reasonably well since the end of the Cold War. The economic reforms initiated in the early 1990s have been carried forward by successive governments and the economic landscape has been transformed in many ways. The digital revolution has positively impacted the delivery of goods and services, and this process has only seen gains in the pandemic. The political landscape has also undergone a sea change. In 2014, Indians voted in a majority government for the first time since the Cold War ended. In terms of foreign policy, India has transitioned from a reactive or coping strategy in the early post-Cold War era to one that is driven by initiatives taken with the intention of proactively shaping policy and the environment. Since 1998, successive governments have added the nuclear, American and maritime dimensions, which have made our stated policy of multi-alignment more viable. National security doctrines of strategic importance and a clearer enunciation of the limits to restraint when the homeland is attacked also reflect a change in the mindset.

Yet, we failed to fully ride the wave of globalization or set sail on the tide of export-led growth which would have led to greater economic progress. Policy reforms for the economy sometimes do not fully translate into action and we have not yet built a true partnership between the government and businesses. We have been less successful than our peers in building a modern infrastructure and a superior industrial base, and remain on the outer bands of the global supply chains. We have been unable to develop meaningful indigenous capacities in key defence technologies essential for national security, and we have been unsuccessful in scaling up civilian technologies to a level that will majorly impact our economy—and if this is not addressed in the coming decade, we face the spectre of slipping into techno-colonialism. Our relations with neighbours remain hobbled because of our inability to find solutions for historical disputes even after seventy-five-plus years, and also because of our limited ability to deliver on pledged assistance. Our national security is still grappling with how to apply new technology to our military and critical organizational reforms essential to the art of modern warfare. In brief, we have done well in the past two decades, but the deficiencies we still face may not have allowed us to reap the full benefits of the many positive directions that foreign policy is taking in terms of its maritime orientation—with its new footprints in Africa and elsewhere—and its readiness to assume greater regional responsibilities in dealing with challenges.

Recent events are likely to accelerate developments that we are seeing at the global and local levels. During this decade, China might well surpass the United States of America as the world's leading economy. America may retain superiority in technology and military power, but unless the country's capacities can be enhanced through economic rejuvenation, its ability to dominate the Western-led global order may be challenged. Although Americans believe that their military operations in Iraq and Afghanistan have not damaged their global standing, it is likely that trust and faith in the US from its allies and partners might erode—and it may not be able to retain allies (such as Turkey) or check adversaries (such as Iran). China sees the situation evolving to its advantage. The country is not content to leave it to luck or chance; it intends to use new technologies and growing military power to accelerate the American decline. In the coming decade, China is likely to become more confident in the deployment of pressure in its proximity, more willing to provide the means to wean away the more distant nations from Western influence, more prepared to play divide and rule with the West, and more ready than ever to stare down the current hegemon. China seems to have truly joined the battle of wills at a global level with America.

Russia's invasion of Ukraine in early 2022 demonstrates the fragility of the current global system and is a reminder that no relationship or strategy is permanent. Expectations of an early end to the conflict have been replaced by fears that there will be a protracted war with neither side appearing willing to yield. The West is unable to tolerate the dismemberment of a European state. Russia is unwilling to change course for the present, despite the burden of sanctions. For now, the endgame remains elusive and although, eventually, a modus vivendi will be found, the implications of this conflict for our region, and for India, will be immense.

For a start, given the global dependence on Russia for resources and on Ukraine for food, and the possibility of global recession if this war does not end soon, India may need to rethink its economic policy to achieve the target of sustained 8 per cent annual growth. For another, a hard assessment of Sino–Russian relations can no longer be avoided because the probability that Russian dependence on China will increase has become more likely. The question of whether Russia can be absolutely and implicitly trusted on matters relating to our national security, in a new situation of Russia's greater dependency on China, will need an answer. India's diplomacy has risen to the short-term challenge posed by this war, but over the longer run, as one of the contributors in this book describes it, the challenge for us will be to balance equities on both sides without losing our autonomy or being diverted from our strategic objective of atmanirbharta.

—⚏—

The essays in this volume, written by notable strategic experts and thinkers, look at whether India is ready for the new challenges that might come its way in this decade. They cover regional and functional challenges of national security, challenges of a kind that we might need to prepare for and suggest possible solutions for policymakers to consider. The essays are a way of looking into the future—always a venture fraught with risk, but with the idea of suggesting ways and means for India to prepare for eventualities, should they arise.

Our immediate strategic challenges will be China and Pakistan. Two of India's leading subject-matter specialists—Jayadeva Ranade and Vikram Sood—write about them and what India should do to meet the situation. Jayadeva Ranade contends that China's journey to replace the Americans as global hegemon must, inevitably, start by seeking unipolarity, and demanding this status in Asia and the Indo-Pacific. This is what China has been proactively doing for the past decade in terms of creating the building blocks of Asian hegemony—through the Belt and Road Initiative, by creating alternative financing and development mechanisms to wean countries of the region away from others and towards Beijing, by using leverages of all kinds to compel regional competitors to acquiesce to its power and by weakening regional groupings in order to create a new Sino-centric world. In the process, China appears to be eroding the American alliance system that has underpinned the Asian balance for seven decades, and is attempting to strangulate new emerging concepts like the Indo-Pacific that Beijing considers to be a nascent challenge to its vision for this region. China is an ascendant and confident power to our north.

Jayadeva Ranade suggests that the country will not merely pose a territorial challenge to India in the coming decade—in an effort to change the strategic balance in Asia—but, at a larger level, it will pose a civilizational threat that is intended to weaken India internally and damage its credibility regionally. We may expect to see limited military operations and more widespread psychological operations, as well as greater interference in our internal affairs in this decade. Beijing might utilize our economic dependence in core sectors, like pharmaceuticals, electronics and communications, or close off access to rare earths and other critical materials in an effort to hamper our economic growth. Ranade believes that weaning the Indian economy off Chinese dependencies in critical areas should not be postponed any longer. Yet, the current situation of strategic competition and rivalry between China and America is also a strategic opportunity for India—if we can leverage our position as a swing state in this new dynamic. We need to have clarity about our expectations and demands from both. The objective is to work with like-minded countries to shape Chinese behaviour in a less aggressive direction, but this is possible only when India develops new capacities in technology to play a truly stabilizing role in the Indo-Pacific.

Pakistan, our other neighbour to the west, is, according to Vikram Sood, not a failing state but a faltering one. This might be a more dangerous situation for India to confront because, as he writes, Pakistan has made its choice of a policy of unremitting enmity towards India and may be preparing to deal with New Delhi in two dimensions. The first, according to the author, is through the instrument of terrorism, but under high-technology conditions. The application of new technologies, including in cyberspace and through unmanned vehicles, is expected to act as force multipliers. The second dimension is likely to be a two-front challenge from Pakistan and China, where the former might be content to accommodate the latter's hegemonic interests and allow its territory to be used by

Beijing to mount a challenge from the seas and ocean to India's south, all in return for financial and military assistance. This would thus encircle India from three sides—the north, the west and the south.

The prospect of fighting a two-front conflict or dealing with a hybrid terror attack are not new, but with Afghanistan having come under Pakistan's control, they are free to devote time, resources and energy to dealing with India. The prospects of Pakistan regaining lost ground with the Arab and Muslim states to its west by playing the Islamic swing-state card needs to be factored in as well, since this will adversely impact our new relationships in that region and affect regional balance. India needs to be vigilant and nimble here. In this context, Sood, in his essay, has also tantalizingly inserted Turkey's neo-Ottoman ambition as another potential axis that we might need to be concerned about. We should prepare for a situation where China has concluded that India could be taught a lesson with help from Pakistan in order to subordinate the only serious, long-term potential challenge to its Indo-Pacific hegemony, and where Pakistan is confident that China will guard its back as Islamabad executes the policy of techno-jihad.

India has been planning and developing its capacity to deal with such situations, but it also requires support in the international and foreign policy domains if it is to neutralize these threats. Arun Singh and P.S. Raghavan, who have many years of experience and deep knowledge about the United States of America and Russia respectively, share their thoughts about how these two major powers can help Delhi maintain strategic independence in the face of challenges from China and Pakistan. Arun Singh writes that the era of Sino–US engagement may have run its course. Both are now seeking to shape the architecture of global and multilateral frameworks. This might hold greater prospects for the consolidation and strengthening of Indo–US partnership. He characterizes this as an irreversible trend in this decade because the Americans have taken a strategic view of

India. This is an inherent opportunity to rework our engagement with the US and to recover ground lost earlier to China in terms of economic engagement. This could also mean more opportunities for deepening collaboration in defence and high-technology areas with Washington. The geostrategic compulsions that are likely to enhance the quality of this partnership are also bolstered by the common ground that we share as democracies and open societies. Yet, we should not take this relationship as inevitable or look at it through rose-tinted glasses.

Arun Singh properly outlines the dilemma that shared values and common political systems might pose. If, on the one hand, it could bring important advantages for India in both the geopolitical and technology areas, it might, on the other, also reduce India's flexibility—something that has served our interests well in the past. One important point that the author posits is the need for both countries to navigate the differences on the climate-change issue, bearing larger strategic convergences in mind. How does India balance the benefits of deeper partnership with American demands for the greater accommodation of its interests—not simply in strategic terms, but also in terms of trade and services? Could the US allow sufficient space for Indian industry in the new reordering of the global economy—by reshoring to India instead of home-shoring? Does the new situation in Afghanistan mean that the US might return to its old policy of valuing Pakistan in terms of her utility for America's homeland security? Will this mean that the Americans will hold on to Pakistan and use India to balance China? Arun Singh offers his perspective on such matters, which are likely to shape Indo–American relations in this decade.

P.S. Raghavan deals with our other strategic relationship—with the Russian Federation. With his understanding of Russia and the evolution of India's Russia policy, Raghavan aptly notes, with some regret, that in the past twenty years, the sharpening of New Delhi's focus on the Indo-Pacific appears to be mirrored by the dimming of its attention to the Eurasian supercontinent. Russian concerns over the emergence of a new disruptive US-led geopolitical structure (Indo-Pacific/QUAD) and India's role in this American adventure, paired with our country's concerns about the Sino–Russian partnership as well as Russia's nascent moves with Pakistan, have tended to overshadow the important fact that no other country has defended India's interest at critical times with such commitment, nor supplied such levels of military hardware and transferred such sensitive defence technologies as Russia has done. He correctly observes that this is because of underlying strategic convergences and, more importantly, strategic trust, which need to be unearthed and brought back to centre stage. Some elements of renewal, including India's interest in the Russian Far East and willingness to invest in its energy sector, are seen as positive signs, but there is also a requirement to develop new opportunities in partnership with Moscow, especially on the connectivity front through the International North–South Transport Corridor, which has become important after the changed situation in Afghanistan. Among the other questions that Raghavan has posed is the tantalizing one of whether India, which enjoys favourable relations with both Washington and Moscow, can play the role of a bridge, because even a limited thaw in Russo–American relations will be beneficial to New Delhi.

The military dimensions of the challenge confronting India in this decade have been outlined by three experts who have held senior positions in India's armed forces. Lt General Rakesh Sharma agrees with Jayadeva Ranade and Vikram Sood about the increasing threat from the burgeoning nexus between Pakistan and China. But, more significantly, he argues that the nature of warfare is changing fundamentally because new technologies have taken the act of war beyond the purely kinetic, and future wars may be devoid of all human interface altogether. Moreover, the lines between war and peace are blurring. War, he opines, will be waged to gain strategic advantage, and no longer with expectations of outright victory. More specifically, in the Indian context, technology has flattened the Himalayas and changed our strategic geography. We need to prepare for a long-term and permanent Chinese influence over the Himalayan states, Pakistan and possibly even Myanmar. China is preparing for future wars by developing lethal autonomous weapon systems, electromagnetic-spectrum warfare capabilities and space-based weapons. This, in Lt Gen. Rakesh Sharma's view, calls for nothing less than a revolution in our strategic thinking. There is a need for jointness, for combined arms planning and strategy, for rapid experimentation with new technologies and with indigenization of deterrence capabilities to dissuade and punish China or Pakistan, should they engage in adventurism, as well as military doctrines in new areas including the cyber world, unmanned vehicles and outer space. He calls for a revolution in military doctrines, a re-evaluation of our capabilities under new high-tech conditions of warfare, and a greater synergy between the political and the military dimensions of national security.

In his piece on the trajectory of India's maritime security challenges, Vice Admiral Shekhar Sinha makes the central point that the sea-blindness of India's ruling elites for nearly a millennium, as a result of the reorientation of security perspectives towards land boundaries owing to successive invasions from the northwest, has at last been redressed. The entire idea of India's neighbourhood is being redefined in maritime terms. The Indian Ocean is being relooked at from both geo-economic and geostrategic angles. Chinese behaviour in the South China Sea, its growing capacity to deploy force beyond the western Pacific, and its maritime Silk Road strategy, make it India's foremost maritime security challenge. Vice Adm. Sinha believes that India's geographical advantage in the Indian Ocean is being systematically undermined by Chinese initiatives in

Djibouti and Gwadar, and the deployment of People's Liberation Army (PLA) ships right to the western extremities of the northern Indian Ocean. Being cognizant of this challenge is only the beginning for, as Vice Adm. Sinha writes, the counter-strategy must be to substantially strengthen our naval capacities in new areas, such as in the underwater maritime domain, and to defend our geostrategic space against hybrid methods, including the use of fishing vessels to restrict movement of our naval fleet. We must also impose costs on Chinese actions that infringe on our national security, as well as engage with China, the United States and others in building new security structures in the Indian Ocean. He urges readers to see the QUAD and other outreach efforts by India to major and smaller players in the Indo-Pacific in this larger context.

A key question that is central to India's capacity to deal with the challenges of this decade in air and in space is at the heart of Air Marshal Raghunathan Nambiar's writing—namely, as to whether a country like ours can afford not to have its own aviation and aerospace industry. And whether this situation can be allowed to persist? He posits that aerospace power is critical in contactless future warfare, and especially important in dealing with Chinese aggression in the Himalayas or a challenge on the high seas. He notes that China has developed fifth-generation fighter aircraft, and has aggressively pursued missile and drone technologies, apart from building advanced indigenous technological capabilities in Multiple Independent Re-entry Vehicle (MIRV), hypersonic glide vehicles and missile shields. It has also successfully managed to keep its weapons of mass destruction outside multilateral arrangements.

India, on the other hand, remains dependent on external sources in all these areas. According to him, we need to overcome a triple challenge—the lack of technology, financing and managerial skills. Despite the advancements by our northern neighbour, we continue to spend on immediate operational exigencies instead of long-term strategic solutions. Even relatively simple research and development programmes stretch on for years, thus rendering any achievements almost immediately obsolescent due to delays. Defence offset and other policy measures appear to be conducive to indigenization of capacities, but acquisition procedures and slow growth in the government–defence industry interface continues to hamstring our efforts. Air Marshal Nambiar recommends a massive infusion of capital by the Government of India into targeted sectors, such as aircraft (including drone) design, and development and manufacturing—in partnership with private players—which are hobbled by the high costs of defence R&D.

Professor Prabhat Ranjan expands upon this very theme in terms of outlining the critical technologies for India's security till 2030. He says that the world is on the cusp of merging the industrial revolution with the autonomous revolution. A combination of machines and computers will have potentially revolutionary implications on how future conflicts will unfold. India, he states, urgently needs to develop strong indigenous technologies in at least five critical areas, including, inter alia, sensors, computing and communications. Without even a rudimentary semiconductor industry, we are hitting a dead end in electronics. Without enhancing computing capabilities, especially by developing quantum technology, we will hobble our military capabilities. Without a leap in communications technology, including optical or laser communications and Low Earth Orbit (LEO) constellation-based communications, we may not be able to stand up to the challenges that China might pose. He correctly posits that this is not due to a lack of roadmaps, including the Technology Vision 2020 that was laid out in 1996, but by the deeper malaise that India has been unable to overcome—namely the lack of progress in implementing good ideas, which has left the country totally dependent on imports.

A new dimension that is gaining traction in recent years relates to the potential security challenge of shared rivers. India and China are both critically water-deficient, and climate change will exacerbate the situation for both countries. There is, however, one big difference. Uttam Sinha states that the critical contrast between the two countries is that China, as an upper riparian, is more water secure, while India's major river systems, the Indus–Sutlej and the Brahmaputra—and even some of the tributaries of the Ganga, for that matter—have their headwaters in the Tibet Autonomous Region of China and thus receive a large portion of their waters from outside our territory. The hydrological equation gives China a huge strategic advantage that can be translated into political leverage and bargaining with India. The problem is compounded by the impact of climate change, because the Chinese intend to divert surplus waters from rivers to quench the thirst of parched lands further north, and have just announced in March 2021 a massive hydroelectric project on the Brahmaputra/Yarlung Tsangbo. The project conceives of eleven hydropower stations generating a capacity of 60 gigawatts of power—three times more than the Three Gorges. Uttam Sinha perceptively highlights the limits of cooperation between China and India on transboundary rivers. The scope is confined to limited information-sharing on just two rivers—Sutlej and Brahmaputra—and that too only during the flood season.

Thus far, China has refused to expand the scope of such arrangements with India or enter into more formal treaties with any other lower riparian state. Uttam Sinha also situates the hydro-relations with China in the context of the larger political problems between the countries. The riparian affairs between the two countries may, therefore, increasingly be influenced by the prevailing political dynamics and strategic considerations, or what analysts describe as a 'hydro–political–security complex'. In this complex, factors like availability, distribution, quality and competing uses will not only contribute to regional water insecurity but also influence peace and stability in Asia. In this essay, the author offers a sensible assessment based on statistics about the potential impact that the damming of the Brahmaputra inside Tibet might have on India. He believes that this might be mitigated to a very large degree by the country creating more water development footprints in Arunachal Pradesh, particularly through building more water storage capacities to mitigate dry season flow and thereby exert down-riparian prior-appropriation rights. This, he feels, is also important from the point of view of China's claim to the Arunachal territory and the prospect that greater economic integration in the border region as an effective way to neutralize China's claim. Again, as with the technology issue, the problems lie not in conception or policy, but in execution, and this will need to be addressed across the board if New Delhi is to meet the strategic challenges it is likely to face in this decade.

There is no inevitability in either China's rise or in America's decline. Nor can it be predicted with any certainty that by 2050 China will be the hegemon. However, any forward planning in policy formulation for India will need to take these assumptions into account. The intention is to educate the reader about the potential challenges that confront our nation, and possible avenues to mitigate them and shape our security environment to our advantage. This ought to begin with the basic premise that India needs to be prepared for a decade of uncertainty, where the Sino–US rivalry might evolve into a bipolar order that limits our flexibility in terms of choices of policy and technology. Policies that enable us to leverage our position as the swing state need to be formulated so that we do not get trampled in the global competition between China and America—but rather, ensure that we derive benefit were this situation to arise.

All the contributors to this volume are also clear that India's options will be hobbled unless and until we become innovators of new technology. Reducing dependencies on both friend and adversary in critical technologies lies at the core of our future strategic autonomy in this age of uncertainty. In short, unless the government and industry—working in tandem, with proper financing mechanisms and focused policy—immediately kick into action, we might be placed in the position of subordinating ourselves to either China or America. Fundamental military reforms are at the take-off stage, and a smart military that is capable of delivering asymmetric responses to threats is necessary to attract friends and deter adversaries.

Our domestic efforts will need to be bolstered by smart partnerships with others. While building new friends, we need to keep old partners like Russia by our side, engage all countries, including China, and resolve outstanding matters with our smaller neighbours which have hobbled foreign policy for decades. All of this to ensure that we are better placed to deal with the real challenges of this uncertain decade.

CHAPTER 1

China's Major Strategic Threats to India till 2035

JAYADEVA RANADE

In recent years, India has effectively countered China's increasing aggressiveness, while trying to keep relations stable. However, the nature of Beijing's threats to New Delhi over the next fifteen years will be quite different from those faced by other nations. Dictated by geography, its rise and changing global power politics, India will face a range of challenges—including military, economic and diplomatic, in addition to water-security issues.

As China's national strength has grown, so have its efforts to carve out a position for itself at the helm of global affairs. In keeping with its belief that the US and the West are in decline following the global economic downturn of 2008 and now the COVID-19 pandemic, China has assessed that the time is right to make an overt bid for global leadership. The pointer is its reiteration of 'political and strategic mutual trust', and its call for promoting a 'more just and reasonable international order' in the joint statement issued on 4 February 2022 after the Xi Jinping–Vladimir Putin summit in Beijing. So was the emphasis against 'hegemony'. China sees its emergence as the unchallenged power in Asia as a first step to ensure that no one stands in the way of its ambitions.

In keeping with its quest for global supremacy, Beijing has adopted increasingly aggressive policies with most of its neighbours. Soon after taking power in 2012, Xi Jinping, who considers himself a 'child of Red destiny'—very unusually—publicly announced the 'China Dream'.[1] This goal—known as the first centenary goal—includes the country's ambition of recovering all the territories it claims to have 'lost' through the imposition of unequal treaties by hostile foreign powers.

In 2017, Xi laid down the timeline for realizing the China Dream, saying it should be achieved by 2021—the centenary of the founding of the Chinese Communist Party (CCP). He also announced a second centenary goal: to establish China as a 'major world power with pioneering global influence' by 2049, the hundredth year of the founding of the People's Republic of China (PRC).

This clearly implies that the country aspires to rival, if not surpass, the United States in the exercise of global influence and power. As part of this effort, Beijing has begun recommending China's 'model of governance' as a superior alternative to Western democracies, especially since the COVID-19 pandemic. Beijing has also made repeated calls for a 'community of common destiny for mankind' implying the dominance of Chinese values as the world heads into a new era. Though these policies firmly place the United States in China's crosshairs, it is India that will be the first to directly confront the challenges they pose.

Under China's first centenary goal, it identifies its 'lost' territories on the basis of a Qing dynasty map that is taught in schools across the country. The map, published in 1954 in *A Brief History of Modern China* (see map) impinges on the maritime domain of a number of China's neighbours, including India, Japan, Vietnam, Philippines, Thailand, Brunei and Indonesia.

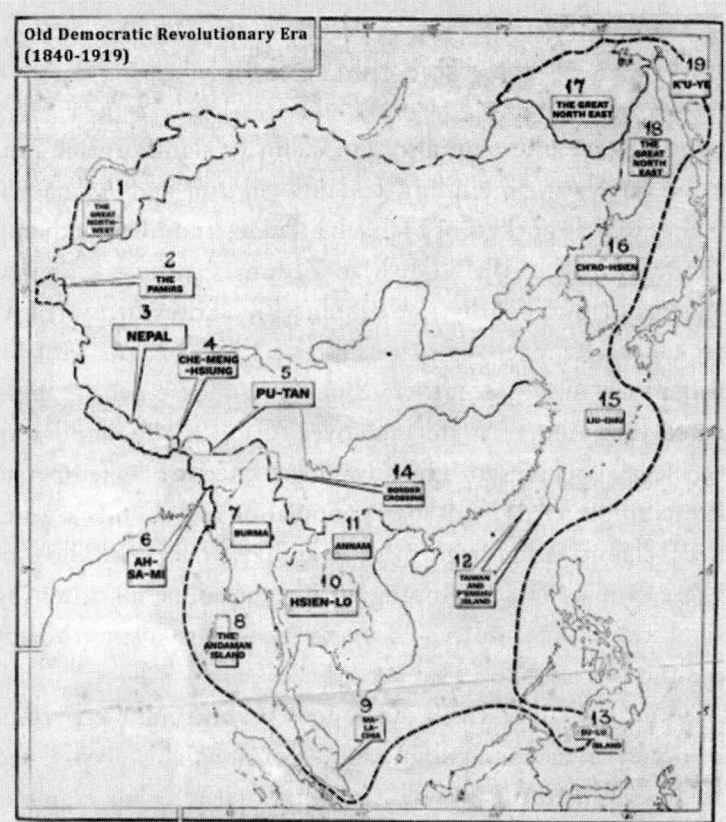

The Great North-West, according to the Chinese text in the map, was seized by Imperialist Russia under the treaty of Chuguchak, 1864. It covers huge segments of the present day Soviet republics of Kazakhstan, Kirgizstan and Tajikistan.

The Pamirs was secretly divided between Britain and Russia in 1896

Nepal went under the British after independence in 1898

Che-Meng-hsiung (i.e. present day Sikkim) was occupied by the British in 1889

Pu-Tan (i.e. the whole of Bhutan) went under Britain after independence in 1865

Ah-Sa-Mi (i.e. whole of Assam, NEFA and, Nagaland) was given to Britain by Burma in 1826

Burma became a part of British empire in 1886

The Andaman Islands went under Britain

Ma-LI-Chia (i.e. the whole of present day Malaysia and Singapore) was occupied by Britain in 1895

Hsien-lo (i.e. the whole part of Thailand) was declared "independent" under joint Anglo – French control in 1904

11. Annam (covering present day North and South Vietnam Laos and Cambodia) was captured by the French in 1885

12. Taiwan and Penghu islands were relinquished to Japan in accordance to the treaty of Shimonoseki 1895

13. Su-Lu islands were occupied by the British

14. Border Crossing-The region where the British crossed the border and committed aggression

15. Liu-Chiu (i.e. Ryukyu Islands) was "occupied by the British"

16. Ch'ao-Hsien (i.e. present day North and South Korea)

17. And 18. The great North-East, covering a huge area of the Soviet Far East, was given to Russia under the treaties of Aigun (1858) and Peking (1860)

19. K'u-Ye (i.e. Sakhalin) was divided between Japan and Russia.

In India's case, the map also lays claim to significant chunks of settled territory—including Ladakh, Sikkim and Arunachal Pradesh, as well as pockets of Himachal Pradesh and Uttarakhand. The first chairman of the CCP, Mao Zedong, has been criticized on websites maintained by the People's Liberation Army (PLA) for not taking Arunachal Pradesh in the 1962 war. At least on three occasions—most recently in May 2021—these websites have advocated that China should take over Arunachal Pradesh from India's 'illegal' occupation. The advantages cited are its temperate climate, its ample fertile land, sparse population and abundant water resources, claimed as enough to generate power for the whole of southwest China. With Xi Jinping setting a deadline for achieving these ambitions, the country's efforts to recover its 'lost territories' are bound to increase.

With India, China's rivalry also goes beyond the recovery of territories; it contains a civilizational dimension! This deep-seated conflict has surfaced occasionally, but unmistakably. For example, China has consistently contested use of the word 'Indian' in 'Indian Ocean'. Its double standards were, however, exposed when Vice Admiral Yuan Yunbai,[2] speaking at the Shangri-la Dialogue in 2015, justified China's claim over the South China Sea on the grounds that the name included 'China'!

This pronouncedly negative attitude towards India pervades the top echelons of the CCP. As far back as 2015, an article captioned 'Six Wars that China Is Sure to Fight in the Next Fifty Years' listed the country's third war as 'The War for the "Reconquest" of Southern Tibet' (Arunachal Pradesh).[3] The article, which aroused wide interest especially in Asia because of the specifics it cited, was published in *Wen Wei Po*, a China-owned Hong Kong daily. The article, published on 8 July 2013 says:

[T]he best strategy for China is to incite the disintegration of India. By dividing into several countries, India will have no power to cope with China. China should at least try its best to incite Assam province and, once conquered, Sikkim to gain independence to weaken the power of India. This is the best strategy. The second-best plan is to export advanced weapons to Pakistan, helping Pakistan to conquer Southern Kashmir region in 2035 and achieve its unification. While India and Pakistan are busy fighting against each other, China should undertake a blitz to conquer Southern Tibet. India will not be able to fight a two-front war. China can retake Southern Tibet easily, while Pakistan can control the whole Kashmir.

China often floats proposals through the media outside the mainland to retain an element of plausible deniability. A similar view was expressed in greater detail in a seventy-page article posted in September 2021 on the popular Chinese portal Zhihu.

More recently, in October 2020, one of China's most influential think tanks candidly assessed that India and China 'were doomed to have a serious collision of interests or even military conflict from the time of their independence'.[4] While the think tank—which is directly subordinate to China's foreign intelligence arm—hinted that both countries would try to avoid a full-scale conflict, it said that the contest over the border is highly likely to move from 'reconciliation through dialogues' to a new stage featuring 'contention for control with real power'.

The author—Hu Shisheng—added that as both armies continue to advance their control to their respective perceptions of the border, this will inevitably lead to standoffs and clashes. The conflict would then probably escalate from 'cold weapons to firearms', till, in course of time, 'the bottom line of tolerance will become a red line lying between the border troops of both countries'.

The article goes on to assert that the contest for influence and dominance 'between China, India and their neighbours' was more complicated than the border issue. As their national strengths grow, India and China 'would have an increasing overlap of interests in the same area'.

Other Chinese publications and the official state media reflect similar views. In January 2021, an article titled 'It is Extremely Difficult for China and India to Be a Family' was posted on the popular Guancha portal.[5] The article said that from 1949, the era of 'Hindi–Chini Bhai Bhai', to the war in 1962, 'the historical trend of China–India relations has been doomed'. Listing why China and India cannot be 'friends', it said: 'If India dares to provoke China so much when it is so weak, can India not threaten China if it becomes strong?'

Russia's war in Ukraine is a complication for Beijing and particularly Xi Jinping. The longer it drags on the more stringent the sanctions on Russia are likely to become and the risk of China getting hit with sanctions increases. Protracted conflict in Ukraine will also exhaust and diminish Russia. In addition to domestic dissatisfaction as Russia gets isolated internationally, there are already reports that Russia is unable to obtain the microchips, microprocessors and other vital components required for the manufacture of advanced or hi-tech weaponry. Xi Jinping is, additionally, facing domestic criticism for the support to Putin. Despite that, he expressed support for Putin during his call to him on his birthday on 15 June. The situation is unlikely to improve and the internal criticism aimed at Xi Jinping is unlikely to dissipate. However, if China does get targeted by sanctions, then Xi Jinping will be in a very precarious position. The Party could ask him to step down or he could become even more aggressive.

This is only a harbinger of things to come. With Xi Jinping making a strong bid for a third term at the helm of affairs, India should prepare for continued pressure on a range of critical issues.

Immediate Territorial Threat

Given China's growing territorial claims, the most immediate risk to India will be military. While China has settled its land borders with Russia and Myanmar, its 4,057-kilometre-long border with India remains an outstanding issue. (China's borders with Vietnam and North Korea are yet to be settled too.)

Since 2012, when Xi Jinping took over China's top three posts of general secretary of the CCP, chairman of the Central Military Commission (CMC) and president of the People's Republic of China, Beijing has made clear its intentions along India's northern borders.

In April 2013, immediately before Li Keqiang's first visit to India as premier, the PLA stepped up its intrusions. The incursion at the Depsang Plains—near India's strategically important post of Daulat Beg Oldi at the base of the Karakoram Pass—was especially significant as it was larger in both scale and duration. A month later, the *China Youth Daily* (*Zhongguo Qingnian Bao*), whose circulation is higher than the CCP's official newspaper, *People's Daily*, published a lengthy article justifying China's claim on Ladakh.

The following year, in 2014, the PLA carried out an extended intrusion at Chumar[6] in Ladakh. This incursion commenced prior to Xi Jinping's arrival in India on his first visit as China's president and continued till well thereafter. There is clear evidence that both these incursions, coinciding as they did with high-level Chinese visits, were premeditated.

Later, in early 2017, reliable sources had privately confided to this author that while the top echelons of China's political and military leadership had decided to 'teach India a lesson', they had—in the first quarter of that year—agreed to defer action. While action was deferred, it was nonetheless clear that China's objectives to 'humiliate' the Indian government, stall the country's rise and secure its own territorial objectives continue to remain.

Probably not linked with these plans, or because PLA officers had been energized by the preparations for major action, Beijing recommenced the construction of a road on Bhutan's Doklam plateau in June 2017.[7] This violated the 2012 tripartite agreement between India, China and Bhutan, compelling India to block China's aggression. The resulting face-off between both armies lasted seventy-three days. Since then, China's military media has been reporting an increased number of exercises by the PLA and PLA Air Force (PLAAF) on the high-altitude Tibetan Plateau.

In view of the steadily deteriorating bilateral relations, and with the absence of forward movement at the summits held in Wuhan in April 2018 and Mamallapuram in October 2019, it was clearly discernible that China was preparing to take punitive military action against India by 2020-21.[8]

In May 2020, China's façade of being a 'friendly' neighbour was fully exposed and its long-term intentions became clear when it suddenly intruded in the Ladakh sector and subsequently amassed troops along the entire Line of Actual Control (LAC).[9] On 15 June 2020, in the midst of this military pressure, Chinese foreign minister Wang Yi and the spokesman of the PLA, Western Theatre Command, made formal announcements of China's claim on Ladakh.

Later, on 7 March 2021, Wang Yi's carefully worded statement at a press conference on the sidelines of the National People's Congress (NPC) explicitly placed the onus for the confrontation on Indian provocations. While he said that China was ready to resolve disputes through negotiations, he stressed on the country's sovereignty and territorial integrity. Significantly, except for Wang Yi, no Chinese leader has publicly commented on the situation along the border. During his visit to Lhasa in July 2021, Xi Jinping made only an oblique reference.

Meanwhile, China's military exercises in Tibet continue and the PLA is making medium- to long-term preparations to boost defence-related infrastructure along the border. The construction of a railway line between Shigatse, Tibet's second-largest city, and Yatong, across the Sikkim border, is under way. An electric railway line linking Shigatse and Lhasa with Nyingchi and Metok across Arunachal Pradesh was completed in June 2021. China's 14th Five Year Plan (2021–2025)—adopted at the plenary session of the NPC that ended on 11 March 2021—has also approved the construction of new border infrastructure. This includes twenty 'multipurpose' border airports,[10] a high-speed railway linking Chengdu with Lhasa, in addition to the upgrading and extending of national highways along China's Himalayan border. In at least six counties bordering India, the traditional grazing lands of Tibetan nomads have begun to be cleared for conversion into military camps.

In addition to boosting military infrastructure along the frontier, China is also moving to repopulate its borders with settlers and security personnel. It has completed construction of the 628 planned 'model xiaokang', border defence villages, officially described as 'making every village a fortress and every household a watch post'. These villages could nibble at the territories of China's neighbours, as has happened in the case of both India and Bhutan. An example is China's reported construction of a village opposite Kibithu in Arunachal Pradesh.[11]

The absence of progress at the commander-level talks between the two countries further suggests that China's military pressure will be protracted and could expand to other areas along the LAC. In the near to medium term at least, Beijing will ensure that the PLA stays in the areas it now occupies. Scrutiny of the Chinese media shows no sign of any moves by the leadership to defuse the situation or reduce tension, except on Beijing's terms. This can lead to occasional armed clashes. India must take cognizance of this.

CPEC: Chinese and Pakistani Territorial Ambitions

The China–Pakistan Economic Corridor (CPEC) has significantly altered the strategic geography of the subcontinent. The CPEC—the first leg of Xi Jinping's flagship Belt and Road Initiative (BRI) to be operationalized—fuses the military power of China and Pakistan, solidifies their convergence of interests and merges their territorial ambitions. With the CPEC, China has reversed its hitherto ambiguous stance on Kashmir and effectively endorsed Pakistan's occupation of territories over which India claims sovereignty. These include Pakistan-occupied Kashmir (PoK), Aksai Chin, Gilgit-Baltistan and the Shaksgam Valley.

China is leaving no stone unturned to secure its investments in the corridor. Since the CPEC's announcement, it has repeatedly told Indian interlocutors—at the highest levels, at Track-1 and Track-2 exchanges, think tanks, academic conferences, etc.—that India should ease tensions with Pakistan, resume talks, resolve the Kashmir issue and only thereafter look to improve ties with China.

Pakistan is actively working to help China secure its goals. At least since April 2020, a colonel-ranked officer from the Inter-Services Intelligence (ISI), Pakistan's intelligence agency, has been posted in China's PLA headquarters, ostensibly for purposes of 'better coordination'. In November 2020, Pakistan announced its decision to grant Gilgit-Baltistan—through which the Karakoram Highway runs—the status of a full province. The message to India could not be clearer: from now, China's growing territorial and financial stake in Pakistan will make it a significant player along India's northern and western borders.

That China is prepared to intervene militarily if it perceives a threat to the CPEC or its interests was evident when it reorganized and restructured the PLA in 2016. Indicating the growing significance of the Tibet and Xinjiang regions, China merged the PLA's former military regions of Lanzhou and Chengdu into one unified Western Theatre Command. The command, which encompasses over half of China's land area and more than a third of its land-based military, is now the largest of the PLA's five commands, and has more manpower and weaponry. Its tasks include 'protecting China's borders, eliminating threats in Xinjiang and Tibet, as well as in Afghanistan and other states that host training bases for separatists and extremists, and protecting Chinese workers and the assets of the China–Pakistan Economic Corridor'. The command also encompasses the Qinghai region, enabling the training of troops in high-altitude warfare and acclimatizing them for rapid induction into Tibet. The command poses a real and potent long-term threat to India. Unfortunately, New Delhi seems to have missed its significance, otherwise the developments since May 2020 could have been thwarted.

The military component of the CPEC has been clear from the beginning. It includes the establishment of a fibre-optic cable to ensure quick and secure communication between the headquarters of the PLA's South Xinjiang Military District in Kashgar and Pakistan's GHQ (general headquarters) in Rawalpindi. This link has now been extended to Islamabad, Karachi and Gwadar. Plans also provide for the extension of the Karakoram Highway[12] to Gwadar port to provide the military with seamless connectivity. There are also plans to link China's South Xinjiang Railway with Pakistan's Punjab Railway.

Significantly, China began developing the Gwadar port only after Pakistan ceded 'sovereign rights' over Gwadar to it. China has also established an electronic eavesdropping station near Gwadar to monitor naval and shipping activities in the Arabian Sea, extending its reach as far as the Gulf of Aden. It is only a matter of time before PLA Navy warships berth regularly at Gwadar and Karachi. In fact, China's military media already refer to Gwadar as a 'logistics base' and Karachi as a 'naval base'!

Sino–Pak naval cooperation poses a long-term threat to India's west coast as well as to Indian shipping that goes through the Gulf of Hormuz and the Arabian Sea. This maritime threat is elevated by the presence of China's naval base at Djibouti, as well as the four others that are being developed/operated by China on Africa's east coast. If the recently signed long-term Sino–Iran 'Strategic Partnership'[13] fructifies, China's military capabilities in the region will increase significantly.

China is already building frigates for Pakistan. A Chinese media report further proposed that it sell its Liaoning aircraft carrier to Pakistan once China's fourth aircraft carrier is ready. China is also expected to sell its Unmanned Underwater Vessels (UUV) and submarines to Pakistan, enhancing the maritime threat to India. As China expands its navy to include at least four aircraft carriers by 2035, it is imperative that India accelerates the development of the Andaman and Nicobar Islands as well as Lakshadweep into full-fledged air, missile, naval and surveillance bases. This will be an effective barrier for the Chinese navy. With Xi Jinping having announced his deadlines, the time for India to do this is short.

China also revised the priority for allocating its latest J-20 'stealth' fighter aircraft and accelerated their production. Although these fifth-generation fighter jets were first earmarked for delivery to China's Eastern and Southern Theatre Commands, the Western Theatre Command began receiving them much earlier than planned, along with the Eastern Theatre Command. The Chinese Air Force now has two hundred J-20 aircraft in service. Indicating the deep collusion of interests between China and Pakistan, the Chinese media has alluded to the fact that its J-17 fighter aircraft—an older version of fighter jets—are being kept ready for 'lending' to Pakistan 'when' conflict occurs. After April 2021, this nexus went a step further with reports that China's JF-17 aircraft, co-produced with Pakistan, are being upgraded and equipped with the fourth generation PL-10 air-to-air missile.

China's Military Strategy: Propaganda Onslaught and Cyber Offensive

China's military strategy extends beyond conventional warfare. Its current doctrine incorporates learnings from the West's operations in Libya, Iraq, Afghanistan, and now Ukraine. Prior to the initiation of conflict, it plans to deploy PLA Political Commissars and other personnel with forward troops to 'soften' the population in the adversary's border areas. Pro-Beijing elements in the adversary country that have access to the media will be used to spread China's version of events, laced with propaganda and disinformation.

This propaganda onslaught is to be followed by a massive cyber offensive intended initially to disrupt communications between the political and military leaderships, and between the higher and lower formations of the armed forces. This will later expand to attacks on public utilities like power plants, railway stations, hospitals and web-linked services to disrupt normal life and build pressure on the leadership to yield. The PLAAF will then initiate the opening phases of conflict, together with China's missile force, followed by an offensive by the ground forces. India has to be ready for such a coordinated onslaught. Hardening of cyber defences needs to be a priority.

Subverting Democratic Societies from Within

China has often adopted Sun Tzu's maxim to wage war by other means. In addition to the importance the CCP attaches to spreading its narrative globally, it has deployed the United Front Work Department (UFWD)[14] to penetrate democratic societies.

The UFWD—which the CCP calls its 'magic weapon'—works closely with China's security services and foreign ministry to co-opt and weaken governments and civil societies in target countries by creating internal fissures. Since 2016, when Xi Jinping took over as head of the Central Small Leading Group on UFWD, there has been a doubling of the department's budget and personnel, along with a visible uptick in its efforts to influence individuals and organizations worldwide.

A detailed expose of the UFWD's modus operandi in Australia was publicized in April 2019 by the Fairfax–Four Corners Report. Though specific to Australia, it is corroborated by reports from other countries. Such activities have been uncovered in the US, the UK and Europe too.

Over the years, the UFWD has spread its tentacles in India, operating below the counter-intelligence radar to create powerful pro-China lobbies. Its operatives—including those at the Chinese Embassy and consulates—use all manner of inducements to target and suborn opinion makers, especially the intelligentsia, media houses, politicians, think tanks, academics, students, government officials, businessmen, etc. They are known to lavish cash on their targets, fund fully paid trips to China, and use the denial of a visa as an ever-present disincentive for those who speak against Beijing's policies and actions. The three Confucius Institutes and more than two dozen Confucius classrooms that function in India without government approval are active platforms for Chinese propaganda. The United Front selects their teachers and the subjects taught conform with China's approved version. The extent of the UFWD's success was particularly visible in some of the reporting by the Indian media during the 2017 Doklam crisis and the clashes at Galwan in May 2020.

Insurgent groups in India's northeast and in sensitive areas like Sikkim have long been cultivated by the United Front. A clear indication of its penetration was the warning issued to India by Liu Zongyi, secretary general of the Research Centre for China–South Asia Cooperation at the Shanghai Institutes for International Studies.[15] He said: 'If India supports secessionist forces in China, the latter could as well support separatist forces in northeast India in an-eye-for-an-eye manner … One of the measures could be not recognizing Sikkim as a part of India.' Such threats, made daily during the Doklam face-off in 2017, have often been repeated since. It is known that China continues to maintain contact with the insurgent groups in India's northeast who travel to Kunming to pick up arms and ammunition.

Economic Factors

For decades, China has eyed the Indian market and, over time, made serious inroads as well. It has ingressed critical sectors of the Indian economy and successfully built a pro-China lobby, especially in the business sector, without Indian officials awakening to the extent of the damage done. Today, the persistent and successful efforts by China's leading telecom and technology companies—namely, Huawei and ZTE—have placed India's critical communications in the control of Chinese companies, leaving this vital sector vulnerable to penetration. India has only now taken cognisance of these vulnerabilities, and decided to bar Huawei and ZTE from trials for 5G communications technology. The dangers of such vulnerabilities, however, have not yet permeated through the government system. Disregarding the fact that an estimated 50,000 Chinese hackers are deployed to target the government and business computers in India and abroad, some businesses continue to advocate that Huawei be allowed to bid for 5G.

New Delhi's failure to establish manufacturing and innovation in high-end microchips, microprocessors, semiconductors, wafers, etc., and build capacity in computer hardware is costing us dearly. This has resulted in inordinate dependence on Chinese chips, routers and more that are widely used in communications infrastructure and in most public utilities. The fact that even government communications providers such as MTNL and BSNL are dependent on Chinese equipment[16] is a matter of serious concern. These components are known to have 'backdoors' that allow hostile actors to spy and disrupt facilities.

Many instances of hacking and surveillance of sensitive government computers as well as the disruption of public utilities such as electricity supply have occurred due to the weaknesses in our cyber infrastructure. To help India develop its own capabilities, it needs to provide tangible incentives to Indian companies like Wipro—one of the very few computer hardware manufacturers—to rapidly start fabricating high-end microchips, microprocessors and semiconductors. If necessary, the government should facilitate collaboration with companies like Taiwan's Taiwan Semiconductor Manufacturing Company (TSMC) and South Korea's Samsung, among others.

Another area of concern is the degradation of India's capacity in high-precision engineering. For example, Indian power generation and distribution companies have sourced turbines, generators, etc., from China instead of acquiring them from Indian manufacturers. While Chinese products are undoubtedly cheaper and their supply lines far quicker, this has hollowed out indigenous industry. Inordinate dependence on others, particularly inimical countries like China, for essential infrastructure will only increase our vulnerabilities.

Similarly, India's pharmaceuticals sector is dependent on foreign, mainly Chinese, suppliers for vital ingredients. Nearly 70 per cent of active pharmaceutical ingredients come from China. India's pharma industry used to produce these ingredients domestically, but has, for some years, preferred to import them because it reduced their manufacturing costs. The implications of this are now evident and even advanced and friendly nations have begun to hoard life-saving supplies for times of crisis.

The sharp rise in Chinese imports by Indian businessmen and traders because of their lower prices has had a deleterious impact on cottage, small and medium enterprises at home. Business deals are sweetened with loans from Chinese financial bodies on apparently easy and attractive terms. Today, many of India's leading industrialists and business houses are under sizeable debt to Chinese entities.

Having ignored the fine print, which usually provides for arbitration or settlement in Chinese courts, Indian businesses will suffer if they default on their loans. China has repeatedly used trade as a weapon—it has done so with the Philippines in 2010, Japan in 2013 and Taiwan in 2021. It is, therefore, imperative that India move rapidly towards total indigenization—atmanirbharta—in critical sectors, while developing alternative global supply chains for vital products.

Diplomatic Factors

Beijing has never hesitated to pull out all stops to expand its influence and achieve its global ambitions. It has increasingly used its USD 14 trillion economy to make inroads into the resource-rich African continent and the Middle East. Besides, it has deftly used its financial muscle and the lure of its markets to divide the European Union (EU), and, at least till the outbreak of Russia's war in Ukraine, drive a wedge between Europe and the US. Countries, especially those with weaker economies, are particularly vulnerable to Beijing's inducements.

China will use all these elements of power, its constituency of support in world organizations, along with its permanent membership in the United Nations Security Council (UNSC), to block India's admission to the UNSC, the Nuclear Suppliers Group (NSG) and other international organizations that it perceives could raise the country's global profile.

Similarly, China will persist with its efforts to whittle down India's influence in the South Asian Association for Regional Cooperation (SAARC) and Bay of Bengal Initiative for Multi-Sectoral Technical and Economic Cooperation (BIMSTEC) and keep it boxed in within South Asia. It will strive to further reduce India's influence in China-led organizations like Brazil, Russia, India, China, and South Africa (BRICS), Shanghai Cooperation Organisation (SCO), etc. With Pakistan, China will further enhance its long-standing support, including in the diplomatic and military arenas. This includes 'protecting' Pakistan from any indictments by the international community for harbouring terrorists, like removing it from the Financial Action Task Force (FATF) list. Beijing is also likely to keep raising the Kashmir issue at the UNSC to pressure India into resolving its territorial issues with Pakistan.

China has made deep inroads into Nepal, Sri Lanka, Myanmar and the Maldives using its considerable wealth, backed by its diplomatic and military clout. It has now enhanced its efforts to make similar inroads into Bangladesh and Bhutan. While the Trans-Himalayan Regional Corridor (THRC) and the Bangladesh–China–India–Myanmar Corridor (BCIM) will yield short-term economic advantages to those who sign on, the societies and economies of India's vulnerable northeastern states will be at considerable risk. Additionally, New Delhi could lose markets and see its influence wane amongst its neighbours.

China could use its influence in Africa to neutralize India as a potentially powerful rival, and parley Pakistan's influence in the Muslim world to restrict India's reach and expand its own influence in the oil-rich region. Interestingly, in October 2020, China revealed its apprehension that India is trying to prevent its rise by disrupting the groupings created and led by China—such as BRICS and SCO.

Despite this unrelenting push, the road ahead will not be smooth for China. With the American administration deciding on a policy of strategic competition with China and the US Senate passing the bipartisan 'Endless Frontier Act' on 8 June 2021, Beijing will confront a major obstacle. In addition, the US's Tibet Policy Support Act, 2021, challenges Beijing's bid to determine the Dalai Lama's reincarnation. The US and the West are also contesting China's efforts to gain influence in Europe, the Middle East and Southeast Asia. Already the China–EU Comprehensive Agreement on Investment, concluded in December 2020 and greeted with fanfare in China, has been frozen because of doubts about the Asian giant's behaviour.

The surge in global anti-China sentiment post the Covid pandemic will restrict US and European markets to China. Pressure from the US and the EU on China will also increase consequent to the country siding with Russia in its invasion of Ukraine. Closer to home, Bangladesh has indicated that there are limits to Chinese influence and pressure; there is anger in Nepal at China's aggressive push on its territorial claims, and there is uncertainty in the Maldives. Importantly, India, Japan, Australia, Vietnam, Indonesia and Singapore will not willingly acquiesce to China's dominance.

India's political, diplomatic and military leadership will need to discard its defensive mindset and assertively counter China. India must continue to build its relationship with the US and France, while keeping Russia close for the time being. Ties within the neighbourhood and with countries in the region, such as Japan, Vietnam, Indonesia, Australia and Singapore, need to be reinforced. Taiwan will be a useful partner for economic and technology cooperation. India must not hesitate to raise China's 'unfriendly' actions in international fora and counter the growing Sino–Pakistan nexus in the diplomatic domain.

Science and Technology

In its quest to become a global superpower, China has for years focused on acquiring a leading position in science and technology, with an emphasis on military applications. Faced with growing US pressure since 2013 to disrupt its technology sector, China has focused on niche areas of frontier science, assiduously built domestic talent and stepped up its efforts to lure high-end scientists and researchers to work in the country. It has allocated significant outlays for science and technology (S&T), and has sought assistance from foreign countries and overseas Chinese to establish world-class laboratories and universities to advance cutting-edge research.

These efforts have been redoubled since 2017, when Xi Jinping spelt out the country's national goals—among them to join the ranks of the world's most technologically advanced nations by 2025. Since then, visits by China's senior leadership to S&T research institutes have increased, and greater emphasis has been placed on research, innovation and the development of indigenous technologies.

Today, the number of Chinese students graduating in STEM subjects from the US is estimated at around 46,000 undergraduates, 40,000 master's students, and approximately 36,000 students in PhD programmes.[17] Given China's push in the sector, the number of graduates (aged twenty-five to thirty-four) is expected to increase 300 per cent by 2030, compared to just 30 per cent in the US and Europe.[18]

On 11 March 2021, the NPC plenum approved China's '14th Five Year Plan (2021–2025) and Long-Range Objectives through the Year 2035 for National, Economic and Social Development of the People's Republic of China'. The plan proposes to increase R&D spending by at least 7 per cent a year between 2021 and 2025. Since China's scientific community is specifically concerned about basic research, the share of basic research is proposed to be increased from 6 to 8 per cent over the next five years.

For India, this plan is especially significant. It sets out China's strategic intent, and identifies core areas of national security and development. It focuses on strategically important scientific programmes, with a number of major projects dedicated to artificial intelligence (AI), quantum information, integrated circuits, internet of things, biomedicines, development of organelles, life and health sciences, brain science, biological breeding, as well as air, space, deep-earth and deep-sea research.

Many of these frontier projects have military applications. For instance, China's robotic research is linked with developing 'non-human soldiers'. A number of the projects mentioned in the document have now shifted from the realm of speculation to emerge as imminent threats. India has to recognize the implications of China's S&T focus which will put it under additional pressure.

To strengthen strategic technology, China is formulating the 'Actions for Developing China through Science and Technology' to improve the new 'whole-of-the-nation' system (*juguo tizhi*). This plan will mobilize national resources for specific objectives, including developing strategic weapons technology. China aims to establish a number of national laboratories in certain fields, for instance quantum information, photons and micro-/nano-electronics, network communications, AI, biomedicine and modern energy systems. These labs will lead the way in technology between 2021 to 2025. The plan aims to boost global competitiveness in areas such as robotics, new energy vehicles, aerospace and agricultural machinery. It focuses on transforming China into an advanced manufacturing superpower.

It is important to note that China's strategy of civil–military fusion blurs the distinction between civilian and military research.

Its leading universities, including Tsinghua and Fudan, are engaged in secret research for the PLA. Tsinghua is China's top university for AI and second in the world in the number of high-level papers published. An authoritative report released by the university in 2018 revealed it has established a number of AI research bases, most dealing with military-related research.[19] A range of commercial companies are also involved in AI-focused military applications. The predictive aspect of AI, with its ability to determine the behaviour of military adversaries and anticipate social unrest, is an area of special interest.

Xi Jinping set out clear objectives to complete the modernization of China's military by 2027 and turn the PLA into a 'world-class army' by 2050. The PLA is to be equipped with a strong combat capability that can win any type of war, particularly with the US and Taiwan as primary targets. Before China moves against the US, however, it will try and establish dominance over the South China Sea and regional powers, like India and Japan. In December 2019, the Centre for Security and Emerging Technologies estimated that China's R&D spending on AI for civilian S&T was approximately between USD 90 million and USD 2 billion, based on 2018 data. Its estimated spending on R&D alone for military-related AI was USD 2.7 billion. In November 2020, China's military leadership mandated the PLA to incorporate 'intelligentization', or AI, in addition to 'mechanization' and 'informationization' in the PLA's modernization plans. Reports in China's military media on PLA exercises now frequently mention the application of AI.

In addition to indigenous efforts, China has 'stolen' vast amounts of technology from advanced countries by various means including cyber hacking. Universities and students have concealed their affiliation with the PLA while engaging for years on sensitive defence-related research in British, US and other scientific institutions.

Twenty-two Chinese universities linked to the PLA were uncovered by British authorities in 2021. Since 2019, the US has cracked down on such activities and arrested, or sent home, a number of Chinese researchers.

The possibility of biowarfare has now emerged as a major challenge. China, a world leader in CRISPR gene-editing technology, is known to be working on ways to identify individuals belonging to its ethnic minorities. There are numerous pointers to China's research on biowarfare. These include books like *War for Biological Dominance* (2010) by Guo Jiwei, professor and chief physician at the Third Military Medical University, Army University, and *New Highland of War* (2017) authored by Zhang Shibo, retired general and former president of the PLA National Defence University. And, for the first time, the 2017 edition of *Science of Military Strategy*—an authoritative textbook published by the PLA National Defence University—included a section on 'biology as a domain of military struggle', which includes discussion of 'specific ethnic genetic attacks'.[20]

China's plans to conduct biology experiments in space are an additional worry. The *Global Times* on 14 March 2021 reported a delegate as saying on the sidelines of the NPC Plenum that a single-function biology experiment platform payload is expected to be launched via a Long March carrier rocket by September, while a multifunctional platform supporting biological experiments may be put into orbit by 2022. Cheng Wei, the founder of a private space technology start-up based in Huzhou, Zhejiang province, told *Global Times* that his firm has an ambitious goal of initiating an orbital space biology lab around 2025. It aims to conduct studies relating to changes in humans' vital signs in space to explore the development of future manned space missions and study the feasibility of long-term human stays on the moon or other extraterrestrial bodies.

The COVID-19 pandemic has exposed our unpreparedness to tackle biowarfare, pandemics or nuclear fallout. These dangers must now be taken cognizance of.

Food and Water Security

Looking into the not-too-distant future, where climate change is likely to affect both land and water, China is making serious efforts to ensure food and water security. Anticipating a severe global food shortage by 2030–35, China is aggressively buying farmlands across the world. Since 2010, it is estimated to have invested USD 94 billion in farm activities abroad, purchasing 3.2 million hectares of land on various continents. It is also providing USD 206 billion in annual farm subsidies at home. India, which has an equally large population, will face increasing competition from China to secure scarce food and water resources. The conflict in Ukraine has highlighted the danger of food shortages.

China's plans to construct a number of hydroelectric projects along the lower reaches of the Brahmaputra River (Yarlung Tsangbo) are bound to impact India. In March 2021, China finally put the stamp of approval on these plans.[21] These include the construction of the world's largest dam at the Great Bend of the river. Without specifically referring to the irrigation of China's arid but arable north, the plan ambiguously said these dams will ensure 'national security in many areas and benefit the country and the people'. These dams will, undoubtedly, have an adverse impact on the livelihoods of some 600 million people in the Ganga–Brahmaputra–Meghna basin. Critically, the dam on the Great Bend of the Brahmaputra, which will be three times larger than the Three Gorges Dam on the Yangtze, will give Beijing a strong lever to use against India at a time of its own choosing.

Additionally, the extensive construction activity planned in Tibet will raise temperatures and accelerate the retreat of the region's glaciers which give rise to major Asian rivers, including the Mekong, the Indus and the Brahmaputra, as well as many others that feed into the Ganga, even more. This will reduce the water flow in these rivers, if not dry them out entirely.

Civilizational Competition

As part of its efforts to win the civilizational war with India, China has begun to project that the Buddhism practised in Tibet, China, Japan, etc., is of Chinese origin and that it travelled to Tibet from Mainland China! This rivalry—or jealousy—stems from China's historical view that India's over-5,000-year-old civilization is not only of greater antiquity but also the source of Buddhism, learning, metaphysics and philosophy, as well as the world-acclaimed practice of yoga. In fact, classical Chinese texts refer to India as 'Xi Tian' or Western Heaven! China has been trying, since former president Jiang Zemin's visit to Egypt in 1999, to revise its narrative and claim that its civilization is also 5,000 years old and as old as those of India and Egypt! This is an enduring area of competition.

India, the Dalai Lama and China

In addition to India's unassailable position as the home of Buddhism, the issue of the reincarnation of the Dalai Lama—venerated by 6.5 million Tibetans as a 'living god'—is becoming increasingly important for the atheist Chinese Communists. China's 1995 attempt to 'recognize' and impose Gyaltsen Norbu as the 11th Panchen Lama has failed. Despite the lapse of over twenty-five years, Gyaltsen Norbu is not yet accepted by Tibetans as the Panchen Lama, but is only deemed to be a 'learned monk'. Similarly, Beijing's persistent efforts to discredit the Dalai Lama and undermine his influence have proved unsuccessful.

Worried that restiveness in Tibet could increase or even take a violent turn after the Dalai Lama passes, and that a reincarnate not under Chinese control could become a serious problem—especially with high global anti-China sentiment—the leadership is keen to avoid a situation of two Dalai Lamas, like that of the two Panchen Lamas at all costs.

On his part, the Dalai Lama has announced that he will not be reincarnated under a totalitarian regime and will give clear indications as to where his reincarnation or 'emanation' will be found. He has set the stage for the Tibetan people to continue their struggle to preserve their religious beliefs, customs, language, history and traditions. The United States has backed him with the 'Tibetan Policy and Support Act, 2020', making it official US policy that 'the succession of Tibetan Buddhist leaders, including the succession of the Dalai Lama, be left solely to Tibetan Buddhists to decide, without interference from the Chinese government'.

With the Dalai Lama living in exile in India since 30 March 1959, India will inevitably be drawn into the reincarnation imbroglio. The matter has been complicated by China's efforts to implicitly link the reincarnation issue with the settlement of the India–China boundary. Beijing claims it has always exercised sovereignty over Tibet—a statement contested by Tibetans and, till October 2008, by the United Kingdom as well. Till then, the UK had only acknowledged China's 'suzerainty' and not its 'sovereignty' over Tibet.

Meanwhile, China's position on the Tibet issue has hardened. Consecutive year-long campaigns across the Tibet Autonomous Region (TAR) and other areas to 'educate' the clergy to 'adapt Tibetan Buddhism to socialism with Chinese characteristics' and work against 'the Dalai Lama secessionist forces' have become the norm.

As the search for the Dalai Lama's reincarnation gets underway, Beijing will mount pressure on New Delhi to shut down the

Central Tibetan Administration and other institutions set up by the Tibetans in exile at Dharamshala and elsewhere, and designate them as secessionist outfits. They will warn India not to recognize the reincarnation selected by the Tibetan Buddhists without Beijing's approval as the 'legitimate' Dalai Lama. The majority of Tibetan Buddhists, on the other hand, are very unlikely to accept China's nominee. If, as is likely, the Dalai Lama's reincarnation is born or 'discovered' in India, this will become an additional point of perennial friction. India should adhere to its policy of non-interference in religious matters and accept the choice of the Tibetan Buddhists in the country.

Meanwhile, the UFWD continues its efforts to penetrate the exiled Tibetan community in India and abroad. The Chinese embassy in India has at least two or three persons tasked exclusively with monitoring and penetrating the Tibetan community. The Dalai Lama, other high-ranking Tibetan Buddhist religious personages, different Tibetan Buddhist sects and the Central Tibetan Administration are priority targets for the UFWD and China's cyber hackers. The case of a US citizen of ethnic Tibetan descent working in the US police, who was arrested in 2020 on charges of spying on Tibetans for the Chinese, is an example of the department's reach.

Conclusion

The challenges that loom ahead will test India's resolve, political will and diplomatic and military skills. Given the absence of trust after May 2020, India will have to ensure strict reciprocity in bilateral relations and not yield or show even a hint of deference on matters of territorial integrity and national sovereignty. At the same time, New Delhi will need to try and keep relations peaceful to concentrate on its own important development agenda. It is in China's interest as well to repair the damage caused by its aggression and restore peaceful relations with India if it wants to pursue its ambitious 'Two Century' goals.

Notes

1. At the Chinese Communist Party's (CCP) 18th Party Congress in 2012, he announced the 'China Dream', which includes: making the Chinese people prosperous, making the Chinese nation strong, and 'the rejuvenation of the great Chinese Nation'. He repeated this goal at the 19th Party Congress in 2017 and laid down the timeline for its achievement.
2. Vice Admiral Yuan Yunbai was till 2021 the southern theatre commander of the PLA.
3. The six wars include the Unification of Taiwan (2020–25); the 'reconquest' of the Spratly Islands (2025–30); the 'reconquest' of Southern Tibet (2035–40); the 'reconquest' of Diaoyu Island (Senkaku) and Ryukyu Islands (2040–45); the unification of Outer Mongolia (2045–50); taking back of lands lost to Russia (2055–60).
4. Hu Shisheng and Wang Jue, 'The Behavioural Logic behind India's Tough Foreign Policy towards China', CIR, September/October 2020, http://www.cicir.ac.cn/UpFiles/file/20201103/637399976670524949 1072987.pdf, accessed 20 November 2020.
5. 'Miscellaneous Talks on China–India Relations', Kojiro, 13 January 2021, https://user.guancha.cn/main/content?id=446819&s=fwzwyzz wzbt, accessed 19 January 2021.
6. PTI, 'Chumar Standoff an "Evil Design" of PLA: Ex-ITBP Chief Subhas Goswami', *The Economic Times*, 29 October 2015.
7. 'Recent Developments in Doklam Area', 30 June 2017, https://www. mea.gov.in/press-releases.htm?dtl/28572/Recent_Developments_in_ Doklam_Area
8. Speaking at two separate Air Force Commanders' Conferences in 2017 and 2018, I cautioned that China was preparing to 'teach India a lesson' and this would probably entail military action against India in 2020-21!
9. Official spokesperson's response to media queries seeking comments on the statement issued on 19 June by the Chinese spokesperson on the

events in the Galwan Valley area, 20 June 2020, https://mea.gov.in/response-to-queries.htm?dtl/32770/Official_Spokespersons_response_to_media_queries_seeking_comments_on_the_statement_issued_on_19_June_by_the_Chinese_Spokesperson_on_the_events_in_the_

10. Some of the twenty 'border airports' to be built by 2025 have been identified as those at Tashkurgan (the westernmost point in China and the last stop before the Khunjerab Pass), Shigatse, Lhunze (Longzi), Dingri (Ngari, Ali), Burang/Purang (Ngari), Yadong and an additional runway at Lhasa's Gonggar airport.

11. Kibithu is one of India's easternmost towns with a permanent population. It is located on the last roadhead on the Indian side of the LAC. The Lohit River, a tributary of the Brahmaputra, enters India at Kibithu.

12. The Karakoram Highway is the main overland artery between China and Pakistan. It passes through the Khunjerab Pass into Gilgit-Baltistan, linking China's Xinjiang region with Hasan Abdal in Pakistan's Punjab.

13. On 26 March 2021, China and Iran signed an agreement to increase cooperation and trade over the next twenty-five years. Marking its significance, Iran aired the signing live on state-run TV.

14. The United Front Work Department reports directly to the Central Committee of the CCP.

15. Ai Jun, 'India's Head Is Swollen by Ego to Think It Has a "Taiwan Card" to Play', 6 April 2021, https://www.globaltimes.cn/page/202104/1220346.shtml, accessed 7 April 2021.

16. 'Over 50% Equipment in BSNL Mobile Networks Chinese: Govt', *The Indian Express*, 18 September 2020, https://indianexpress.com/article/business/over-50-equipment-in-bsnl-mobile-networks-chinese-govt-6600371/, accessed 19 September 2020.

17. Jacob Feldgoise and Remco Zwetsloot, 'Estimating the Number of Chinese STEM Students in the United States', CSET, https://cset.georgetown.edu/publication/estimating-the-number-of-chinese-stem-students-in-the-united-states/, accessed 8 July 2022.

18. Andreas Schleicher, 'China Opens a New University Every Week', 16 March 2016, https://www.bbc.com/news/business-35776555, accessed 29 April 2017.

19. These include: the 'State Key Laboratory of Intelligent Technology and Systems'; the 'Intelligent Microsystems Ministry of Education Key Laboratory of the CMC Science and Technology Commission National Defence Frontier Innovation Special Zone'; the 'CMC Science and Technology Commission's High-End Laboratory for Military Intelligence'; 'Tsinghua Brain and Intelligence Laboratory'; and the interdisciplinary 'Tsinghua University Intelligent Unmanned Systems Research Center'.
20. Elsa B. Kania and Wilson VornDick, 'Weaponizing Biotech: How China's Military Is Preparing for a "New Domain of Warfare"', Center for a New American Security, 14 August 2019, https://www.cnas.org/publications/commentary/weaponizing-biotech-how-chinas-military-is-preparing-for-a-new-domain-of-warfare, accessed 7 July 2022; see also Jayadeva Ranade, *Xi Jinping: China's Third New Era,* New Delhi: K W Publishers Pvt. Ltd, 2022.
21. The construction of these dams was approved under China's 14th Five Year Plan and Long Range Objectives 2035. The appointment in February 2021 of fifty-eight-year-old hydroelectric engineer Li Guoyin as minister of water resources ensures the project impetus.

CHAPTER 2

Pakistan: The Inevitability of Enmity

VIKRAM SOOD

Pakistan moved from its dawn to twilight in the last seventy years—with very brief spells of sunshine in between. Created in the name of Islam and as a homeland for the Muslims of South Asia, tendencies towards Islamic extremism were inherent in the new country's leadership. Its new identity had to be Islamic and non-Indian. This became more virulent with time, with a larger percentage of Muslims staying on in India after Partition. This added to the frustration of the new leaders of Pakistan as it threatened the very basis of the country's creation. The dream sold was that Pakistan would be a New Medina, which would lead to a new Caliphate and, with its large population, the country could be the leader of the Islamic world. Muslims in India would be protected by Islamabad—by keeping the Hindus and Sikhs in Pakistan as hostages for good Indian behaviour.[1]

Angered at having been given a 'moth-eaten Pakistan' without all of Punjab, Bengal, Assam and Kashmir, it set about rectifying this injustice by trying to make a grab at Kashmir as its first foreign-policy initiative. A new country without a strategy chose India as its enemy. Also, aggravated by the fact that India proceeded to become a united country, Pakistan's very survival became dependent on sustaining this enmity.

The threat from Pakistan has morphed over the decades. A military grab of Kashmir under the garb of 'freedom fighters' was first attempted in 1947, followed by another in 1965 on similar lines; both were unsuccessful militarily, but Pakistan did gain territory in Pakistan-occupied Kashmir and Gilgit-Baltistan in 1948 because the pushback across the Krishna Ganga was literally stopped midstream. The second attempt in 1965 and the Tashkent Agreement enabled Pakistan to give the impression domestically that they had attained parity with India. This was shattered in 1971 when Pakistan lost East Pakistan (now Bangladesh) and 93,000-odd soldiers became prisoners of war.

This led Islamabad to desperately look for strategic depth in Afghanistan, spurred a Zulfiqar Ali Bhutto-led drive towards assimilating with and leading Islamic nations, and a search for the nuclear weapon. Bhutto had already launched his nuclear weapons programme in March 1972, just months before he came to Simla for talks with Indira Gandhi in July. India, in a remarkable and inexplicable show of magnanimity, had conceded on the negotiating table what it had won on the battlefield. Thus emboldened, Pakistan began sharpening its anti-India stance, equipped with Islam and with the support of Islamic nations and the prospective acquisition of the nuclear bombs—this later helped foster terror under a nuclear umbrella.

Islam and Pakistan

We normally assume Pakistan is a normal democratic state because it has begun to hold elections periodically. However, it is a confused state and has been so from the beginning. The country has been ruled directly by the army through most of the seventy-odd years of its existence, and indirectly the rest of the time. That army, which was professedly very professional and assumed to be secular, over a period of time—especially since the puritanical martial rule of General Zia-ul-Haq—has become a fervent believer in fundamentalist Islam. This aspect affected Pakistan internally and externally. Islamabad thus found it easier to deal with the Afghan Mujahideen fighting their jihad against the Soviet Union, with funds from the US and Saudi Arabia, and jihadi foot soldiers being supplied from the madrassas of northwest Pakistan and Balochistan. It became financially lucrative for the Pakistan Army, as it led the battle and began to adhere to the purity of Islamic precepts.

We must remember that Pakistan was an Islamic idea, where the argument was that Islam cannot coexist with Hindus and the two adherents must live separately. Islam also states that only Muslims must rule over Muslims and that non-Muslims can never do so. Islamic theology refers to Dar-ul-Islam and Dar-ul-Harb where the former is the territory of peace and tranquillity where Islam dominates and the latter is the territory of war and chaos where Islam does not dominate. 'Muslims are expected to bring God's word and will to all of humanity and do so by force if absolutely necessary. Further, attempts by the regions in Da-ul-Harb to resist or fight back must be met with a similar amount of force.'[2] That is the ethos of Pakistan too. Javed Ahmad Ghamidi, a progressive Pakistani scholar of Islam, who was exiled to Malaysia in 2009 for his views, explained a few doctrines that shaped the extremist mindset. One was that only Muslims had the right to govern, and every non-Muslim government was illegitimate. Islamic extremists hold the overthrow of non-Muslim governments to be necessary and permissible whenever possible.[3] There is no word like 'secularism' in the country's lexicon as it does not exist in the Koran.

The second aspect to remember is that those Muslims who lived in what became India overwhelmingly sought the creation of a new homeland, Pakistan. In the 1946 elections, the Muslim League, which was spearheading the Pakistan Movement, won almost all the Muslim seats, under separate electorates on a limited franchise, in what is now Maharashtra and Gujarat and in what became Tamil Nadu and Andhra; with substantial victories ranging from 85 per cent in Bihar to 95 per cent in Bengal including Assam, Central Provinces (now Madhya Pradesh), United Provinces (now Uttar Pradesh).[4] It has been calculated that this translated into 87 per cent of the total Muslim seats. Those living in what became Pakistan had not voted similarly. At the time of Partition, many chose to stay behind as Indians but a sizeable percentage of these Muslims on the Indian side stayed behind because they had no means to cross the newly formed border—they had no address to go to; it was alien territory.

In the run up to the Partition of India, sections of the Deobandi ulema, which included Maulana Ashraf Ali Thanvi, who were in touch with Muslim League leaders including Jinnah, had supported the League's ideals.[5] Another Deoband ulema, Mufti Muhammed Shafi, who migrated to Karachi, Pakistan, in 1948, formed the Darul Uloom Karachi and became the Grand Mufti of Pakistan.[6] While in Deoband, Shafi taught the hadith and was the chief mufti who resigned in 1943 to concentrate on the Pakistan Movement. There were others too sympathetic to the Pakistan movement.

Islam inevitably became the language of politics prior to Independence in 1947. Pakistan was the first state to have been created in the name of Islam; the circumstances of its creation, a bitter partition, contentious issues and a constant fear of the bigger India meant that Islam would only get strengthened in the country. Politically, fundamentalism in Islam began with Zulfiqar Ali Bhutto (the villain of Pakistan in 1971 and the saviour in 1972), when, after an initial foray into Islamic socialism in the post-Bangladesh phase he felt the need to woo both the Arab world and the indigenous Islamic right wing.

The Constitution that he passed in 1973 defined Pakistan as an Islamic Republic, with Islam as the state religion. It also stated that all laws would be in accordance with Islamic injunctions of the Quran and Sunnah, and interpretation was monitored by the Shariat Court and the Council of Islamic Ideology as Bhutto moved closer to the Arab world—chiefly the King of Saudi Arabia and Muammar Gaddafi of Libya. Bhutto was seeking acceptability and funds through increased Islamic credentials. But Islamic groups at home was not satisfied and Bhutto succumbed to their demand to declare Ahmediyas as non-Muslims in 1974.

The move towards fundamentalism sharpened during the martial law regime of General Zia-ul-Haq and the Afghan jihad of the 1980s, leading into a Kashmiri jihad in the 1990s and has continued since. There has been a steady regression in Pakistan towards increasingly fundamentalist practices as a blowback from the Islamist activities of India-specific terror groups. Sectarian mafias operating within the country, to whom political parties turn for support, have been mainstreamed. They may not be able to win elections yet, but they have become an increasingly important factor in the country's landscape.

Zia-ul-Haq had empowered sectarian militant groups to keep a check on the Shia groups backed by Iran. Groups like the Jamiat-e-Ulema Islam—which formed the extreme Sunni Sipah-e-Sahaba (Guardians of the Prophet's Companions)—and the Lashkar-e-Jhangvi, became notorious and feared for their cruelty towards the Shias. Originally, the Barelvi school held sway in Pakistan, but General Zia had changed all that when he empowered Deobandi mullahs, mosques and madrassas during the Afghan jihad.[7]

The end of the Afghan insurgency did not lead to the end of sectarian violence in Pakistan. The 1990s saw the formation of more militant Pakistani Deobandi organizations like the Tehrik-e-Nifaz-e-Shariat-e-Mohammadi (Movement to Implement the Shariah of Mohammad). The Pakistan military was, at that time, also supporting Deobandi organizations like the Harkat-ul-Mujahideen, Harakat-ul-Ansar and later the Jaish-e-Mohammad. These were India-specific terror groups and were joined by the Lashkar-e-Taiba, another Pakistan Punjab-based terror outfit.

Another Deobandi group aided by Islamabad was the Taliban, comprising clerics and students. While they were victorious in their jihad in the 1990s, the Pakistani security establishment lost the kind of control it earlier had over the group, and the militants began to gravitate towards the al Qaeda in the first decade of the twenty-first century. And now, the Taliban sits in the highest echelons of power in Kabul—a religiously endowed movement has geographical territory under its control.

Pakistan was created on the idea of a separate Islamic nation for Muslims. Once this objective was achieved, the mullahs set about Islamizing the polity, while the Muslim League and squabbling politicians lost control of the state to the army. Today, over seven decades after its formation, Pakistan has all the trappings of an Islamic republic managed by the Pakistan Army, which now owns the country. The author Arif Jamal remarked in an interview in September 2013: 'Almost all Pakistani military officers are either nationalist jihadists or Islamist jihadists.'[8] The army will continue to keep the bogey of the Indian threat alive because that assures its privileged position in the country.

Terrorism as a policy option for the Pakistan Army will not change. If at all, it will morph according to circumstances and perceived needs, and adapt newer methods of terrorism. The use of drones has already begun, and we can expect this to become more lethal in the future. Pakistan would have watched very closely the effect of a pandemic on the Indian system and given their commitment to jihad, it will be easy to argue that spreading the pandemic could be an option against India. The fact that this could affect their coreligionists in India is not going to be a limiting factor. The Pakistan Army has been responsible for the killing of the largest number of Muslims on the Indian subcontinent including Afghanistan. What Pakistan did not bargain for was that today radical Islamic groups vie with one another for space to establish their purist credentials in the 'Land of the Pure'.

The last conventional attempt, again portrayed as a mujahideen onslaught, against India in 1999 in Kargil, in northern Kashmir, ended in failure and defeat. But it is only a matter of time before Islamabad turns its attention to Kashmir once again. There is an inevitability about this because the thought that Kashmir will be a part of Pakistan is the dream that keeps the nation together. Their real interest is the water that flows from Kashmir and irrigates the fields of Punjab in Pakistan. Islam was the cover and now it has become a millstone. One can see the signs of an international campaign accompanied by heightened terrorism in Kashmir.

Indian magnanimity of the early years did not prevent events like the Mumbai terror attacks of 1993, 2006 and 2008 and scores of others. This 'soft approach' was viewed by Pakistan as more in keeping with their idea of the 'cowardly Hindu' and a major Indian weakness. This was enough encouragement for Pakistan's continued intransigence.

It took Indians quite a while to understand that hope was no substitute for policy. And that policy depended on assessed threats and national interest. The attitude of the Pakistan government towards India does not evolve with any change at the top. It is the all-powerful military cabal of the army's corps commanders that determines policy in Pakistan. There has been consistency in this from the early days. The army, as is well known, has scant regard for their own elected representatives and often makes this disdain obvious. They cannot be expected to treat India—both the enemy and Hindu—any better. Dreams of eternal peace with Pakistan are delusional.

Pakistan made its choice of a policy of unrelenting enmity towards India and terror under a nuclear umbrella. This would continue into the twenty-first century as a low-cost option for the Pakistan Army. This war of attrition by using jihadi foot soldiers appeared to be successful, in so far as it kept India on the back foot—although it did not bring Pakistan victory. This option too seems to have run its course when the Indian government chose to react with retaliatory attacks in response to terrorist acts in 2019. The next stage could be pre-emptive strikes by India.

While direct, openly attributable terror may be downplayed by Pakistan, there are others in the game. The presence of the Islamic State (Pakistan) (IS[P]) is relatively new. It recently distributed propaganda material—the April 2021 issue of their monthly Urdu journal *Yalghar* (Invasion)—on the social media.[9] These are early days, but it would be tempting for Pakistan to pin the blame of terrorist activity in India on the IS(P) to maintain deniability. The journal is critical of the Taliban, describing it as the ISI's stooge, and is also critical of al Qaeda. It may not be a favourite of the Pakistani system, but would have its uses in the future, provided Pakistan can keep it under some control. It is this aspect—control of such movements—that is difficult to determine. Terrorist groups often break away from their original sponsors and pursue their own vested interests. However, Pakistan will continue to remain a haven for various groups operating not only in the neighbourhood—some of them working in tandem with others, while some against each other—but even further afield. This situation will continue to complicate security in the region.

There is no need to expect most cordial relations with a neighbour, but a working arrangement tends to help all parties involved. The question is, can even this be ever possible with Pakistan. The chances are dim. Pakistan, in its current parlous state, is more a threat to itself, an oppressor in Afghanistan and a nuisance to India. Since geography cannot be altered, Pakistan cannot be relocated, but strategically, it will remain important, especially as an adjunct to China.

Pakistan's Intentions and Capabilities

What we must consider is Pakistan's intentions and capabilities. Its intention is anti-India in every way and its ultimate desire to dismember India. Let us not assume that what the Lashkar-e-Taiba or other jihadis proclaim in Pakistan is something the army disapproves of. On the contrary, it must be remembered that there is an increasing Islamic content in the Pakistan Army, at all levels. The dream is spelt out in Islamic tenets: that Muslims must not be ruled by non-Muslims and should be liberated. Jihad against India is more than a commitment for this lot; it is considered an honour. The dream of the Islamists is to have a final Ghazwa-e-Hind—a holy raid on India. The concept of Ghazwa draws its strength from the concepts of Dar-ul-Uloom and Dar-ul-Harab. A part of this has been explained by Austin Cline in his essay cited in an earlier note. The Pakistani terrorist organization Lashkar-e-Taiba has often spoken of Ghazwa-e-Hind as a means of liberating Kashmir from Indian control. The group's founder, Hafiz Muhammad Saeed, has declared repeatedly that '[i]f freedom is not given to the Kashmiris, then we will occupy the whole of India including Kashmir. We will launch Ghazwa-e-Hind. Our homework is to get Kashmir.' Pakistani propagandist Zaid Hamid has also repeatedly invoked Ghazwa-e-Hind as a battle against Hindu India led from Muslim Pakistan. According to Hamid, 'Allah has destined the people of Pakistan' with victory, and 'Allah is the aid and helper of Pakistan'.[10] Pakistan could seek to be a part of a two-front war by launching terror attacks in India along with cyberattacks from China. Its capacity to launch terror attacks has not visibly diminished, but, if the statements from the Pakistan establishment are to be believed, Kashmir remains the focal point.

The army may be arrogant and adventurous at times, but the generals are unlikely to launch a nuclear strike. The acquisition of nuclear warheads and missiles are more for self-satisfaction than actual use. This inventory helped them in image-building in West Asia in the past, but with better India–West Asia relations, even this may be of reduced value. However, it might be too optimistic to think that Pakistan will forgo the use of these weapons. Any serious study of that country's nuclear policy cannot ignore its renewed efforts to strengthen its nuclear weapon capability.

The Nuclear Option

Pakistan's acquisition of nuclear weapons was meant to counter India's superiority in conventional weapons and give the country some security. It has been frequently touted as the ultimate weapon against India. Apparently, its present holdings of 165 nuclear warheads (compared to India's 150) with a reach of up to 2,750 km (Shaheen III) do not give Islamabad the security it requires. So it continues to look for more material.[11] In recent years, there have been reports emanating from Europe about Pakistan's attempts to acquire more nuclear-grade material and technology. A threat assessment by Norwegian security agencies referred to Pakistan's search for dual-use nuclear technology by evading international regulations under the cover of using this tech for education and health. The 2019 annual report of the Security Information Service of the Czech Republic referred to Pakistan misleading the world while trying to procure internationally controlled items and technologies. The Germans too had disclosed in 2020 that Pakistan continued to engage in the production and proliferation of weapons of mass destruction (WMD) to protect itself against India. The Germans also provided accounts of Pakistan's efforts to steal information and material through cover companies and transport dual-use goods. The UAE, Turkey and China were the favourite launching pads for such activity.[12]

China's role in assisting Pakistan's nuclear programme has been crucial; in fact, there would be no Pakistani nuclear programme without Chinese assistance. The Chinese built the pressurized water reactors (PWRs) at Chashma—the CHASHNUPP-3 and CHASHNUPP-4—and, in November 2017, Pakistan signed a deal with China to build an additional 1,100 MW PWR to be called CHASHNUPP-5. According to a November 2020 imagery report, nuclear weapons facilities had been developed at Chashma, disabusing the notion that the Chinese-assisted reactors were meant for only peaceful purposes. Similar satellite imagery suggests the presence of new centrifuge halls and other support facilities, indicating that there was a 40 per cent increase in the production capacity at the Khan Research Laboratories, Kahuta.

Pakistan's nuclear threshold is well known and looking ahead, there could be a biowarfare threshold or worse—a bioterror option in Pakistan Army's arsenal, working through some of its trusted terror groups.

Afghanistan and the Taliban

The future of the Taliban and Afghanistan, after the US departure in 2021, remains uncertain in terms of which group will control the elected Afghan government: the Taliban by itself, under some Pakistani influence, or will there be endless strife? The one factor that can be taken as given is that there will be continued violence in Afghanistan and one of its fallouts could be the return of al Qaeda to support the Taliban in opposition to the IS (Khorasan). Afghanistan seems destined to move from hybrid theocracy to complete theocracy under Taliban control.

More than two decades ago, Eqbal Ahmad, one of Pakistan's most cerebral political thinkers and analysts, had said that the costs of Islamabad's policies have long been accumulating since 1980, when Zia-ul-Haq had declared Pakistan as a frontline state in the Cold War. 'Those costs—already unbearable in proliferation of guns, heroin and armed fanatics—are likely now to multiply in myriad ways.'[13] Ahmad added that the domestic costs of Pakistan's friendly proximity to the Taliban are incalculable and potentially catastrophic. 'More importantly, the Taliban is the most retrograde political movement in the history of Islam,' he wrote. Strong words, but prophetic.

We now see the Taliban displaying its regressive nature every other day since the Americans have concluded a deal with the organization to enable them leave Afghanistan. This would mean a more emboldened and less amenable Taliban in Kabul. Pakistan's leaders never recognized that they would become susceptible to the culture of violence they had created. There was an opportunity for Pakistan to change policy after 11 September 2001, but its khaki grandees assumed that duplicity would help them win in the end.

As the world watched helplessly as the Taliban strengthened their hold on Afghanistan, the images coming out of Pakistan were not very comforting either. The Haqqani Network has been of immense use to the Pakistani intelligence in a relationship built over nearly fifty years. It was the Haqqani Network that carried out the bombing attack on the Indian embassy in 2008. Islamabad had used its close connections with Sirajuddin Haqqani of the network in the Taliban government to act as an interlocutor to negotiate peace deals with the Tehrik-e-Taliban Pakistan (TTP), which had been carrying out terror activities inside Pakistan.[14] The Imran Khan government has also been forced by circumstance to negotiate a deal with the other

Barelvi militant organization, Tehrik-e-Labbaik (TLP), release its hardliner chief and permit its members to stand for elections. The imagery is that of Pakistan supporting the extreme fundamentalist Taliban government in Afghanistan, dealing with the TTP and TLP for its own domestic survival, while on its way to becoming a fundamentalist Islamic state ruled by the army and the mullahs, in league with China. Today, the Deobandis have political control in Pakistan, despite being outnumbered by Barelvis in the country who are now showing signs of challenging this and seeking a place for themselves. All this makes Pakistan look more and more like becoming an extension of Afghanistan. How Pakistan deals with a Taliban-led Afghanistan in these circumstances will be a major test for the country. One would imagine that they would be unable to handle this adequately, and the region will see violence and terrorism spreading outwards from the Afghanistan–Pakistan area. The Afghanistan situation, with the activities of the Taliban and Pakistan Taliban, is not going to settle down any time soon either.

Western commentary stresses on Islamic movements, chiefly the Muslim Brotherhood and Wahhabi Islam, emanating from the Middle East. The Deoband influence has been in the regions of South and Southeast Asia, which constitute more than 43 per cent of the global Muslim population, while the Muslim population in the Middle East and North Africa makes up roughly 28 per cent of the global figure. Europe today has a sizeable Muslim population, who mostly live in the underprivileged areas on the margins of major urban centres. They are not only from the Middle East, but have also come from Pakistan. Recent protests in Malmo and Oslo have captured headlines, but beneath these stories are Pakistani-inspired individuals or groups, who carry out their campaign for Kashmir on social media. It would not take too much for these various groups to make common Islamic cause.

Internal Disturbances

Internally, as long as the present power equation between the army and politicians continues, instabilities will remain. The army had bet on Imran Khan to ensure their own unchallenged pre-eminence. Instead, his ineptitude and tendency to side with radical followers has strengthened the impression that he himself is an Islamic fundamentalist with greater faith in governance through Shariah rather than democratic principles.

The state of political instability was reflected in the continuing protests that demand greater democratic and economic rights in the Pakhtoon regions in Sindh and Balochistan. The protests have only become more defiant with the passage of time and the government's attempts since then have not succeeded. The protesters have begun to attack the military and even question the dreaded ISI. The army's reactions have been typical—trying to blatantly stifle dissent and criticism in the media and public. In the age of social media, this is hardly going to bring any laurels to the rulers. There does not seem to be any solution to this problem at present.

China's Hold on Pakistan

Prime Minister Imran Khan inaugurated the Karachi Nuclear Power Plant, Unit 2, on 16 June 2021, which also marked the seventieth anniversary of diplomatic ties between China and Pakistan. As usual, the Pakistani leadership extolled the virtues of the China–Pakistan friendship and the economic development prospects of the China–Pakistan Economic Corridor (CPEC). While the economic aspects of the CPEC are discussed often, the military cooperation between the two countries—which involves arms deals, joint exercises and defence pacts—is underplayed.[15]

The strategic value of this arrangement to both China and Pakistan are seen to be immense by both countries. China's objectives may be wider, but both share a common objective of keeping India down. Chinese scholars see India's rise as a major factor in the present state of uneasy India–China relations. Beijing's attitude towards New Delhi has become more aggressive after Xi Jinping signed the CPEC agreement in Islamabad in April 2015.[16] Pakistan hopes that China will help it to get out of its economic morass. This may not happen, and it is more likely that China will concentrate on securing its interests in Gwadar and the Gwadar–Kashgar route. Beijing has vested interests in Pakistan, and so it will remain Islamabad's main source of finance and weaponry across the board.

As China's stranglehold on Pakistan tightens, these problems will get aggravated in the years ahead. India should be looking at China sitting on our western borders. China is not expected to renege on CPEC, and Pakistan has little choice when China demands something from it. For China, Gwadar and Djibouti were parts of its Arabian Sea–Indian Ocean policy and the new agreement with Iran will only strengthen that; this could also mean that Pakistan's swing factor in the region for China will be limited to its ability to hold India back.

In either case, Pakistan can be a surrogate to a China that wishes for control all the way from Xinjiang to the Arabian Sea—Afghanistan and Iran included. With Hambantota, Gwadar and Djibouti under its control, China may indulge in aggressive behaviour in the Arabian Sea, and Pakistan will take advantage of this.

The United States too has, in the past, protected Pakistan for its own strategic reasons during the Cold War and after. Along with China, it too has real-estate interests in the country for geostrategic reasons. However, the US does not know where it stands as its leadership suffers from an attention-deficit disorder every few years. We do not know which way, when and how much the US will swing. The Europeans are too busy sorting out their economic problems, and are somewhat clueless about and very petrified of Islamist terror.

Russians and the Chinese see opportunities for themselves in the region between Pakistan and the Mediterranean, as they perceive a retreating United States.

China has already moved in with a promise to inject anything from USD 280 billion to USD 400 billion into the Iranian oil, gas and petrochemical industries. Pakistan's salience with China will reduce to that extent as Beijing will have direct access to the Gulf, via Afghanistan. Pakistan still hopes to take advantage of this fog. It is thus able to hide its atrocities in Balochistan from the rest of the world, be heavy-handed and ruthless with Pakhtoon restiveness in the Khyber Pakhtunkhwa province. The Pakistan Army will generally endeavour to keep its people in a pressure chamber to suit their Chinese masters, the country's creditors, and themselves. It hopes to be able to keep India on the back foot as it deals with the Taliban in Afghanistan, but operating, so far, from Pakistan.

China will view the unravelling of Afghanistan with some concern, but will be more concerned about its impact on Pakistan. The Afghan resistance to the Durand Line has already created tensions in the region. The Taliban is showing all signs of reverting to hard-line Islamic systems, and this could impact Pakistan, which itself has been moving towards an Islamic Emirates situation. The country now has two terror epicentres. One in the northwest where the Taliban seem to be holding more sway over the TTP and TLP, and the other, the India-specific Lashkar-e-Taiba, Jaish-e-Mohammad and others, who may be temporarily kept under wraps, but could be escalated by the Pakistan army.[17] Besides, sectarian groups still abound. China would worry about Uyghurs of Xinjiang being associated with the Taliban, apart from other Central Asian outfits. Pakistan's inability to control the Taliban could have repercussions on China too.

The Economy

Pakistan's economy requires urgent and deep reforms. Some of these reforms are at the urging of the International Monetary Fund (IMF), but if Islamabad abides by the Fund's suggestions, they will be a massive pain for the common people, who will end up suffering, and the government will become unpopular. If reforms are not carried out, the economic slide will only continue. Presently, Pakistan is incurring debt not to pay for its infrastructure projects but to meet its daily needs and government expenditure. The country's budget for 2021-22 seems to be extremely elastic in its calculations and hinges on impressing the IMF. This is unlikely, and the economy truly faces a disaster. The dependence on debt is so excessive that almost the entire net revenue is accounted for debt servicing, roughly PKR 3.1 trillion, its defence expenditure of PKR 1.37 trillion and pensions amounting to PKR 480 billion. This is more than the cost of running the government. There is also the cycle of petroleum costs and energy prices. Higher import prices will put pressure on energy costs, lead to an inflationary spiral and the IMF will not accept higher tariffs.[18]

This only adds to the debt burden, which exceeds its GDP. The Chinese are understood to have given Pakistan USD 10-11 billion to allow the government to function. The terms of repayment are likely to be stringent. Having spent years in geopolitical contestation with the neighbourhood, Pakistan is now finding it difficult to integrate economically in the region, which is normally the best route for economic revival. Even though commentators earlier have predicted Pakistan's failure as a state, this is not likely to happen. It will be bailed out time and again. But this indulgence will not cure financial profligacy among the country's rulers, especially the military.

The Future

The Joe Biden administration has been aloof so far and the threat of the Financial Action Task Force (FATF) blacklist remains with Pakistan facing serious agricultural problems. Cotton output has been at its lowest in several decades and the IMF has predicted a weak growth rate of 1.5 per cent along with higher rates of inflation and unemployment. Pakistan needs a huge infusion of dollars just to stay afloat; investment and development will come later. Electricity has become far more expensive, there is poor management of water, with the country running perhaps one of the world's most inefficient irrigation networks. In the decade ahead, Pakistan has to concentrate on solving its water problems and drastically improve the level of education. The country is already seeing a massive percentage of dropouts among its children. This percentage increases in higher grades, which means in the years ahead, in an increasingly technological world, Pakistan is setting itself up for a failure.[19] What this means is that an inimical and economically weak neighbour will look for scapegoats and diversions.

The journey ahead for Pakistan, in the next ten years, seems fraught with endless problems, economically and politically. Its only hope is if it regains some strategic relevance to China and the US in the period ahead. China may be stern with Pakistan about financial arrangements and loans, but is unlikely to turn its back on the country. A greater Chinese presence and control in Pakistan will mean a Chinese presence across India's western orders.

Pakistan may not be the military threat that India considered it was. Its obsession with Kashmir has become so overpowering over time that the leaders have pushed themselves and their country into a cul-de-sac. Given this obsession, Islamabad will use every opportunity to use terror and international charity organizations to route funds into India. Pakistani agencies are known to have used such international organizations and charities during the COVID-19 pandemic to channel funds into India. When Pakistan sees itself as economically strong and has a few friends to encourage it, against an India that is seen as weak and vacillating, it will be arrogant and adventurous.

The country's other fixation—to be equal to India, if not conquer it—remains strong. At other times, it will pretend to seek reconciliation. There is also the fear of internal disturbances in Pakistan leading to refugees coming into India. Given the trajectories of the two countries, this spectre could be India's nightmare. The alternative to this is not to seek a quick settlement with Pakistan. That will not work, as each time this is attempted, Islamabad portrays it as a victory. If India can accept the reality of why Pakistan was created by its leaders of the day, then it will become easier to deal with a permanent enemy. We should concentrate on strengthening our own economic and military strengths with this in mind. It is Pakistan that would need to have a normal relationship with India.

Besides, the decade ahead is going to be as tumultuous as it was when it began. This will have repercussions on the India–Pakistan equation as well. With the US moving out of an unsettled and violent Afghanistan, indications are that Turkey has shown willingness to be the security guarantor in Afghanistan. This would be in keeping with President Erdogan's ambitions for a Caliphate stretching from Turkey through Central Asia up to Afghanistan, and Pakistan would happily be a part of this Caliphate providing nuclear safety to the region. Turkey would not be doing this as a member of NATO, but as a kind of an Islamic vanguard. This is a situation that would not be acceptable to Iran and Saudi Arabia.

Given President Biden's inclination to re-engage with Iran—and with China having struck a twenty-five-year, multi-billion-dollar deal with Tehran—it is possible to visualize the complications of the Middle East and their fallout, which will reach our borders. Presently,

India's relations with most countries in the Middle East are cordial and practical, but this can change over time. Indian diplomacy and security will have to remain nimble and vigilant here. Our relations with the region have a bearing on Pakistan's attitude towards India.

For additional complications, the various Islamist groups—the ISIS, al Qaeda, the Taliban, the Tehrik-e-Taliban Pakistan, and the Lashkar-e-Taiba and Jaish-e-Mohammed—would operate with far greater freedom. In their early days, soon after its independence, some Pakistani ulema thought of their country as the lighthouse for Muslims across the world. Lately, this fusion of Islamic and military power has revived dreams of a new Medina, a new Caliphate, among Pakistan's leaders. Erdogan's ambitions in Turkey embellish this dream. Pakistan, as a threat to India, is to be viewed in terms of its intentions and the actions of its allies, rather than its own capacities.

A combined pressure from China and Turkey, both of whom support the Pakistani position, is very much likely in various ways. India will have to remain wary of a two-front subconventional cyber and intelligence attack. Terrorism using modern technology of the decade will be the other factor because the nature of evolving technology is not known. Miniaturized weapons and devices in the age of artificial intelligence and 5G technology will be the threats emanating from an enemy willing and able to resort even to biowar. Support from the West for India, beyond words of comfort, is also not guaranteed.

Pakistan may see in the recent developments in Iran, where the newly elected president is known for his radical beliefs, the evolving situation in Afghanistan with the radical Taliban taking control and, with China having a friendly interest in both, a feeling of having attained its strategic depth. Adventurism could be the result.

Over time, Islamabad's dependence on China will increase, with Beijing having its own strategic interests, thus plying Pakistan with military, economic and technological assistance. The CPEC may settle down to being functional over time—if Pakistan shows independent signs of recovery.

Therefore, though Pakistan itself may not be able to mount a serious military threat without suffering massive losses, together with others and operating under a nuclear umbrella, it could still retain its policy of jihad backed by twenty-first-century technology.

Notes

1. Venkat Dhulipala, *Creating a New Medina—State Power, Islam, and the Quest for Pakistan in Late Colonial India*, New Delhi: Cambridge University Press, 2015, pp. 4–5.
2. Austin Cline, 'Dar Al-Harb vs Dar Al-Islam', Learn Religions, 25 June 2019, https://www.learnreligions.com/dar-al-harb-vs-dar-al-islam-250224, accessed 20 June 2021. The issue of Dar-ul-Harb in the Indian context has been covered extensively by B.R. Ambedkar in his treatise *Pakistan or the Partition of India*, http://www.columbia.edu/itc/mealac/pritchett/00ambedkar/ambedkar_partition/, and commented upon by Dr Anand Ranganathan in his essay 'Ambedkar on Islam: The Story That Must Not Be Told', 14 April 2017, https://www.anandranganathan.com/2017/04/14/ambedkar-on-islam-the-story-that-must-not-be-told/
3. Raza Ahmed Rumi, 'Muslim Clerics Must Reject Notions of Non-Muslim Inferiority', Religious News Service (RNS), 15 December 2016, http://www.religionnews.com/transmission/muslim-clerics-must-reject-notions-of-non-muslim-inferiority/, accessed on 20 June 2021.
4. Robert W. Stern, *Democracy and Dictatorship in South Asia: Dominant Classes and Political Outcomes in India, Pakistan, and Bangladesh*, 2001, Greenwood Publishing Group, ISBN: 978-0-275-97041, Kindle Loc 702–710; and N.N. Mitra, ed., *Indian Annual Register*, 1946, vol. I, pp. 230–231.
5. Venkat Dhulipala, *Creating a New Medina—State Power, Islam, and the Quest for Pakistan in Late Colonial North India*, New Delhi: Cambridge University Press, 2015, p. 104.

6. Mufti Mohammed Taqi Usmani, *Mufti Mohammed Shafi—The Grand Mufti of Pakistan*, 2012 https://archive.org/details/mufti-muhammad-shafi-the-grand-mufti-of-pakistan-by-mufti-muhammad-taqi-usmani.
7. Kamran Bokhari, 'The Long Shadow of Deobandism in South Asia', *New/Lines Magazine*, https://newlinesmag.com/essays/the-long-shadow-of-deobandism-in-south-asia/?c=03, 23 November 2021, accessed 24 November 2021.
8. Interview with Arif Jamal on slain General Sanaullah and the pro-Taliban mindset of Pakistan Army, 28 September 2013, in New Age Islam, https://www.newageislam.com/interview/arif-jamal,-harvard-university/deobandi-taliban-and-the-extremist-mindset-of-pakistani-establishment--when-you-raise-vipers-in-your-backyard,-they-are-bound-to-bite-you,-says-arif-jamal-on-slain-pakistani-general-sanaullah/d/34447, accessed 25 November 2021.
9. Abdul Sayed, 'Islamic State's Pakistan Province Launches New Jihadist Magazine', The Jamestown Foundation, 4 June 2021, https://jamestown.org/program/islamic-states-pakistan-province-launches-new-jihadist-magazine-revealing-struggling-propaganda-effort/, accessed on 21 June 2021.
10. Husain Haqqani, 'Prophecy of Jihad in the Indian Subcontinent', https://www.hudson.org/research/11167-prophecy-the-jihad-in-the-indian-subcontinent, 27 March 2015, accessed on 12 July 2022. See also, Rasheed Kidwai, 'The Complex Narratives of "Ghazwa-e-Hind"', https://www.orfonline.org/research/complex-narratives-ghazwa-e-hind-56257/, 9 October 2019, accessed 8 July 2022.
11. Stockholm International Peace Research Institute, 'SIPRI Annual Report 2021', https://www.sipri.org/yearbook/2021, accessed 7 July 2021.
12. Ashutosh Sharma, 'Is Pakistan Treading the Uranium Route Again?', Ashutosh Sharma Medium Blog, 6 June 2021, https://ashu-ind281.medium.com/is-pakistan-treading-the-uranium-route-again-d466bf6e9d3, accessed 7 July 2021.

13. Dr Eqbal Ahmad, 'What After Strategic Depth', *Dawn*, 23 August 1998, https://eacpe.org/content/uploads/2014/04/What-After-Strategic-Depth.pdf, accessed 17 May 2021.
14. Jeff Smith, 'The Haqqani Network—The New Kingmakers in Kabul', War on the Rocks, 12 November 2021, https://warontherocks.com/2021/11/the-haqqani-network-afghanistan's-new-power-players/?s=03, accessed 12 November 2021.
15. Shruti Jargad, 'Lessons in Friendship: Explaining 70 Years of China–Pakistan Relations', Observer Research Foundation, 31 May 2021, https://www.orfonline.org/expert-speak/lessons-in-friendship-explaining-70-years-of-china-pakistan-relations/, accessed on 10 June 2021.
16. Jayadeva Ranade, 'China–Pakistan Strategic Nexus: Implications for India', Vivekananda International Foundation, 16 April 2021, https://www.vifindia.org/article/2021/april/16/china-pakistan-strategic-nexus-implications-for-india, accessed 8 June 2021.
17. Mohammed Ayoob, 'Is Pakistan Heading Down the Same Path as Afghanistan?', ASPI The Strategist, 23 November 2021, https://www.aspistrategist.org.au/is-pakistan-heading-down-the-same-path-as-afghanistan/, accessed 15 December 2021.
18. Sushant Sareen, 'Pakistan Budget 2021-22: Dodgy Data, Wild Assumptions', Observer Research Foundation, 16 June 2021, https://www.orfonline.org/expert-speak/pakistan-budget-2021-22-dodgy-data-wild-assumptions/, accessed 15 December 2021.
19. 'Pakistan's Future: Geopolitical Dilemmas, Economic Woes and Troubling Fault Lines', VIF–USANAS commentaries by Sushant Sareen and Tilak Devashar, 16 April 2021, https://usanasfoundation.com/webinar-on-pakistans-future-geopolitical-dilemmas-economic-woes-and-troubling-fault-lines, accessed 7 December 2021.

CHAPTER

3

Security Challenges: India–US Relations

ARUN SINGH

India–US relations till 2030 could see two terms of a Joe Biden presidency, or a term and/or a half after 2024 of a Republican or Democratic successor. Driven by the challenges of the moment and the need to galvanize a winning coalition for the elections, each president, and each administration, brings its own unique blend of domestic and international priorities and compulsions. In some cases, as 9/11 did for President George W. Bush in 2001, black swan events can impose their own decisive impact on the agenda.

The trend since Democratic president Bill Clinton's visit to India in 2000, however, would suggest that the consolidation of the India–US relationship should continue, despite any changes in the US presidency. Following the path-breaking Clinton visit—putting an end to the post-1998 Indian nuclear test-related US sanctions phase—it was a Republican, George W. Bush, who completely transformed the relationship through the civil nuclear cooperation agreement, finalized in 2008, and the removing of nuclear-power-related and other high-technology access restrictions on India. His successor, Barack Obama, a Democrat, declared India a major defence partner, articulated his support for India's permanent membership in the UN Security Council, advocated the country's membership of major international export control regimes, and made two (unprecedented for any of his predecessors) visits to India during his tenure—including the first-ever visit of a US president on India's Republic Day (in January 2015).

The erratic and unpredictable Republican, Donald Trump, while critical of India on trade issues, placed the country at strategic trade authorization Level 1 for high-level-technology releases—similar to closest allies and partners. The two countries declared a Comprehensive Global Strategic Partnership during his tenure; started a 2+2 ministerial-level dialogue of foreign and defence ministers—the third meeting was held in October 2020—revitalized the Quad, which included Japan and Australia, and raised it to ministerial-level meetings in September 2019 and October 2020. He also placed emphasis on security in the Indo-Pacific and projected India as a key partner in that strategy, while renaming the Hawaii-based US Pacific Command as the Indo-Pacific Command in May 2018; he also visited India in February 2020, addressed a 100,000-strong crowd in Ahmedabad, and had earlier joined the Indian prime minister at an unprecedented joint appearance before a crowd of 50,000 Indian-Americans in Houston in September 2019.

As a senator, President Joe Biden had been consistently supportive of the India relationship. In an interview with Rediff India Abroad in December 2006, he had said: 'My dream is that in 2020, the two closest nations in the world will be India and the United States.'[1] He was then the ranking member of the Senate Foreign Relations Committee (SFRC) and was set to become the chair of the committee in January 2007, since the Democrats had flipped the Senate in the November 2006 election. Senator Biden had also piloted—along with his Republican counterpart, committee Chairman Richard

Lugar—with an 85–12 vote, the enabling resolution that permitted the moving forward of the negotiations on the breakthrough India–US civil nuclear cooperation agreement. This was eventually signed in October 2008. In the intervening two years, which saw several challenges to the deal in both countries, Biden had been steadfast in his support for the deal in the US Senate, despite opposition from some members of his own party. They included the then senators Barack Obama and Hillary Clinton, who were influenced by concerns of the non-proliferation lobby. During an earlier incarnation as SFRC chair, in 2001, Biden had written a letter to President George W. Bush in August 2001, calling for the removal of economic sanctions against India, which had been imposed since the country's nuclear tests of May 1998.[2]

Speaking at the Mumbai Stock Exchange on 24 July 2013, during his visit to India as US vice president, Biden had reiterated President Obama's articulation that he saw the India–US relationship 'as a defining partnership in the century ahead'. At an event in August 2020, commemorating India's Independence Day, as the Democratic presidential nominee, he said he would 'stand with India' and that an administration led by him would 'confront the threats [India] faces in its own region and along its border'[3] and there would be no tolerance for terrorism, cross-border or otherwise. Speaking at the Hudson Institute on 9 July 2020, Antony Blinken, now the secretary of state, had said that 'strengthening and deepening the relationship with India is going to be a very high priority'.

Four factors have historically impacted India–US relations: the US perception of its global role and challenges, and the resulting choice of strategy and partners; the relevance of Pakistan in this context, and its search for political, military and strategic advantage against India; the prevalence of cooperation or the adversarial relationship in the assessment of China; the strength of the bilateral economic, defence and political relationship.

Global Vision

In the Biden years, the relationship will, no doubt, be impacted by the vision the new administration lays out for its global role and challenges, and the domestic compulsions affecting its foreign policies.

On 3 March 2021, the Biden White House issued an 'Interim National Security Strategic Guidance',[4] pending a more detailed policy document projected for later in the year. The document captured the essence of overall approach, articulated over the past year or so by candidate, and now president, Joe Biden, Secretary of State Antony Blinken, National Security Adviser (NSA) Jake Sullivan and Secretary of Defense Lloyd Austin, among others. It sought to distinguish itself from the Trump administration and provide the organizing principles as the incoming administration and its officials hit the ground running.

In the face of the mounting economic, technological and military challenges from China, the disrupted relations with allies in Europe and Asia—thanks to Trump—and the continued instability in West Asia, and the health and economic disruption caused by the COVID-19 pandemic, the document declared that 'this moment is an inflection point. We are in the midst of a fundamental debate about the future direction of our world.'

It gives an insight into the third major reordering of international relations that the US is attempting since the Second World War. The first was marked by the Cold War, 'containment' of the Soviet Union, global rivalry for influence against communism, establishment of multilateral institutions—such as the IMF, World Bank, General Agreement on Tariffs and Trade (GATT)—to deepen US/Western linkages with other economies. It ended, in US perception, in the defeat and dissolution of the Soviet Union in 1991. Of course, the period witnessed several failures for the US, including in Vietnam, Korea, etc.

The second reordering was marked by the US-led efforts to seal its global preponderance through globalization of production and trade, the declaration of the 'end of history' with the stage ostensibly set for an American-ushered 'liberal international order', including setting up the World Trade Organization, apart from coercively and militarily imposing its unilateral preferences in Serbia/Kosovo (1999) and Iraq (2003). It then turned to the use of economic sanctions against Iran, Russia, etc., when the limits of its military strategies became apparent. The US, again, cannot claim unvarnished success in this phase either, since its policies facilitated the rise of China as a rival; its military interventions in Iraq and Afghanistan did not lead to social and political stability; and under its watch Syria and Libya have become quagmires, and international terrorism continues to be a major threat. Domestically, within America, globalization induced stagnation in 30–40 per cent of the population, led to the rise of Trump, and the sharpening of systemic racism and polarization in US society.

The effort, in this third iteration, is to organize its allies and partners, and the rules for trade and technology access, to deal with China's rise and its unilateral assertions in the South and East China Seas, on the Line of Actual Control with India, in Europe and elsewhere; and to make foreign and trade policy choices more acceptable to the wider American society, to the electoral advantage of the Democratic party.

Search for a China Strategy

China was identified as the main global rival in Biden's interim report and was described as having 'rapidly become more assertive … the only competitor potentially capable of combining its economic, diplomatic, military and technological power to mount a sustained challenge to a stable and open international system'. On 3 March itself, previewing the release of the report, Blinken gave a speech titled 'A Foreign Policy for the American People', where he described the US relationship with China as the 'biggest geopolitical test of the 21st century'.[5]

In an article I wrote in February 2021 for the Institute of China Studies,[6] I had given a detailed assessment of the Biden administration's approach to the challenge from China, its search for a strategy factoring in cooperation, competition and confrontation, the prevarication of several of its European and Asian allies, and the likely Chinese countervailing strategies.

On 10 February 2021, Biden spoke, for the first time after his January 20 inauguration, with President Xi Jinping of China. This was after he had already spoken with several US allies in Europe (UK, France, Germany), Asia (Australia, Japan, Republic of Korea) and Prime Minister Narendra Modi of India. According to a White House press release, 'President Biden affirmed his priorities of protecting the American people's security, prosperity, health, and way of life, and preserving a free and open Indo-Pacific … underscored his fundamental concerns about Beijing's coercive and unfair economic practices, crackdown in Hong Kong, human rights abuses in Xinjiang, and increasingly assertive actions in the region, including toward Taiwan.'[7] Suggesting options for some agenda for cooperation, the note added: '… the two leaders also exchanged views on countering the COVID-19 pandemic, and the shared challenges of global health security, climate change, and preventing weapons proliferation'.

Earlier, on 4 February 2021, deliberately choosing the Department of State for his first visit to any Cabinet agency, to signal 'America is back', Biden had asserted that 'American leadership must meet this new moment of advancing authoritarianism, including the growing ambitions of China to rival the United States'.[8] In a subsequent interview to CBS, aired on 7 February, he said that he was not going to handle relations with China 'the way Trump did ... but there is going to be extreme competition ... We're going to focus on international rules of the road.'[9]

Following Secretary of State Antony Blinken's 5 February telephone call with Yang Jiechi, Chinese Communist Party's director of the Office of the Central Commission for Foreign Affairs, a spokesperson of the State Department said that 'Secretary Blinken stressed the United States will continue to stand up for human rights and democratic values, including in Xinjiang, Tibet, and Hong Kong, and pressed China to join the international community in condemning the military coup in Burma. The secretary reaffirmed that the United States will work together with its allies and partners in defense of our shared values and interests to hold the PRC accountable for its efforts to threaten stability in the Indo-Pacific, including across the Taiwan Strait, and its undermining of the rules-based international system.'[10] Each formulation—support for human rights and democracy, defence of shared values, stability in the Indo-Pacific, a rules-based international system—was clearly and deliberately chosen and projected to show, to both domestic and international audiences, that the incoming administration would press China on these issues, as it worked out its approach to a 'free, open and prosperous Indo-Pacific'.[11] Blinken also tweeted after the call, highlighting that he had raised the issues of concern.[12]

Earlier, on 23 January, within three days of the presidential inauguration, the spokesperson had said that 'the United States notes with concern the pattern of ongoing PRC attempts to intimidate its neighbors, including Taiwan', and urged 'Beijing to cease its military, diplomatic and economic pressure'.[13] This was in response to reports of Chinese military postures and movements in the Taiwan Strait.

During their confirmation hearings on 19 January, Blinken, Defense Secretary Austin and Treasury Secretary Janet Yellen had all sought to lay out the Biden administration's approach to relations with China. Austin had said that Beijing was 'the pacing challenge' for Washington DC, and expressed support for the 'Indo-Pacific' strategy and the Quad grouping (with Japan, Australia and India), activated during the Trump presidency.[14] Blinken said that he agreed with the substance of the previous administration's policies on China, including characterization of Chinese actions in Xinjiang as 'genocide', although there may appear to be differences in tactics and strategy.[15] Yellen said that the US needed to take on China's 'abusive, unfair and illegal practices', and accused it of 'dumping products, erecting trade barriers, giving illegal subsidies ... stealing intellectual property, engaging in practices that give it an unfair technological advantage, including forced technology transfers ... low labor and environmental standards'.[16]

Before Biden's call to Xi, a senior US official was cited in the media as indicating that America would maintain the technology access restrictions on China.[17] The Taiwan representative in Washington DC had a meeting in the State Department on 11 February 2021, and the East Asia and Pacific Bureau tweeted: '… the US is deepening ties with Taiwan, a leading democracy and important economic and security partner'.[18]

The Biden administration clearly feels it is under pressure to be seen as taking a tough line on China. President Trump had, during his campaign over 2015-16 and his presidential tenure over 2017–20, built up a narrative critical of Chinese economic, trade and intellectual property practices, and unilateral military assertions in the Indo-Pacific. A hard line on China could be a campaign issue in the 2022 mid-term Congressional elections, and the 2024 presidential one. Competition with China could also provide the peg for some bipartisan support in Congress for the administration's preferred economic, technology or infrastructure spending measures. Several bills to fund R&D and infrastructure are working or have worked their way through US Congress, citing the China challenge.

At the same time, the administration had also sought holds on court proceedings regarding the Trump ban on some Chinese apps, including TikTok and WeChat, and later rescinded them, although it ordered a more detailed review of data flows and other challenges from such apps. The commerce secretary, Gina Raimondo, refused to specifically commit during her confirmation hearing to keep Huawei on the entity blacklist, and her approval was initially put on hold by the Republican senator, Ted Cruz. In a subsequent response, Raimondo conveyed that the information she had seen so far did not suggest that Huawei should be removed from the list. The administration has said that it is reviewing the grounds for several of the late-term Trump decisions on China, but leaks have indicated that negotiating advantage provided by the current tariff and technology restrictions would not be unilaterally given up. At the same time, it was reported that the administration had withdrawn the Trump-era rule requiring educational institutions to report their hosting of the Chinese government-sponsored Confucius Institutes.[19]

The new team is clearly working its way through the strategy to be adopted in the global rivalry with China. For now, there seem to be similarities to the EU characterization of China (in its 2019 'EU–China—A strategic outlook' document) variously as 'a negotiating partner, with whom the EU needs to find a balance of interests, an economic competitor in the pursuit of technological leadership, and a systemic rival promoting alternative models of governance'.[20] In addition, the US now sees China as a geopolitical rival competing for economic, technological and military space in Asia first and elsewhere subsequently.

During his visit to the Pentagon on 10 February 2021, Biden had said, '... We need to meet the growing challenges posed by China to keep the peace and defend our interests in the Indo-Pacific and globally.'[21] He also referred to the Department of Defense-wide China task force Secretary Austin had set up 'to look at our strategy and operational concepts, technology, and force posture, and so much more ... drawing on civilian and military experts ... to provide ... recommendations ... on key priorities and decision points ... [to] chart a strong path forward on China-related matters'.[22] The task force has since completed its work and moved into the implementation phase.

The columnist David Ignatius wrote in *Washington Post* on 12 February that the administration, supported by Blinken and Sullivan, is exploring a plan for 'techno-democracies' to work together to prevent the dominance of global technology by an authoritarian China. The goal would be to 'set the rules and shape the norms that govern the use of technology',[23] and this would be accompanied by continued pressure on allies and partners against using Huawei for 5G and denying China access to the West's most advanced technologies. Another proposal was to set up an International Technology Finance Corporation to support technology development in the West or fostered by the West. It could be argued that we are seeing the germination of ideas for new multilateral structures or modification of rules in existing ones, such as the WTO, to respond to the challenge from China.

Earlier, Trump had thrown the gauntlet to China. The country was recognized as a major global rival in the National Security Strategy of December 2017. The document said: 'China seeks to displace the United States in the Indo-Pacific region, expand the reaches of its State-driven economic model, and reorder the region in its favor.'[24] It went on to list an entire litany of economic and geostrategic grievances against China, including its efforts to enhance its adversarial influence in Europe, Africa and the western hemisphere. The US National Defense Strategy of January 2018 had spoken in a similar vein.

This had been after some flip-flops in the earlier part of 2017. On 2 December 2016, as president elect, Trump had spoken over the phone with Taiwan president Tsai Ing-wen, the first such conversation at that level since 1979. The chill that followed in the US–China relations thawed a bit when 'First Daughter' Ivanka Trump visited the Chinese Embassy in Washington DC on 1 February 2017 for the Spring Festival celebrations. Trump then had an orchestrated phone call with Xi on 9 February 2017, after which it was put out by the White House that he agreed, at the request of President Xi, to honour the 'one China policy'.[25] Chinese president Xi was invited to the Trump Florida resort, Mar-a-Lago, in April, and the American president, in turn, visited China in November. The aim then was to get some cooperation on North Korea and some concessions on trade that Trump could sell domestically as a major win.

This approach had been supported by sections of the business and policy communities invested in the China relationship. Post December 2017, however, there was broadly a 'whole-of-government' approach with the vice president, secretary of state, secretary of defense, national security adviser, attorney general, FBI director and a host of subordinate officials coming out with a series of coordinated policy pronouncements critical of China. The exceptions to this were Treasury Secretary Steven Mnuchin and the adviser to the president, Jared Kushner, who were seen as continuing to focus on the advantages stemming from cooperation. Former US national security adviser John Bolton wrote in his memoir of his White House years that Trump, in a meeting with Xi, on the margins of a G20 summit in June 2019 in Osaka, asked his Chinese counterpart to buy more farm produce from the US to help him electorally.[26]

There was also a 'whole-of-society' approach with the administration's messages directed at US business, universities, governors, think tanks and the entertainment industry to recognize the dangers emanating from China and not give into blandishments, or short-term financial or profit needs. China's authoritarian system under President Xi was described as a challenge to US-espoused democratic values; its predatory economic and forced technology transfer practices were chronicled as a challenge to US technological leadership; its unilateral military assertions in the East and South China Sea and elsewhere were assessed as a challenge to a rules-based international order. A series of measures were adopted to deny technology and financing access targeting Chinese technology companies, those linked to its military, those involved in internationally illegal construction activity in the South China Sea, and constraints were placed on the operation of the Chinese media and Confucian Institutes in the US. Apart from this, its consulate in Houston was closed, sanctions were placed on Chinese officials involved in the crackdown and human rights violations in Hong Kong and Xinjiang, and higher-level government contacts were authorized with Taiwan.

The Obama–Biden administration, over 2009–16, had also vacillated on China, initially calling for 'strategic reassurance', but eventually gravitating to 'pivot' and 'rebalance', recognizing the growing economic, technological and military challenge, including because of Chinese unilateral assertions in the East and South China Seas, and militarization of certain features. Eventually, even the 'rebalance' could not be done with any impact, since the US remained preoccupied in Europe, on account of Russian actions in Ukraine, in West Asia, because of the continuing instabilities in Iraq and Syria, and tensions between Iran on the one hand and Israel, as well as Saudi Arabia and UAE on the other. The US also did not effectively challenge Chinese militarization of some South China

Sea features and limited itself to occasional 'freedom of navigation' sailings, challenging Beijing's claims.

Despite the broad convergence in the US system now about the challenge from China, there are, nevertheless, differences among US policymakers about the specifics of strategies to be adopted. Unlike the approach to the Soviet Union, 'containment' is ruled out because of deep Chinese interlinkage with the Western and global economy. In an article he had co-authored in the September/October 2019 issue of *Foreign Affairs*, National Security Adviser Jake Sullivan had argued that while the 'era of engagement with China has come to an unceremonious close … each will need to be prepared to live with the other as a major power … coexistence will involve elements of competition and cooperation'.[27]

The Biden team has also signalled that it would want to work out a common front with its allies and partners on China, so that the strategy could be more effective. This will not be easy, although, from the US perspective, there were gains made through articulation of common positions on China during the G7, US–EU and NATO summits in June 2021. America's European allies, including Germany and France, are canvassing against a solid anti-China front, hoping to keep opportunities open for their business interests. Speaking at an Atlantic Council event on 4 February 2021, French president Emmanuel Macron argued for 'strategic autonomy' for Europe in its China decisions.[28] The EU, at French and German prodding, finalized a Comprehensive Agreement on Investment with China in December 2020, despite NSA-designate Jake Sullivan tweeting at the time that the new administration would 'welcome early consultations with our European partners on our common concerns about China's economic practices'.[29] No doubt, the Trump years have left a lingering impact on the European assessment about US reliability. Western countries and their allies have also, so far, not shown a united front against China's selective targeting of Norway,

Sweden, Australia, Republic of Korea and Japan, at various times, through coercive economic measures. Europe has also, until now, not presented a united front against Chinese pressure on Lithuania, following its decision to allow a Taiwanese representative office. US and European businesses have not cut down on investments in China over 2020, despite the pandemic and various measures adopted by the Trump administration.

US–China relations have a come a long way since the initial outreach in 1971 as part of American attempt to sharpen the Sino-Soviet split to alter the global balance in its favour. In the India–Pakistan conflict that year, US sided fully with Pakistan, despite the genocide in East Pakistan (now Bangladesh), also as a signal to China that it stands with its friends and allies. The US approach for a long time was guided by the expectation that 'integrating China into the international mainstream' would lead to political and economic liberalization. Vice President Walter Mondale, during a visit to China in 1979, said that the 'rise of China is in US interest'. President Reagan, in a National Security Decision Directive (NSDD 120) issued in 1984, before the visit of Chinese Premier Zhao Ziyang, said that the 'US seeks a strong, secure and stable China that can be an increasing force for peace, both in Asia and the world'. Washington DC facilitated China's entry into the WTO in 2001, and funding from multilateral development institutions. Reagan had also authorized the sale of military equipment to China, increased cooperation to boost its civil nuclear programme, loosened control on exports of technology and helped establish research efforts in many cutting-edge areas. More than 70,000 US companies are present in China today and generate revenue of more than USD 550 billion. Chinese students in US universities number around 400,000 and make up a third of all foreign students.

China will also seek to influence the outcome of the debate in Washington DC. Speaking to the influential US National

Committee on US–China relations on 2 February 2021, Yang Jiechi said: 'Solidarity and enhanced coordination and cooperation are the only way ... to tackle global challenges effectively... [The] Trump administration adopted misguided policies.' He argued that attempts at 'decoupling' and a 'new Cold War' go against the trend of the times, and 'a new type of international relations characterized by mutual respect, fairness, justice and win-win cooperation' should be established, and efforts made 'for building a community with a shared future for mankind'.[30]

The US, under Biden, has to work out an approach towards China, mindful of the existing multifaceted interlinkages and advantages from cooperation, and yet, also remember the challenge to US pre-eminence from the Chinese political system and technological progress. Many of its allies, while concerned about China, do not see the same security threat and want to hedge, thus avoiding taking clear sides. In an article in *Foreign Affairs* in its July/August 2020 issue, Singapore prime minister Lee Hsien Loong wrote: 'Asia-Pacific countries do not wish to be forced to choose between the United States and China.'[31] Many US allies in the region, while concerned at growing Chinese military capacities, do not share American concerns on authoritarian models of governance.

The specifics of the new administration's China policy will, therefore, only congeal over time in response to emergent challenges, factoring in US domestic politics and reactions of its allies and partners. The era of 'engagement' is, however, over. The search is on for a new balance between cooperation, competition and confrontation. New architectures of security and other multilateral frameworks would be sought out or rules modified to influence the new game in an era of flux, uncertainty, across-the-board competition, multipolarity and intense great power rivalry. China will play its own hand too, through the Belt and Road Initiative (BRI), Asia Infrastructure Investment Bank (AIIB), New Development

Bank, Forum on China Africa Cooperation, the 1+17 (now 1+16 after Lithuania's exit in May 2021) process with a group of central and eastern European countries, and other outreach programmes in Latin America and West Asia.

Domestic political compulsions and American efforts to preserve its pre-eminence in the global context will drive a search for partners and institutional architectures in the 'Indo-Pacific' to 'shape the environment around the rise of China'. The 'Interim National Security Strategic Guidance' declared that the US will 'deepen partnership with India'. The new team has repeatedly emphasized the relevance of the Quad with Japan, India and Australia. On 12 March 2021, the four countries held a virtual summit meeting, the first time at this level, and in an early phase of the new administration, revealing the priority it attaches to this grouping in its Indo-Pacific strategy. Secretary of State Blinken had also held a foreign minister-level meeting in February. The March Summit resulted in several concrete decisions: a joint effort to produce one billion COVID-19-related vaccines for supply in the Indo-Pacific region, and setting up joint working groups on climate and on new and emerging technologies. An in-person Quad summit was held in Washington DC in September 2021.

These will provide India an opportunity to explore further deepening of defence cooperation and technology partnerships, and 'trusted, secure supply chain' relationships.

Trade and Economic Issues

One distinguishing feature of this guidance, particularly from that of even the Obama administration, was the way it elaborated on the planned approach to international economic engagements. Issued under the authority of the president, it asserts that the US, in its international engagements, would 'redefine America's interests in terms of working families' livelihoods, rather than corporate profits or aggregate national wealth'.

Clearly Joe Biden has absorbed the lesson from the Trump victory in 2016, with the latter having got seventy-four million votes in 2020, eleven million more than in 2016, despite all the criticism of his polarizing and whimsical behaviour and decision-making. In the globalization of production and trade, led by the US since the dissolution of Soviet Union in 1991, the American economy benefited in the aggregate. However, only the elite benefited, whereas 30–40 per cent of the population in the middle saw their wages stagnate, longevity come down, death rates and drug addiction go up. This was the segment drawn to Trump and has largely remained loyal to him since. He continues to dominate the Republican party, despite his electoral loss, and has raised prospects of a 2024 rerun.

At her confirmation hearing in US Senate on 25 February, the nominee for US trade representative, Katherine Tai, said that America would not be seeking only efficiency in global production through trade policies and negotiations, but would also be adopting a 'worker-centric' approach.[32] This echoed the comments of her Trump presidency predecessor, Robert Lighthizer, who had criticized the unbridled pursuit of efficiency for offshoring of US jobs.

The Interim Guidance goes on to declare that the US would 'only pursue new trade deals after … investments in American workers and communities'. During his presidential campaign, Biden had repeatedly promised that any new trade deals would come only after an increase in competitiveness of the American worker through investments in infrastructure, skills and technology. In his 3 March 2021 speech, Secretary of State Blinken had articulated that US would 'fight for every American job, and for the rights, protections and interests of all American workers'.

While not adding new tariffs so far, unlike Trump, Biden has not rescinded the earlier ones as yet either, except one worked out through mutual concessions with the EU, and has issued executive orders calling for 'Buy American'.

The guidance also says that 'in today's world, economic security is national security'. This is a theme oft-repeated by the National Security Adviser Jake Sullivan. There is an intensified search for 'trusted, secure supply chains', to break the Chinese current advantages in rare earths, pharmaceutical ingredients and emerging technology areas such as AI and 5G.

Interestingly, in response to a question, US Trade Representative (USTR) Catherine Tai said that she preferred the term 're-shoring' to 'onshoring' since the former allowed for trusted supply-chain relationships. In March itself, the office of the United States trade representative had issued a fact sheet on the president's Trade Agenda, asserting, inter alia:

> President Biden will pursue a fair international trading system that promotes inclusive economic growth and reflects America's universal values ... [T]rade policy must respect the dignity of work and value Americans as workers and wage-earners, not only as consumers ... [T]rade agenda will support long-term investments to strengthen domestic production of essential medical equipment, expand industrial capacity and bolster preparation to tackle future public health crises ... Trade must protect and empower workers, drive wage growth, and lead to better economic outcomes for all Americans ... Workers will have a seat at the table as the Biden Administration develops new trade policies that promote equitable economic growth by including strong, enforceable labour standards in trade agreements that protect workers' rights and increase economic security ... [T]rade agenda will include the negotiation and implementation of strong environmental standards that are critical to a sustainable climate pathway ... The Biden Administration recognizes that China's coercive and unfair trade practices harm American workers,

threaten our technological edge, weaken our supply chain resiliency, and undermine our national interests ... Policies that promote equitable global economic growth and increase global demand benefit American workers, manufacturers, farmers, ranchers, fishers and service providers by expanding the customer base. The trade agenda will include a review of existing trade programs to evaluate their contribution to equitable economic development, including whether they reduce wage gaps, increase worker unionization, promote safe workplaces, tackle forced labor and exploitative labor conditions, and lead to the economic empowerment of women and underrepresented communities.[33]

Speaking at an AFL-CIO (American Federation of Labor and Congress of Industrial Organizations) townhall on 10 June 2021, Tai reiterated that US would follow a worker-centric trade policy, and that workers would be at the table when trade negotiations are pursued. These comments reveal the trend in the Biden presidency's approach to trade and economic relationships.

There is an inherent opportunity for India to further rework its geo-economic engagement with the US, to its economic and geopolitical advantage. The two countries should consider starting a strategic commercial dialogue, going beyond the USTR's normal preoccupation with market access issues based on current patterns of production. New areas of supportive interactions should be explored in emerging technologies, through in-depth dialogue between business and governments in both countries. The US could benefit from India's skilled workforce and tech entrepreneurs in meeting Chinese competition. Further, Indian IT companies have built up expertise in skilling and in setting competency standards, including for skill sets relevant for new and emerging technologies. They could partner with the American government and other entities in contributing to skill development in high-tech areas where the US continues to be short of workers relative to demand. India's fintech sector has made significant advances as well, including towards inclusivity, and could contribute to taking on monopolies in the US and helping underserved communities.

The existing Global Comprehensive Strategic Partnership provides the framework for trusted, secure supply chain arrangements. The US has variously described India as a 'pre-eminent US partner in the Indo-Pacific',[34] a 'net provider of security' in the region, and that it sees the rise of India to be in its own interest. It should, therefore, allow sufficient space for Indian industry in the new reordering. As India looks to expand output through production-linked incentives, or to attract foreign investment, access to major markets would incentivize business. The new US approach also provides India with potential opportunity to regain ground lost earlier, including to China, in the uncritical rush towards globalization and cost reduction, unmindful of security, equity and employment.

At the Tai hearing, Senator John Cornyn of Texas, co-chair of the Senate India Caucus, called for building a strategic economic partnership with the country. The moment must be seized by both sides. Otherwise, we will remain bogged down, like the senators from Montana, Louisiana and Washington did, in talking about market access for apples, pulses and shrimps. The growing strategic partnership will then not have the ballast of a more solid economic interlinkage.

Afghanistan/Pakistan

Developments in Afghanistan will also have a bearing on India's security. The guidance document had reiterated that 'the United States should not, and will not, engage in "forever wars"', and that the country would work to 'responsibly end America's longest war in Afghanistan, while ensuring that Afghanistan does not again become a safe haven for terrorist attacks against the United States'.

The US withdrew all its military troops from Afghanistan by 31 August 2021, marked by a chaotic and rushed exit, a collapse of the government structure it had supported since 2001, a military takeover by the Taliban, now dominated by hard-line elements, including designated terrorists with earlier and continuing links with the al Qaeda. Questions remain about how effectively it will be able to tackle subsequent terrorism-related challenges through an 'over the horizon' presence.

As vice president in the Obama administration, Biden had pushed for a substantial draw down of US military presence. President Obama eventually did not take this advice, mindful of the negative political blowback for him from any subsequent terrorist attack on US soil, or a collapse of the Afghan governance structure that the Americans had spent 'blood and treasure' building since 2001. Trump, on the other hand, had come into office promising to end US military presence in Afghanistan. Even he could not bring the number of troops below 2,500—despite an agreement with the Taliban—since there was not much progress in the intra-Afghan reconciliation talks, and Taliban violence against Afghan civilians and government targets had continued.

Biden had inherited this situation, including a 1 May ostensible deadline for the withdrawal of all US troops as per the US–Taliban agreement. He had indicated that the 1 May deadline was not feasible, but also said that he would want US troops out of Afghanistan before the end of the year, and subsequently set a deadline for September. The administration indicated that it was reviewing the specific commitments made under the agreement by both sides. Clearly, it was in a bind. If it withdrew, as it eventually did, without progress in reconciliation, and with continued violence, there would be no guarantee that its counterterrorism requirements would be addressed. If the US-supported Afghan governance structure collapsed, as it eventually did, it would majorly dent US credibility in the international context.

Today, its rivals, Russia and China, are calculating their next steps in the global competition, assessing eroding US political will and credibility for any sustained force posture and engagement. Russia has since put forward proposals for European security, seen as a pushback against NATO actions and enlargement since 1997. On the other hand, if the US had not withdrawn, it would have owned the next phase of the strategy in Afghanistan. The Taliban had indicated that if the Americans did not meet its deadline, it might once again start attacking US forces. The country would then have to also escalate and counterattack.

To bypass the impasse, the US had come up with three planks of a new approach: calling for an intra-Afghan summit in Turkey, with the presence of top leaders of all major factions; asking the secretary-general of the United Nations to convene a meeting of foreign ministers of the US, Russia, China, India, Iran and Pakistan to get a regional buy into the process; presenting a US-drafted reconciliation framework document to speed up negotiations between the Taliban, the Afghan government and others. In a letter to the then Afghan president Ashraf Ghani, Secretary of State Blinken sought to generate pressure on him for compromise by writing that 'we are considering full withdrawal of our forces by 1 May, as we consider other options' and added to it by suggesting that after US withdrawal 'the security situation will worsen and that the Taliban could make rapid territorial gains'.[35] Ghani had resisted power sharing with the Taliban or the creation of an interim governance structure, arguing that any such framework should emerge only through an election. Sensing the environment, he had proposed a ceasefire, setting up of an interim government and an early election for a new government in Kabul. The Taliban did not accept this framework, and essentially waited for full US withdrawal even as it escalated attacks on the ground while not directly targeting American forces.

The US and others are now grappling with the need to provide humanitarian assistance, given the dire social and economic situation in Afghanistan, while not working through or strengthening the Taliban regime, which is not inclusive of minority ethnic groups, has placed restrictions on education of girls and the ability of women to work, and has not shown a clear break with terrorist groups.

The positive developments in India–US relations, and the political and economic equities New Delhi had developed within Afghanistan since 2001, were reflected in India being included in the regional group that had been suggested by US. However, the American withdrawal, without a stable reconciliation framework, has created negative security implications for India.

Pakistan did not find any mention in the guidance. Historically, the US–Pakistan relationship has oscillated between incentivizing and pressurizing, depending on whether the US is valuing or is frustrated by the cooperation it is getting from Pakistan for its objectives. This was done initially against the Soviet Union, and later in the Afghanistan context. Today, Pakistan will be valued if it can deliver on US terrorism-related concerns. It will be criticized, and demands will be made within the American system, for scaling back support if it fails. India will need to carefully watch as this dynamic plays out, making sure that it is able to preserve the US relationship and prevent Pakistan from getting any assurances against India's interests. The US will continue to find a need to engage with Pakistan because of its nuclear weapon capabilities, and the presence of terrorist groups in the Afghanistan–Pakistan region. There were reports earlier of the US seeking some presence in Pakistan to enable it to better respond to threats from Afghanistan. In an op-ed in the *Washington Post* on 21 June 2021, the then Pakistan PM, Imran Khan, said that '… Pakistan is ready to be a partner for peace in Afghanistan with the

United States—but as US troops withdraw', Islamabad would not give bases for operations in Afghanistan. Otherwise, he claimed convergence with US interests in seeking stability in Afghanistan and terrorism-related threats.

US-Russia Relations

The Biden administration had explored the possibility of bringing in more stability in its relationship with Russia. The president took the initiative to schedule a meeting with President Vladimir Putin in Geneva on 16 June 2021. In separate press conferences after the meeting, both he and Putin avoided sharply polemical tones, acknowledged the continuing differences, but also a willingness to find a common ground on areas such as arms control. There were, however, no immediate prospects of a rollback of any of the sanctions imposed by the US. In fact, in several Sunday morning TV appearances on 20 June that year, NSA Sullivan indicated that more sanctions were in the works, based on an earlier pipeline, related to Ukraine, human rights issues, etc.

Disagreements on Ukraine, perceptions related to the Russian cyber hacking of US political, economic and government entities, and the treatment of political opponents, will hinder any overall positive movement, especially since these are now politically charged issues in the US, closely monitored by members of Congress and others. Russia had recalled its ambassador for 'consultations' after Biden referred to Putin as a 'killer' in a TV interview, but there was agreement on his return after the Biden–Putin meeting. There had also been a build-up of Russian forces along the Ukrainian border that year, prompting statements of concern from the US, France and Germany; but it was drawn down as the date of the Biden–Putin meeting neared.

US–Russia relations entered an intensified adversarial phase with the Russian invasion of Ukraine on 24 February 2022. US has used this challenge to its global and European standing by consolidating NATO, reinforcing trans-Atlantic coordination, providing political support and arming Ukraine to prevent any easy Russian victory and seeking to weaken Russia in the medium to longer term with severe financial, trade and technology sanctions. At this stage, it does not seem likely that the US will be able to normalize relations with a Putin-led Russian governance structure.

This development posed a test also to the US–India relationship, since India, with its defence cooperation and historical relationship with Russia, did not support sanctions against Russia, did not go along with US-led votes critical of Russia in multilateral structures including in United Nations Security Council and General Assembly, even while it distanced itself from Russian actions by repeatedly expressing support for 'sovereignty and territorial integrity' of countries and calling for dialogue and end to conflict.

Recognizing the primacy of the longer term, Chinese challenge to its global and Asia-Pacific interests and role, despite current Russian actions challenging the European security architecture, the US administration has sought to manage the current differences with India keeping in view the longer-term convergences. In recent comments, the US national security adviser has said that they are playing the 'long game' with India. The secretary of state has said that India's relations with Russia had developed with India when US was not willing to be that kind of a partner, but was now willing to take the relationship to a deeper level of confidence.

However, the developments in the Russia–Ukraine context, its impact on Russia's relations with Europe and the US, would need to be watched closely. There are voices in Europe calling for due weight to be given to Russia's security concerns, or opposing further sanctions on Russia, which are also causing energy and inflationary challenges to European countries themselves and globally. However, if the slide in Russia's relations with the West is not mitigated early enough, there will be growing challenges for India in its attempts to balance its equities on both sides.

Confrontational US–Russia relations will be a challenge for India, since major defence purchases from Russia, including of the S-400, will come under adversarial scrutiny, especially as New Delhi does more and more business with the US in the framework of the Indo-Pacific, and gets more defence supplies, technology and intelligence sharing. Russia, on account of its own China-related strategies, has continued to oppose any strategic framework based on the 'Indo-Pacific' construct. Moscow's articulation appears aimed at questioning the need for or advantage in the consolidating India–US relationship. Russia would be worried about a potential further decline in its relative share of arms supplies to India, and see the consolidating US partnerships globally as a challenge in its own relative position vis-à-vis America.

It would be important for the US to recognize its own interest in ceding geopolitical space to India—mindful of its historical relationship with Russia, with nearly 60 per cent of the country's defence inventory being of Russian origin—so as not to reinforce history-based suspicions and perceptions in India of the US being an unreliable partner. A recent American Seventh Fleet 'freedom of navigation' activity off Lakshadweep, unilaterally asserting the US interpretation of international law, in violation of Indian provisions, and making a public statement of it, has reminded New Delhi of past US challenges to India's national interests.

Some Jarring Notes

India would also need to watch carefully how the US advocacy on climate change plays out. Biden had called for a summit of major economies and 'emitters' on 22 April 2021.[36] His Cabinet-level special envoy, John Kerry, has been calling for 'enhanced ambitions'. India has been proactive in rapidly increasing renewable energy, including wind and solar, in its energy mix. It has also taken several initiatives, including the International Solar Alliance and Coalition for Disaster Resilient Infrastructure. As the debate progresses on this, it would be important that the principle of 'common but differentiated' responsibility is kept firmly in view, along with that of historical emissions, climate justice, and the need of developing countries for access to technology and finance for mitigation and adaptation.

In sections of the Democratic party in the US, there is criticism of some of the actions of the Indian government on the Citizenship (Amendment) Act, National Register of Citizens, Jammu and Kashmir, etc. The US faces its own challenges of systemic racism and voter suppression. The two governments would need to navigate any differences keeping in mind the overall strategic convergence. The Biden team has said that any differences on these issues would be addressed as a 'dialogue among friends'.

Prognosis

The overarching priority for the US to deal with the economic, technological and military challenge from China will provide the convergence for the advancing of the US–India Comprehensive Global Strategic Partnership. Businesses and governments in both countries could seize this moment to build new, trusted and secure supply chain relationships, including in critical and emerging technologies. This would deepen economic interlinkages to the geo-economic advantage of both. Both would also gain by managing their differences on Russia and Afghanistan by showing understanding for their varying domestic and geopolitical compulsions.

Despite his victory in November 2020, Biden faces some domestic headwinds. The Senate is evenly divided, and conservative

Democratic senators are joining Republicans in holding back progress on some of the progressive agenda that Biden supports on the economy, voting rights, etc. There is a growing humanitarian and political crisis of illegal immigrants from Guatemala, Honduras, and El Salvador on the US–Mexico border, prompting criticism of the administration as being 'soft' on the issue. The former president Donald Trump continues to dominate the Republican party and Republican fundraising. Republican-majority legislatures in several states have passed laws restricting voting facilitation and sustaining the partisan projections of a 'stolen election' in 2020. There is talk of Democrats losing control of the Senate and perhaps even the House in the 2022 mid-term elections. Trump could make a renewed bid for the presidency in 2024.

Should all this happen, there would be another turnaround in many of the US domestic and foreign policies. But its approach on China, Russia and Afghanistan–Pakistan can be expected to continue. So would its approach to the India relationship, which has enjoyed bipartisan consensus since 2000, through Republican and Democratic administrations.

Notes

1. Aziz Haniffa, 'In 2020 the Two Closest Nations in the World Will Be India and US', Rediff.com, 5 December 2006, https://www.rediff.com/news/2006/dec/05inter.htm, accessed 13 February 2021.
2. George Gedda, 'Biden Pushes End to India Sanctions', Associated Press, 28 August 2001, https://apnews.com/article/7db49bd4371acb8b387e8a46f81f6b40, accessed 13 February 2021.
3. Sriram Lakshman, 'Joe Biden, Kamala Harris Reach Out to Indian Americans on Independence Day', *The Hindu*, 16 August 2020, https://www.thehindu.com/news/international/joe-biden-kamala-harris-reach-out-to-indian-americans-on-independence-day/article32367161.ece, accessed 13 February 2021.

4. Joe Biden, 'Interim National Security Strategic Guidance', 3 March 2021, https://www.whitehouse.gov/wp-content/uploads/2021/03/NSC-1v2.pdf, accessed 21 March 2021.
5. Antony Blinken, 'A Foreign Policy for the American People', 3 March 2021, https://www.state.gov/a-foreign-policy-for-the-american-people/, accessed 21 March 2021.
6. Arun K. Singh, 'US–China Relations in the Post-Trump Phase', ICS Analysis, no 128, February 2021, https://www.icsin.org/uploads/2021/02/24/5d73d221fbebf85d3187a344502e132f.pdf, accessed 21 March 2021.
7. 'Readout of President Joseph R. Biden, Jr. Call with President Xi Jinping of China', White House, https://www.whitehouse.gov/briefing-room/statements-releases/2021/02/10/readout-of-president-joseph-r-biden-jr-call-with-president-xi-jinping-of-china/, accessed 13 February 2021.
8. 'Remarks by President Biden on America's Place in the World', White House, https://www.whitehouse.gov/briefing-room/speeches-remarks/2021/02/04/remarks-by-president-biden-on-americas-place-in-the-world/, accessed 13 February 2021.
9. 'Biden Says "I Hope to God I Live Up To" the Job of Being President', interview by Norah O'Donnel, CBS Evening News, CBS, 8 February 2021, https://www.cbsnews.com/news/biden-interview-president-live-up-to-job/, accessed 13 February 2021.
10. 'Secretary Blinken's Call with PRC Director Yang', United States Department of State, https://www.state.gov/secretary-blinkens-call-with-prc-director-yang/, accessed 13 February 2021.
11. 'New Zealand Waitangi Day', *Mirage News*, 6 February 2021, https://www.miragenews.com/new-zealand-waitangi-510651/, accessed 13 February 2021. See also Ananth Krishnan, 'US, China Spar as Top Diplomats Hold First Call', *The Hindu*, 6 February 2021.
12. Antony Blinken (@SecBlinken) tweeted, 'In my call with my counterpart in Beijing, Yang Jiechi, I made clear the U.S. will defend our national interests, stand up for our democratic values …', Twitter, 6 February 2021, https://twitter.com/SecBlinken/status/1357886400675393537.
13. Ned Price, 'PRC Military Pressure Against Taiwan Threatens Regional Peace and Stability', United States Department of State, https://www.

state.gov/prc-military-pressure-against-taiwan-threatens-regional-peace-and-stability/, accessed 13 February 2021.
14. 'Confirmation Hearing of Lloyd Austin to be Secretary of Defense', United States Senate Armed Services Committee, 19 January 2021, https://www.armed-services.senate.gov/imo/media/doc/Austin_01-19-21.pdf, accessed 13 February 2021.
15. 'Confirmation Hearing of Antony J. Blinken, Nominee for Secretary of State', United States Senate Committee on Foreign Relations, 19 January 2021, https://www.foreign.senate.gov/imo/media/doc/011921_Blinken_Testimony.pdf, accessed 13 February 2021.
16. 'Confirmation Hearing of Dr Janet Yellen for Secretary of the Treasury', United States Senate Finance Committee, 19 January 2021, https://www.finance.senate.gov/imo/media/doc/JLY%20opening%20testimony%20%20(1).pdf, accessed 13 February 2021.
17. Michael Martina and David Brunnstrom, 'U.S. to Look at More Restrictions on Tech Exports to China', Yahoo Finance, 11 February 2021, https://finance.yahoo.com/news/u-look-more-restrictions-tech-022929685.html, accessed 13 February 2021.
18. East Asian and Pacific Affairs Bureau (@USAsiaPacific) tweeted, 'Great to see @TECRO_USA Rep. Bi-khim Hsiao today. The U.S. is deepening ties with Taiwan, a leading democracy and important economic and security partner.' Twitter, 11 February 2021, https://twitter.com/USAsiaPacific/status/1359612332096315393.
19. Brendan Cole, 'GOP Slams Biden Reversal of Trump-era Rule Targeting Chinese "Propaganda" on Campuses', *Newsweek*, 10 February 2021, https://www.newsweek.com/china-confucius-institute-propaganda-tom-cotton-1568157, accessed 13 February 2021.
20. European Commission, 'Joint Communication: EU–China—A Strategic Outlook', 12 March 2019, https://ec.europa.eu/info/sites/info/files/communication-eu-china-a-strategic-outlook.pdf, accessed 13 February 2021.
21. 'Remarks by President Biden to Department of Defense Personnel', White House, https://www.whitehouse.gov/briefing-room/speeches-remarks/2021/02/10/remarks-by-president-biden-to-department-of-defense-personnel/, accessed 13 February 2021.

22. Ibid.
23. David Ignatius, 'Biden's Ambitious Plan to Push Back Against Techno-Autocracies', *The Washington Post,* 12 February 2021, https://www.washingtonpost.com/opinions/bidens-ambitious-plan-to-push-back-against-techno-autocracies/2021/02/11/2f2a358e-6cb6-11eb-9ead-673168d5b874_story.html, accessed 13 February 2021.
24. Donald Trump, 'National Security Strategy of the United States of America', December 2017, http://nssarchive.us/wp-content/uploads/2020/04/2017.pdf, accessed 13 February 2021.
25. 'Readout of the President's Call with President Xi Jinping of China', White House Archives, https://trumpwhitehouse.archives.gov/briefings-statements/readout-presidents-call-president-xi-jinping-china/, accessed 13 February 2021.
26. Julian Borger and Maanvi Singh, 'Trump Was Willing to Halt Criminal Investigations as "Favor" to Dictators, Bolton Book Says', *The Guardian,* 18 June 2020, https://www.theguardian.com/us-news/2020/jun/17/john-bolton-book-trump-china-accusations-dictators, accessed 13 February 2021.
27. Kurt M. Campbell and Jake Sullivan, 'Competition without Catastrophe: How America Can Both Challenge and Coexist with China', *Foreign Affairs,* September/October 2019, https://www.foreignaffairs.com/articles/china/competition-with-china-without-catastrophe, accessed 13 February 2021.
28. 'President Macron on His Vision for Europe and the Future of Transatlantic Relations', Atlantic Council, 4 February 2021, https://www.atlanticcouncil.org/news/transcripts/transcript-president-macron-on-his-vision-for-europe-and-the-future-of-transatlantic-relations/, accessed 13 February 2021.
29. Jake Sullivan (@jakejsullivan), 'The Biden–Harris administration would welcome early consultations with our European partners on our common concerns about China's economic practices', Twitter, 22 December 2020, https://twitter.com/jakejsullivan/status/1341180109118726144.
30. 'Full Text of Yang Jiechi's Speech at the Dialogue with National Committee on US–China Relations', China.org.cn, 3 February 2021,

http://www.china.org.cn/world/2021-02/03/content_77184203.htm, accessed 13 February 2021.
31. Lee Hsien Loong, 'The Endangered Asian Century: America, China, and the Perils of Confrontation', July/August 2020, https://www.foreignaffairs.com/articles/asia/2020-06-04/lee-hsien-loong-endangered-asian-century, accessed 13 February 2021
32. 'Hearing to Consider the Nomination of Katherine C. Tai, of the District of Columbia, to be United States Trade Representative, with the Rank of Ambassador Extraordinary and Plenipotentiary', United States Senate Committee on Finance, 25 February 2021, https://www.finance.senate.gov/imo/media/doc/Katherine%20Tai%20Opening%20Statement%20for%202.25.2021.pdf, accessed 28 February 2021.
33. 'Fact Sheet: 2021 President's Trade Agenda and 2020 Annual Report', Office of the United States Trade Representative, https://ustr.gov/sites/default/files/files/reports/2021/2021%20Trade%20Agenda/Online%20PDF%202021%20Trade%20Policy%20Agenda%20and%202020%20Annual%20Report.pdf, accessed 9 March 2021.
34. 'Secretary Blinken's Call with Indian External Affairs Minister Jaishankar', United States Department of State, 29 January 2021, https://www.state.gov/secretary-blinkens-call-with-indian-external-affairs-minister-jaishankar/, accessed 9 March 2021.
35. Antony Blinken, 'Letter to Ashraf Ghani', https://tolonews.com/pdf/02.pdf, accessed 9 March 2021.
36. 'US: Joe Biden Signs Climate Directives, Announces April Summit', Deutsche Welle, 27 January 2021, https://www.dw.com/en/us-joe-biden-signs-climate-directives-announces-april-summit/a-56365062, accessed 28 February 2021.

CHAPTER

4

Russia and Eurasia in India's Calculus

P.S. RAGHAVAN

It is only over the past two decades or so that a recognition of maritime opportunities and challenges has permeated India's foreign policy and strategic thinking. China's naval and economic expansion into the Indian Ocean, the rhetoric surrounding India's Indo-Pacific engagement with the US and, more recently, the military face-off across the Line of Actual Control with China, have sharpened the focus on the country's strategic challenges in the maritime domain. At the same time, they have somewhat dimmed public consciousness of the cross-cutting nature of the strategic challenges for India in the Eurasian landmass to its north and west.

The Setting

The India–China military confrontation, which erupted across the Line of Actual Control in mid-2000, triggered a major debate on India's foreign policy options. As the face-off dragged on for months, sections of the media and academia urged New Delhi to make the 'strategic choice' of an unequivocal alignment with the US as the only viable course to meet the Chinese challenge. The rhetoric surrounding the Quad dialogue (India, US, Japan and Australia) and the Malabar naval exercises (now including the same four countries) has reinforced this thought, combined with the perception—of fairly wide prevalence in the Indian strategic community—that Russia, weakened by Western sanctions and a flagging economy, was too beholden to China to be of any help to India vis-à-vis that country.

At the same time, in the midst of tensions with China, and when India was still in the grip of a devastating second wave of COVID-19, India's defence and external affairs ministers travelled to Moscow for multilateral meetings. The former attended the 'Victory Day' anniversary of the conclusion (for Russia) of the Second World War. It was a signal of the importance that the Indian government attached to India–Russia relations; more immediately, it provided the opportunity for the defence minister to discuss with his Russian counterpart bilateral military–technical cooperation. It was reported that the discussions included the prospects of fast-tracking deliveries of the S-400 air defence system, and supplies of MiG-29 and Su-30 fighter aircraft. The minister publicly confirmed that his Russian hosts had reassured him that current contracts would not only be executed, but would be expedited.

There were some indications of Chinese pressure on Russia to hold military supplies to India in abeyance as long as the military face-off continued, since Beijing is also a strategic partner of Moscow. Russia quietly let it be known that the supplies to India would continue. Meetings of the Shanghai Cooperation Organization and of the foreign ministers of Russia, India and China (RIC) in Moscow provided the opportunity for bilateral meetings of the Indian and Chinese defence ministers and of the foreign ministers on 'neutral' territory.

The dichotomy between India's engagements with Russia and China was highlighted by the signals from Russia of an intensification of Russia–China relations. President Vladimir Putin spoke expansively in October 2020 of Russia sharing military technologies with China, adding that a military alliance could not be ruled out, though it was not immediately on the agenda.[1] This was read as a warning to India, as well as to the US, and did not go down well in India. New Delhi's irritation was heightened by Russian foreign minister Sergey Lavrov's public remarks about India being drawn into 'anti-China games', by devious Western 'Indo-Pacific strategies', to undermine the India–Russia partnership.[2] Such public statements soured the atmosphere of Lavrov's visit to Delhi in April 2021, when both sides seemed to be merely going through the motions of declaring the robustness of their partnership. Lavrov went on to Pakistan from Delhi, received a warm reception and reiterated Russian concerns about the creation of a 'disruptive US-led geopolitical structure' in the Asia-Pacific.

A reconciliation of perspectives was signalled by telephone conversations between the Russian president and the Indian prime minister in April and September and their decision to establish a 2+2 foreign and defence minister dialogue mechanism. During a visit to Moscow by the Indian external affairs minister in July, discussions covered the long-planned connectivity project from India to Afghanistan and Central Asia through Iran, as well as resource-development projects in the Russian Far East, and a Free Trade Agreement between India and the Eurasian Economic Union. The chaos in Afghanistan, following the precipitate withdrawal of NATO forces from that country, provided more common ground for cooperation. Finally, the summit meeting in December 2021 between President Putin and Prime Minister Narendra Modi sought to restore the narrative of strong India–Russia relations.

Over the last two decades, the course of US–Russia relations has impacted the India–Russia engagement in many ways. In the first decade of this millennium, India–Russia relations added new dimensions, contemporaneously with a growing vibrancy in India–

US relations, despite the growing friction between America and Russia. After the Russian annexation of Crimea in 2014, when US–Russia relations degenerated to new levels of acrimonious hostility, India came under pressure from both Russia and the US to take positions in support of one against the other. India did not subscribe to the US sanctions against Russia, but the secondary sanctions legislation, CAATSA, posed a direct threat to India–Russia defence cooperation. The outcome of the ongoing confrontation between Russia and the US in Ukraine will influence the course of India's relations with both the countries.

The India–Russia Partnership

Relations between the two countries flow from the decades-old India–USSR relations, which were shaped by Cold War equations. Russia's political support for India at critical times and its military supplies were particularly valuable. After a brief hiatus in the post-Cold War years, India and Russia declared (in 2000) a Strategic Partnership, which included a commitment to economic and political multipolarity in the world order, shared perspectives on major global issues and intensified defence cooperation. The last involved Indian purchases of advanced Russian weapons systems, including fighter aircraft, tanks, artillery, armoured vehicles, missile systems, naval vessels and submarines. In later years, more sophisticated weapons platforms and technologies were added to the mix, including through joint development and production. The joint venture BrahMos, which started with the manufacture of an anti-ship supersonic missile system designed in Russia, has since developed more advanced missile systems in India for use in land, sea and air. The nature of weapons suites and technologies transferred by Russia remains shrouded in secrecy, but it is known that no other country supplies to India the level of military technologies that Russia does.

Soviet/Russian-origin weapons and equipment form the backbone of India's present military capability—in quantitative terms, a dependence of 60–70 per cent. Over the next several decades, their operational efficacy, including repair, refit and upgrades, will need Russian involvement. This logic drives India to more defence purchases from Russia, alongside strong efforts over at least a decade to diversify sources of military acquisitions. The latest arms transfers report of the Stockholm International Peace Research Institute (SIPRI) records that Russia supplied 46 per cent of India's arms imports in the five-year period between 2017 and 2021. Though this proportion is falling, India's second-largest supplier, France, had only a 27 per cent share, with the US at third, with 12 per cent.[3]

Energy is another sector of expanding India–Russia cooperation. Since 2000, Indian companies have invested an estimated USD 15 billion in hydrocarbons projects in Siberia and the Russian Far East. Further investments of USD 2-3 million are reported to be under negotiation. India's draft Arctic policy indicates interest in Indian presence in the Russian Arctic, through participation in renewable and non-renewable energy projects. The document also draws attention to reserves of mineral deposits—copper, phosphorus, niobium, platinum-group elements and rare earths—in Russia and other Arctic countries.[4]

The Russian hydrocarbons sector also has investments in India. In 2017, a consortium led by Russia's oil major, Rosneft, acquired India's second-largest oil refinery, along with its downstream retail fuel business, making it India's biggest private fuel retailer. This was Russia's largest foreign investment ever (at about USD 12.9 billion) and India's largest inward investment. Expansion of refining capacity, and the increase of fuel retail outlets, is under way.

After the multinational Nuclear Suppliers' Group permitted international civil nuclear cooperation with India (without obliging it to accede to the Nuclear Non-Proliferation Treaty), Russia became the first (and, so far, only) beneficiary of this waiver, because other countries were unwilling to accept the provisions of India's liability legislation. Six nuclear power plants of 1,000 MW capacity are being constructed in Tamil Nadu. Two are in operation, two are in advanced stages of construction, and construction of another two commenced in June 2021. As per a 2018 Action Plan for collaboration in nuclear energy, another six plants will be constructed on a new site, maximizing the localization of manufacturing equipment and components in India.[5] Russia extends credit on attractive terms for the equipment and services for the projects. Given the limited uranium reserves in India, Moscow's commitment of fuel supply for the life cycle of every plant is valuable. The collaboration, therefore, helps to undergird India's international commitments to reduce the fossil-fuel content of its energy mix.

India's search for diversification of supplies of critical minerals—both for industry and for strategic applications—has intensified in the wake of the supply disruptions that the COVID-19 pandemic caused. As host to about 30 per cent of global natural resources, Russia provides opportunities for sourcing and investment. A consortium of Indian state-owned enterprises is scouting around in multiple countries, including Russia, for viable projects.

The debate over India's choices of strategic partnerships needs to examine how dependent these strands of India–Russia cooperation are on the state of political relations between the two countries. Economic and commercial activities could normally thrive independently of bilateral political relations, as long as they are not of unremitting hostility. In general, the more broad-based the economic and commercial relations are (involving more jobs and local economies), the greater the incentive for both countries not to take policy actions inimical to the interests of each other.

But high-technology defence transfers belong to a distinctly different category. Sharing of sensitive technologies between countries is based on strategic convergences and credible assurances that these technologies will not be shared with other, potentially hostile countries. The receiving country also needs a credible assurance that the same (or a superior) version of the weapons platform is not being supplied to its adversary. In this sense, defence cooperation cannot be considered tactical or transactional. A number of analysts miss this critical difference between civilian trade and high-technology defence trade in their analysis of the 'dispensability' of Russia in India's strategic calculus.[6]

The US Factor

The burgeoning India–US strategic partnership from the early 2000s was inspired by shared interests in trade, investment and technology, cultural links and the Indian diaspora in the US. But an important strategic underpinning to the relationship was shared perspectives on China. The US saw a strong, democratic India as a potential counterpoise to a fast-rising China, which would soon threaten its global dominance. This perspective motivated Washington to tweak the global non-proliferation regime, opening the door to international civil nuclear cooperation with India, and to expanded India–US civilian and military cooperation.[7] US defence exports surged from near zero to about USD 20 billion in a decade.

The geopolitical environment in the early years of this century accommodated the contemporaneous growth of India's relations with both the US and Russia. The erosion of the exclusivity of New Delhi's relations with Moscow accorded with the thrust for multipolarity that the post-Cold War situation encouraged. The flow of weapons platforms and military technologies from Russia continued apace. Though defence imports from the US increased sharply, they did not as yet include the more sophisticated weapons platforms, since the procedures for the US to dismantle all the technology controls—the 'foundational' agreements—took years to conclude. In the early 2000s, Russia supported India's efforts with the US and France to secure liberation from the 'nuclear apartheid' of technology-denial regimes. On the other side, US president George W. Bush requested President Putin in 2002 to intercede with the leaders of India and Pakistan to defuse tensions between them, and later praised him for his efforts.[8]

In the afterglow of the India–US nuclear deal, when US–Russia relations were deteriorating rapidly, there was greater pressure on India to shift away from Russia and towards the US position on major international issues. The pressure became more intense after the breakdown of US–Russia relations in 2014 (when Crimea was incorporated into the Russian Federation). India refrained from criticizing the annexation and resisted US blandishments to join the economic sanctions regime against Russia. But then came the more potent Countering America's Adversaries Through Sanctions Act (CAATSA), which essentially closed the US market to any country involved in 'significant' defence transactions with Russia. The air defence system, S-400, fitted this description. As US officials admitted openly, CAATSA was intended, beyond 'punishing' Russia, to wean major arms importers away from Russian equipment and towards US-made systems.[9]

India did conclude the contract for the S-400. There are indications that the US may waive the application of CAATSA for this purchase. Nevertheless, the Damocles sword of CAATSA continues to hang over future India–Russia defence projects. Russia's concern also is that the intensifying India–US military-to-military cooperation and the confidentiality embedded in their defence agreements may, besides inhibiting purchase of Russian hardware, threaten the confidentiality of Russian technologies vis-à-vis its adversary. Politically, Russia sees an increasing Indian tendency to support US initiatives or equivocate on matters relating to Russia in international fora.

Challenges in Central Asia

India's interests in Central Asia informed its accession to the Shanghai Cooperation Organization (SCO)—then including Russia, China, Kazakhstan, Kyrgyzstan, Uzbekistan and Tajikistan—in 2017, despite unease about many aspects of its structure and political outlook. Central Asia, which is sandwiched between Russia and China, is a strategically important region for India, as it borders Iran, Afghanistan and Pakistan-occupied Kashmir. The region is today dominated by Russia and China. It is important for India to be present here to monitor the Russia–China dynamics in it. Central Asia is also a source of strategically important resources, including uranium, copper, titanium, yellow phosphorus and zinc. As countries in the region seek to increase their autonomy of action from Russia and China, they have welcomed strengthening connections with India, which has had economic and cultural links with the region from the time of the Silk Road.

To link up effectively with the region, connectivity is key. India's direct overland route to Central Asia is blocked by political and security issues in Pakistan and Afghanistan. An alternate route, which has been under negotiation between India, Russia and Iran since 2002, is the International North–South Transport Corridor (INSTC), a multimodal trade corridor from India's west coast to Iran and onwards to Central Asia (with spurs to Afghanistan and Russia, and a connection to Europe). The project was revived after the international nuclear deal of 2015 with Iran led to the lifting of UN sanctions against that country. India has developed a container terminal in Iran's Chabahar port, inaugurated in December 2017, and is committed to establishing a 610-km rail link northward from

Chabahar to Zahedan, which would be a bridgehead to Afghanistan and Central Asia. There is a reciprocal interest: for the landlocked countries of Central Asia, Chabahar becomes the shortest route to the sea—the alternatives being ports in Russia, Turkey or Bandar Abbas in Iran. Uzbekistan is already working on a transit rail link through Herat (Afghanistan), connecting to Zahedan. India has joined the Ashgabat Agreement to establish a seamless multimodal transport and a transit corridor through Central Asia, synchronizing with other regional transport corridors including the INSTC.

Connecting to Afghanistan is an immediate objective. It provides Afghanistan an alternative to the dependence on Pakistan and its Karachi port for transit to the sea. With India–Afghanistan political relations expected to go through a difficult phase after the Taliban takeover, keeping mutually beneficial economic lines open becomes more valuable.

According to some estimates, with the full operationalization of Chabahar Port and INSTC, India's trade with Eurasia could grow to USD 170 billion, from a figure of under USD 15 billion today, because this shorter route, replacing the sea route to Rotterdam and St Petersburg, would reduce transit time and freight by up to 50 per cent each, as dry runs have shown. Indian and Russian leaders periodically promise to provide governmental support to significantly increase bilateral trade from the current paltry figure of about USD 10 billion. An operationalized INSTC could double the trade within a year. The Free Trade Agreement under negotiation between India and the Eurasian Economic Union could provide further impetus to this process.[10]

INSTC has other economic and strategic spin-offs. It would offer not only India, but all of South, Southeast and East Asia a cost-effective trade route to Central Asia, Russia and Europe, avoiding both China and the lengthy sea route in the process. The Chinese Belt and Road Initiative (BRI) involves the creation of transport corridors, connecting China with Central Asia, Russia and Europe. By connecting with the BRI corridors in Central Asia, INSTC would open the BRI for the use of countries other than China. In the long-term, it may also serve the strategic interests of the US and its allies to connect with Afghanistan and Central Asia, without having to go through the territory of Russia.

Recent developments, including Chinese ambitions, Turkey's resurgence and the US withdrawal from Afghanistan, are transforming political and economic realities in Central Asia, further complicating India's strategic challenge in the region.

The tacit arrangement between Russia and China in Central Asia has hitherto been that Russia would be the net security provider, while China would be the dominant economic influence. With growing investments in the region, China is acquiring greater political clout and there are indications that it will take direct action to protect its security interests as well. The apprehension about instability in Afghanistan spilling over into the region may accelerate this process. There have been persistent reports of Chinese discussions on closer security cooperation with Central Asian countries, including 'neutral' Turkmenistan.[11] There are increasing reports of the deployment of Chinese private security contractors in the region.

These moves have caused unease in Moscow, and find mention in the Russian media and academia, but their special relationship has prevented official Russian articulation of the disquiet. Popular sentiments against Chinese exploitation of local labour and land have periodically found public expression in most Central Asian countries, including in Kazakhstan.[12]

Tajik (and Russian) concerns were aroused in mid-2020 by the publication in the official Chinese media of a historian's view that the entire Pamir region in the Himalayas was rightfully Chinese (surrendered in the nineteenth century to the Russian empire by 'unequal' treaties), and hence should be returned by Tajikistan to

China. Official Tajik remonstrations, asking the Chinese government to dissociate itself from these views, apparently got no response. Seen against this background, the building of military infrastructure by China in the Pamir mountains may have ominous ulterior motives.

A new challenge to both Russia and China in the region is an advancing Turkish footprint. Over the past decade, Turkey has been expanding its strategic options, exploiting its geopolitical, demographic, economic and military leverages. After Russia's annexation of Crimea in 2014, Turkey's location on the Black Sea heightened its importance to both Russia and the North Atlantic Treaty Organization (NATO), of which it is a member. President Recep Tayyip Erdogan has leveraged this enhanced importance by injecting a mix of cooperation and defiance into both relationships. Turkey's close economic and defence links with Russia coexist with its harsh criticism of the annexation of Crimea and cooperation with Ukraine on advanced military technologies. On the other hand, Turkey collaborates with Russia and Iran to promote a political settlement in Syria, while being sensitive to US interests in northeast Syria.

Turkey's critical contribution to Azerbaijan's decisive military victory over Armenia in the war over Nagorno-Karabakh in October–November 2020 provided it with a springboard to the Caspian region and beyond, reinforcing its ongoing efforts to link up with the Turkic-speaking peoples of Central Asia. The recent Azerbaijan–Turkmenistan agreement on the delimitation of the Caspian seabed opens the prospect of evacuating oil and gas to Europe through Turkey. In the recent military skirmish on the Tajik–Kyrgyz border, Turkey offered assistance to the Turkic-speaking Kyrgyz. Ankara also offered its troops to secure Kabul airport after the Americans left. Its relations with Pakistan have historical roots.

Turkey has, therefore, thrust itself forcefully into the Eurasian region, where its interests will converge or conflict with those of

China, Iran and Russia—with each of which it has complex, multi-layered relations. India's relations with Turkey have deteriorated in recent years; its diplomacy has to reorient the country's approach to Turkey, bilaterally and regionally, to deal with these new challenges.

The Russia-China Embrace

As Moscow keeps an eye on US influence on Indian policy, New Delhi in turn is concerned about the surge in Russia–China relations, which have acquired near-alliance status.

Sino–Russian relations had already started warming in the early 2000s, with the amicable settlement of their long-standing border disputes. The Chinese demand for Russian natural resources, raw materials and military technologies created economic complementarities. The two countries also shared opposition to Western ideas of democracy propagation, humanitarian interventions and regime change. Strategic analysts generally assumed, however, that their turbulent history of acrimonious rivalry and border disputes would always restrain the intensity of their political embrace. This restraint became untenable, when a virtual breakdown in Russia–West relations drove Moscow to seek Beijing's political and economic support.

Russia and China coordinate their positions closely in most international fora, and often present a united front against the US and its allies. Their trade and investment links have intensified, including in sectors that Russia considers sensitive.[13] Defence cooperation includes Chinese acquisitions of the S-400 air defence system and Su-35 aircraft, as well as the joint development and manufacture of other military platforms.[14] To demonstrate solidarity against Western actions in their respective neighbourhoods, the two countries have held joint naval exercises in the South China Sea and the Baltic Sea. Their joint military exercises are increasingly extensive in scope and sophistication, involving advanced equipment and joint command and control systems. In a joint statement celebrating the Twentieth Anniversary of the 2001 Russia–China friendship treaty, Presidents Xi Jinping and Putin declared that relations have reached the highest level in their history: '... not a Cold War-type politico-military alliance', but exceeding 'this form of interstate interaction'.[15]

At the same time, their relationship does have some wrinkles and there are differences in their strategic perceptions on some regional and international issues. The texture of Russia–China relations is also sensitive to the nuances in the engagement that each of the countries has with the United States.

Russia supported China in its rejection of the 2016 decision of the Permanent Court of Arbitration on its territorial claims in the South China Sea, but remains neutral on the merits of the Chinese claims. It has sustained close relations with China's strategic rivals. Its partnership with Vietnam includes weapons sales, a Free Trade Agreement with the Russia-led Eurasian Economic Union, joint exploration for energy in the South China Sea and plans to reopen a Russian naval base in Cam Ranh Bay. Before Quad activism soured relations, President Putin supported former Japanese prime minister Shinzo Abe's effort to resuscitate Russia–Japan relations, by expressing willingness to explore compromises for a resolution of their Kuril Islands dispute. He invited Indian, Japanese and Korean investment in the Russian Far East to dilute the Chinese presence there.

China opposed the economic sanctions after the Russian annexation of Crimea, but stopped short of endorsing the annexation, and went on to exploit the breakdown in Russia–Ukraine relations by stepping up its defence cooperation with Ukraine. Chinese companies have been hesitant to invest in Russia, except in projects of strategic value to China, mainly in the Arctic. President Putin has expressed his support of China's BRI, but the Chinese have largely ignored his exhortation to select BRI projects in Eurasia in consultation with the Eurasian Economic Union. China concludes project agreements bilaterally with Eurasian Economic Union countries. Moreover, most BRI connectivity projects have taken a southern route to Europe through Central Asia and the Caucasus, bypassing Russia.[16]

China has also taken its brand of brash wolf warrior diplomacy to Russia. Russian officials and business representatives increasingly complain about the overbearing attitude of their Chinese counterparts. In a series of outspoken tweets, a researcher of an institute affiliated with the Russian foreign ministry listed several instances of Chinese treatment of Russia and Russians not consonant with their ostensibly close relations.[17]

Russia's latest National Security Strategy (NSS), which President Putin approved in July 2021 (succeeding the NSS 2015), also provides some hints on thinking about China. NSS 2021 incorporates President Putin's 'vision' of a Greater Eurasian Partnership (GEP). Unveiled by President Putin in 2015, it envisages a Russia-coordinated effort to draw countries of Eurasia into economic partnership, moving towards integration at a pace, and to the level, that individual countries consider compatible with their interests. At the heart of this concept is a cooperative order, in which no country would impose its dominance. Russian analysts have identified the importance of drawing India, China and Japan into this effort. They have also explicitly pointed out that India–China tensions are driving India into US's embrace; persuading China to give up its hegemonistic inclinations would, therefore, be critical to the success of such a venture.[18]

NSS 2021 also stipulates that all 'critical information infrastructure facilities' of the country, including those using advanced artificial intelligence and quantum computing technologies, should 'prioritise use of Russian technologies and equipment'. Contrary to the general impression that Russia will go along with Chinese vendors and Information Communications Technology solutions, this injunction equates all foreign supplies of critical technologies as potential national security risks.

Can the US Bring China-Russia Relations Back into Play?

The Russia–China partnership may have its chinks, but the strong glue that binds its cracks is the hostility between them and the US. China has benefited from the fallout between Russia and the US over Crimea, extracting concessions on hydrocarbons supplies and advanced military technologies, in return for its support of Russia in international forums. Early signals from the Biden Administration—before the war in Ukraine altered priorities—that the US would now focus more strongly on China as its principal strategic adversary, portended a readjustment of Russia–China equations, with Beijing needing Moscow's political support, and therefore acknowledging Russia as a more equal partner.

In his candid remarks to the media after his conversation with President Putin in June 2021, President Joe Biden said he got the impression that Russia needs a modus vivendi with the US, because it is being 'squeezed' by China. Its flagging economy and surging Chinese power are in danger of denting its great power ambitions, by reducing it to a junior partner of China.[19] On the US side, a modus vivendi with Russia would reflect the geopolitical wisdom of making peace with a lesser challenger to prevent it from strengthening the principal adversary by alliance with it.

A logical corollary of this thinking would be an American strategy aimed at weakening some of the Russia–China bonds. A researcher from the Council on Foreign Relations has laid out a detailed prescription for this. Writing in *Foreign Affairs*, Charles Kupchan points out the cracks in the Russia–China edifice—among them, China's challenge in Central Asia and the Arctic. According to him, US efforts to 'tame' China should include luring Russia away from it. This should start with the US jettisoning its 'democracy versus autocracy' narrative, which unites Russia and China against the West. Washington should encourage India to help pull Russia away from China, by waiving sanctions on purchase of the S-400 system. Further, America and its allies should help reduce Russia's economic dependence on China by restraint in the use of sanctions and by working towards a diplomatic resolution of the conflict in eastern Ukraine. The US and Russia should also lead the strategic stability dialogue, launched recently, towards an arms control arrangement, that also eventually pushes China to accept limits on its missiles, which should be in Moscow's interest as well. Finally, the US and Russia should stave off Beijing's creeping ambition in the Arctic, and check its growing influence in Central Asia, the broader Middle East, and Africa. Kupchan's view is that the present US policy leaves China free to pursue its expansion in the Pacific, confident of Russia's support. Putting the China–Russia relationship 'back into play' would divert some of China's attention to its continental flank. It would be an important step towards building a multipolar order, thwarting China's ambitions for a 'Sinocentric international system'.[20]

The Biden–Putin meeting in June 2021 seemed to hint at a US desire for such a geopolitical rebalancing. President Putin appeared to reciprocate, but made the point that, for such a geopolitical rebalance to be sustainable, it should incorporate suitable security guarantees for Russia, so that it does not constantly have to anticipate and counter moves to threaten its territorial integrity and constrain its external influence—which is how Russia sees NATO's expansion, weapons deployments and military exercises and other US policies across Europe and Asia. Bilateral discussions in the months after the Geneva summit covered strategic stability, transborder cybercrimes and the important subject of security guarantees in respect of Ukraine.

A US–Russia modus vivendi that could eventually bring the Russia–China relationship 'into play' may make great geopolitical sense, but would involve a deviation from the course that the US and NATO have set in recent years, and in which stakeholders in the US and in Europe have made heavy political and economic investments.

For years now, there has been bipartisan support in American political circles for policies directed towards circumscribing Russia's international influence and degrading its military strength. President Putin has been a particular target: the desire for a regime change in Russia is never far from the surface in the American political discourse. Among NATO's European members too, there are many whose historical experiences, economic priorities and political ambitions incline them towards pressure on Russia, rather than accommodation with it.

A combination of these factors, possibly together with some domestic influences in Russia, resulted in a breakdown of the US–Russia dialogue and the consequent launch of the 'special military operation' in Ukraine by Russia.

The Impact of the Russia–Ukraine War

Russia's 'special military operation' in Ukraine abruptly shifted global attention from post-COVID-19 challenges and a deepening US–China rift to the ferocious Russia–West confrontation.

The war has spawned a number of narratives: of an unprovoked Russian aggression, Putin's imperial ambitions, a shambolic military campaign, inexplicable battle tactics, substandard equipment and poor troop morale. All these propositions merit rigorous analysis, but the continuing fog of war makes it difficult to evaluate them objectively. From the very outset, Russia was decisively worsted by Ukraine and the West in the information space; it is therefore impossible at this stage to get an accurate picture of the extent of Russia's losses or to establish the truth of the various human rights violations attributed to Russian troops.

The US and NATO unequivocally condemned Russia's action and extended strong political, diplomatic, economic, military and intelligence support to Ukraine and its armed forces. NATO's hands-on intelligence support is credited with helping the Ukrainian forces to score major battlefield successes against the Russians, including sinking a large warship and targeting Russian generals in the field. The West unequivocally condemned Russia's action, and sought to isolate Russia internationally and to throttle its economy with harsh sanctions.

After nearly three months of a seemingly lethargic campaign, Russian forces did eventually take military control over much of eastern and southern Ukraine. NATO arms supplies continued to encourage Ukrainian efforts to push back the Russian advances, and a bilateral Russia–Ukraine dialogue in search of a negotiated settlement, initiated in the early stages of the war, petered out.

The objectives spelt out by some NATO leaders—of a decisive military defeat for Russia, pushing it back to the pre-2014 borders with Ukraine, and a 'strategic defeat for Putin', perhaps including his unseating—promise a long-drawn-out war of attrition. On the other side are elements in the US and Europe, calling for a negotiated settlement that does not seek to 'humiliate' Russia. Domestic political and economic developments in the US, Europe and beyond added disparate voices to this debate.

The concerted effort to isolate Russia internationally did not attract the anticipated levels of support. In particular, the portrayal of the confrontation as one between democracies and autocracies did not find resonance. As former national security advisor Shivshankar Menon points out in *Foreign Affairs*, many of the world's biggest democracies did not see the war through this prism: they did not explicitly condemn the Russian invasion or join the US-led economic sanctions. This was true for most Latin American countries, including the democracies of Brazil and Mexico, and a large part of Asia and

Africa. Much of the world (apart from NATO and some other US allies) views the conflict as a contestation over the European security order—not as an existential threat to the global order.[21] This was even more graphically illustrated by the vote and statements of countries on the UN General Assembly resolution for expelling Russia from the Human Rights Council. As many as eighty-two countries abstained or opposed the expulsion of Russia. A survey quoted in the *Economist* illustrates another line of division in the global responses: between the rich and less-rich nations. Most of the rich nations in North America and Europe are 'West-leaning' (i.e., oppose Russia's action); they account for more than 70 per cent of the world's GDP, but only 36 per cent of the world's population. This means that around two-thirds of people live in countries whose governments are either neutral or 'Russia-leaning'. Even accepting that India and China—two populous countries—skew the statistic somewhat, this is still a significant figure. The *Economist* concludes (wistfully?) that Mr Putin's campaign in Ukraine 'has met widespread condemnation in the West ... But for now, by no means does everyone regard him, and his country, as pariahs'.[22]

This meant that Russia was not isolated from many international fora (despite its expulsion from the Human Rights Council). BRICS and SCO meetings were held. Indonesia resisted pressures and invited Russia to the G-20 Summit that it will host in November 2022. Leaders of US allies Saudi Arabia and UAE publicly shunned US overtures and connected with President Putin to coordinate the OPEC+ oil production targets with him.

The economic sanctions also did not achieve their immediate goal. The 'nuclear options' of freezing Russia's foreign exchange reserves and 'de-SWIFTing' its major banks were meant to bring the Russian economy swiftly to its knees. But, after the initial panic in the markets, the Russian economy 'shrugged off the sanctions', because of interest rate action and capital controls by its central bank, as well as soaring revenues from continued export of oil and gas. Russia reported a current account surplus of about USD 96 billion from January to April 2022, compared to about USD 28 billion over the same period last year.

The ruble recovered in strength, and was hailed in the Western business media as the 'most valuable' emerging market currency. Russians, said the *Economist*, are spending 'fairly freely' in cafés, bars and restaurants once again.[23] The key interest rate, which was abruptly hiked overnight from 9.5 per cent to 20 per cent after the sanctions, was progressively lowered, until it was back at 9.5 per cent. The Russian economy will still experience a major GDP contraction and supply shortages, due to the withdrawal of foreign suppliers. But this would mean a deferred shock, while the rest of the world felt the pain almost immediately, in soaring energy prices, commodity disruptions and food shortages. The sanctions did not achieve the 'smart' objective of hitting Russia and cushioning the impact on sanctions-imposing countries.

Energy proved to be the Achilles heel of the sanctions. Russia's dominant role as supplier of energy inputs to the Western world—oil, gas, coal and uranium—made it nearly impossible to cut off foreign currency flows into Russia or to fully choke off its banks' access to the outside world. The European Union depends on Russia for over 60 per cent of its energy needs (gas, oil and coal). The first five packages of EU sanctions covered only coal imports from Russia. The sixth package, including drastic cuts in seaborne and pipeline oil imports, took many weeks to reach a consensus—and was finally adopted with a revised schedule and a number of national carve-outs. The result was that Russia raked in revenues of over USD 65 billion in the first quarter of 2022—an 80 per cent year-on-year growth!

The US did not stop uranium imports from Russia, because it would have increased electricity prices in US homes. The UK committed to end oil imports only by the end of 2022, and has not yet decided on phasing out gas imports. Meanwhile, even as the European Commission was talking about cutting off Russian oil imports, the US treasury secretary warned against a full European ban, reacting to economists' predictions that this would cause crude oil prices to jump to over USD 185 per barrel. The political objective of choking off Russia's oil revenues collided with the domestic imperative of capping gasoline prices.

The Russian energy dilemma is likely to stalk Europe even after the war (whenever and however it ends). To wean itself away sooner from Russian fossil fuels, it must fast track its programmes for alternative energy sources—at higher cost and accepting interim shortfalls. A sudden surge in building solar and wind energy capacities would put immense pressure on the prices and supplies of steel, aluminium and other raw materials—and Russia is a major producer and exporter of most of them.

India's Independent Line on the War

India's public responses to the Russian invasion and its votes in the UN Security Council, General Assembly and other international organizations drew comment and criticism, within the country and outside. There was intense pressure from the US and other strategic partners in the West to join them in condemning the invasion and to vote with them on resolutions to this effect. India steadfastly abstained on all the resolutions. The official explanation for these votes had four main points: one, that respect for sovereignty and territorial integrity of states is an essential element of the international order [i.e., Russia had violated them]; two, a constructive way forward has to be found respecting these principles; three, that it is regrettable that diplomacy was given up [an admonition to both sides]; and four, that India's first priority was to ensure the safety and security of Indian students stranded in Ukraine [which would require the cooperation of both sides].

The criticism in India was that the government had sacrificed legality and principles at the altar of pragmatism. The pragmatism flowed from the importance of the strategic partnership with Russia, both for defence cooperation and for dealing with the challenges in the Eurasian landmass, which the US withdrawal from Afghanistan has further complicated.

A procession of foreign dignitaries came streaming into India, hoping to leverage the bilateral relations to extract a condemnation of Russia's war on Ukraine. India's official representatives largely stuck to the position articulated in the Security Council and other UN forums.

In his bilateral interaction with President Biden at the India–US 2+2, Prime Minister Modi did not directly respond to his interlocutor's reference to Russia's 'horrific assault'. He said the situation in Ukraine was 'very worrying' and that he had urged Russia and Ukraine to engage in direct talks for peace. In subsequent interactions with Western leaders, he called for a return to diplomacy and a negotiated settlement, recognizing that there can be no victors in this war. In his opening statements with Quad leaders at their Tokyo summit in May 2022, he did not mention Ukraine at all.

The totality of India's statements and actions could be summarized in three basic points: one, India acknowledges that Russia's action in Ukraine violates international law, but will not be pressured into a public condemnation just to please its other partners; two, India's response reflects geopolitical interests that flow from its history and geography, which are distinct from those that drive the war in Ukraine; three, India's position is not one of passive neutrality; it is protecting and furthering interests—and these interests do not conflict with India's shared strategic interests with other partners. India's Western partners appeared to have absorbed this message, judging from the atmosphere and outcomes of the India–US 2+2 meeting, the Quad Summit and high-level bilateral meetings in Berlin, Paris and Copenhagen.

In India, analysts in the media and academia were divided in their assessments of Russia's actions and India's official responses. This division was reflected in a public opinion poll in India, quoted in the *Economist*. Forty per cent of the respondents approved of President Putin's decision to go to war, while 60 per cent disapproved. In a popularity rating of the Russian and Ukrainian leaders, President Zelenskyy scored 63 per cent, while President Putin got 54 per cent.

Consistent with its posture of not condemning the invasion of Ukraine, India did not subscribe to the economic sanctions against Russia. War conditions limited the opportunities and routes of commercial exchanges. The exception was crude oil. Indian state-owned and private companies lapped up deeply discounted oil from Russia. Commentators in the West criticized this as 'back-filling' sanctions, but the fact that European countries continued buying much larger quantities of Russian oil and gas demolished this argument. In fact, given the concern that the US treasury secretary expressed about prospects of a steep spike in crude prices, such purchases by India could be seen as ensuring some check on the prices. Indian analysts have logically surmised that private companies would not have ventured into the Russian market without securing some assurance beforehand that their extensive business interests in the US and Europe would not be impacted by it.

Stressing Convergence, Managing Divergence

India's public response to Russia's war in Ukraine demonstrated an important element of the strategic partnership: that each country is sensitive to the core concerns of the other, even if they do not have the same views. There are many examples of this from the Cold War years, but two from the recent past were India's muted response to Russia's annexation of Crimea in 2014, and Russia's rejection of Chinese and Pakistani attempts to 'internationalize' the Indian Constitutional amendments relating to Jammu and Kashmir in 2019.

Going forward, India–Russia relations will continue to be buffeted by global geopolitical tides. Geography, economics and the politics of Eurasia create overlapping interests. As Indian officials have been at pains to explain to their Western partners, India's shared interests with Russia, and in Eurasia, need not clash with those of its other strategic partners.

India and Russia share aspirations for a multipolar world, though their concept of it, and perceptions of their own roles in it, vary. Their international strategies are guided by their respective perspectives on their geopolitical opportunities and challenges. Unlike during the Cold War years, their interests are not congruent. A mature approach should involve emphasizing convergences and managing differences, so that they do not impact core national interests. It also means vigilance to ensure protection of interests. President Putin has said that Russia does not transfer to any other country the military technologies shared with India. This is an assurance that India must constantly verify in respect of the weaponry and technologies that Moscow supplies to Beijing, as also the nature of their intelligence-sharing arrangements and joint space-based surveillance. As Russia pursues its economic and geopolitical interests with Pakistan, India needs to monitor the sharing of military tactics and strategic doctrines in their defence cooperation. At the same time, Russia should welcome India's political and economic initiatives in Eurasia, which would promote its strategic and security objectives and work to dilute Chinese dominance of the region.

In the post-Cold War world, with its diversity of national capacities and aspirations, countries would have shared interests with a number of others, but rarely a total congruence of interests. This is particularly so for a country in India's complex geography. This situation, of convergence not amounting to congruence, has been recognized in the context of the India–US partnership by a task force on India–US relations, set up in 2015 by the US Council for Foreign Relations. Observing that an alliance model is not appropriate for India, it suggested that the US should treat relations with India as a joint venture, which would not preclude other partnerships of either party.[24] This is an equally appropriate template for India–Russia relations in today's world. They have shared geopolitical, defence, economic and energy interests. Each may also have conflicts of interests, flowing from obligations of other partnerships; they will need to manage them through bilateral reconciliation.

Emphasizing convergence of interests also means exploiting opportunities for mutually beneficial economic cooperation. The leaders of India and Russia have actively encouraged a broad-based economic cooperation architecture to ensure strong mutual stakes in the relationship that would incentivize each partner to be sensitive to the core concerns of the other. These efforts have, in the recent past, come up against fears in the Indian business community of being caught in the complex web of US sanctions against Russia, which may threaten their access to Western markets. Depending on the nature of the sanctions regime after the current war, such concerns could be accentuated. The effort to broad-base the India–Russia relationship is also hampered by unhelpful stereotypes about each other—projected in their media, academia, business communities, and even political circles and officialdom.

In India the narrative is that Russia has been significantly weakened by Western sanctions and its own economic infirmities. This impression could be strengthened after the war. In Indian industry circles, Russia is still associated with the clunky technologies of the Soviet era. On the other side, Russians are theoretically aware of India's economic progress, but cannot bring themselves to believe that the country in which their forefathers helped set up basic industries, now exports innovations and technologies to many developed countries. This mutual ignorance, in addition to the logistical hurdles, explains the paltry bilateral trade and investment exchanges (other than in hydrocarbons). There could be some improvement in these areas: the constriction of Western supplies during the war has led a number of Russian companies to look to India for inputs for industry. The blockades in the Black Sea have led enterprising traders to explore the multimodal freight route from Russia to India, through Iran. This may speed up the operationalisation of the INSTC, which has been caught up in bureaucratic negotiations over years.

On the fear of sanctions, Indian diplomacy needs to impress on the US that India–Russia economic cooperation serves the larger US objective of giving Russia an alternative to China and ensuring a strong India as a counterpoise to China. INSTC would serve the same purpose. Similarly, strangling India's defence cooperation with Russia defeats that objective. Diversification of military supplies necessarily has to be a gradual process if it is not to introduce vulnerabilities in the short term.

Academia and media in both countries take their analyses of each other from Western sources, which accentuates the distortion of perceptions. Both countries need better public communications about the content and direction of their bilateral relations.[25]

Russia and the Indo-Pacific

Russia's strong allergy to India's Indo-Pacific engagement is a direct consequence of US–Russia hostility. Moscow sees the Quad dialogue as a step towards an Indian quasi-alliance with the US, which would disengage the country from Russia. India has consistently sought to allay this apprehension. At a meeting with President Putin in Vladivostok, PM Modi announced an 'Act Far East' initiative, which would extend a line of credit of USD 1 billion to fund projects in the Russian Far East, signalling a strong Indian interest in continued economic engagement with the region. It was also decided that a maritime corridor would be activated for trade between Vladivostok and Chennai. India's message is that the partnerships it is seeking in the Indo-Pacific are to prevent Chinese hegemony in the region, which should be in Russia's interest as well. In fact, it is consistent with President Putin's own idea of the Greater Eurasian Partnership, which Russia's National Security Strategy 2021 has again endorsed. It also accords with the idea of a multipolar Asia outlined by India's external affairs minister.[26] It is only when there is a significant thaw in US–Russia relations that Russia would be receptive to this idea.

Black Swans and Grey Rhinos

The war in Ukraine, following a US–Russia dialogue gone awry, was as unexpected in its launch and execution, as in the response of Ukraine and NATO. As it reaches the end of its fourth month, the 'endgame' is elusive.

Russia will remain Europe's largest country—geography cannot be escaped. Neither can its complex centuries-old cultural and economic interlinkages with Europe be wished away. It will remain host to about 30 per cent of the globe's natural resources. The experience of sanctions has shown that global dependence on Russia's energy, agricultural and commodity resources cannot be easily substituted. The historical ambition of Russia, from the imperial age to the communist era and the Putin years, has been to achieve and sustain the role of a great power. When it has slid into a lesser role, the country has, over time, leveraged its size, geography, military strength and resources wealth to retrieve its status.

It should follow from this that, sooner or later, a new modus vivendi may have to be forged with Russia. The issue at the core of this war—that a stable security architecture in Europe cannot be built without accommodating the legitimate interests of all its constituents—will have to be addressed. This was the point that President Macron made, when he was arguing against humiliating Russia.

A Russia–Ukraine dialogue, catalysed by Turkey, appeared to be moving in this direction. According to Russian foreign minister Lavrov, Russian and Ukrainian negotiators initialled a document on 29 March, providing for Ukraine to become a 'neutral, non-aligned and non-nuclear state', guaranteed by all stakeholders (essentially NATO and Russia), in which foreign countries would not deploy weapons or conduct military exercises, without the concurrence of all guarantor states. Lavrov also claimed that the Ukrainians had agreed to leave Crimea and Donbas out of the purview of these security guarantees, implying that Ukraine may agree to a separate, special status for them. The contents of this document were not confirmed by Ukraine, though its foreign minister did acknowledge that some progress was made. The climate changed abruptly in the first week of April, after the discovery of alleged gross human rights violations by Russian forces on the outskirts of Kyiv. The dialogue petered out and the neutrality document was no longer mentioned.

Russian actions and Western rhetoric now point to a more prolonged war of attrition, particularly if the goals of 'strategic defeat' and regime change in Russia continue to be pursued. The rhetoric is reinforced by new 'revelations' about the state of President Putin's health and his estimated longevity in office (and in the world). Most of them quote faceless intelligence sources, though a couple of known intelligence faces (like the former head of the British MI6) have recently surfaced. It is difficult to totally dismiss such reports. Equally, given the near-impenetrable wall of secrecy behind which the Kremlin operates, reliable intelligence is difficult to get. It is not uncommon for rumour-based 'intelligence' to feed into policymaking. Even assuming that it could be engineered, regime change could have unpredictably messy consequences in a country of Russia's size, complexity and nuclear weapons capabilities.

Russia's continued thrust into eastern Ukraine and NATO stepping up the range and lethality of weapons to the war zone have aroused fears of the conflict spinning out of control. Targeting of military facilities and transport infrastructure in western Ukraine, in an effort to disrupt new weapons supplies, often brings missile strikes perilously close to NATO's border. The US director of National Intelligence warned the Senate Armed Services Committee (10 May) that the conflict could take 'a more unpredictable and potentially escalatory trajectory', including the possible use of nuclear arms—an escalation scenario with potentially disastrous consequences.

A war of attrition could have important consequences for the Eurasian region, Russia–China relations and the US focus on the Indo-Pacific. The Central Asian countries have clearly been uneasy about the potential political and economic impact on them of Russia's action in Ukraine. But they have been careful not to criticize it and have publicly demonstrated their close relations with Russia, at meetings chaired by Putin or in telephone conversations with him. They would be alert to signs of weakening Russian influence in the region—political, military and economic—as a result of the war.

The impact of the war on Russia–China relations is another important factor. At the commencement of the war, it was widely put out that the relationship was now at its highest level. The Putin–Xi joint statement of 4 February 2022 was quoted as proof: it describes Russia–China relations as 'superior to political and military alliances of the Cold War era', declaring that 'there are no "forbidden" areas of cooperation'.[27] It was also asserted that Putin and Xi Jinping had agreed in advance on the timing of the invasion, so that it would not divert the international focus on the Beijing Winter Olympic Games. There is no real evidence for these assertions. Russia and China routinely use hyperbolic formulations to describe their relationship:

the joint statement of June 2021, quoted earlier, describes the bilateral relationship in similar terms. As for prior consultation before the invasion, it would be most uncharacteristic of Putin. All his major operations (e.g., Crimea in 2014 and Syria in 2016) have been launched with the utmost secrecy—even his close aides were not kept in the loop. The story of the Russian–Chinese alliance and prior coordination suited the narrative of democracy versus autocracy for the war. China has, in fact, been rather circumspect in its public posture on the war: while making the right noises supporting Russia's right to indivisible security, and voting with Russia on the UN Security Council on the issue, it has not made any public move to support Russia economically, other than purchasing discounted Russian oil, like India has done. Chinese banks have been careful about fresh exposure to Russian projects. China would have drawn lessons from the Western financial sanctions against Russia, to insulate Chinese financial institutions from similar measures in the future.

Putin telephoned Xi Jinping immediately after commencement of the military operation; it is significant that their next conversation was nearly four months later—on 15 June. The Kremlin said Xi 'noted the legitimacy of Russia's actions to protect fundamental national interests in the face of challenges to its security created by external forces'. There is considerable daylight between this formulation and that in the official readout of the Chinese foreign ministry, which said Xi 'emphasized that China has always independently assessed the situation on the basis of the historical context and the merits of the issue, and actively promoted world peace and the stability of the global economic order', adding that China could play a role in pushing for 'a proper settlement of the Ukraine crisis in a responsible manner'. A weakened Russia more dependent on China after the war would suit Beijing, but it is a moot point whether regime change in Moscow would. At the same time, a negotiated settlement that increases Russia's political and economic space in global affairs is not necessarily in China's interest.

The declarations that NATO is in for the long haul in Ukraine promise a heightened intensity of US and European attention to Russia in the coming months and years. This raises the question of the extent to which this would dilute the US focus on its rivalry with China and on the initiatives in the Indo-Pacific. The longer the haul, the greater will be the disquiet in many parts of Asia about this.

President Putin has had almost total control over the foreign and security policy of Russia over the past two decades. He has the constitutional mandate to seek re-election for another two terms. Putting aside unverifiable rumours about his longevity, it is not clear whether he will use it. The centralization of power in the Kremlin means that a leadership transition could result in a recalibration of Russia's foreign policy, in ways difficult to predict. A new president may have greater room for compromise with the external powers with which Russia is engaged in conflict. On their part, the 'success' of regime change may permit a more flexible approach to Russia's stated security concerns. This is one of the many unknowns of the present situation.

The known and unknown of the current global geopolitical flux make it very difficult to predict the post-war course of the India–Russia relationship. At the core are the configuration of four triangles of relationships: US–Russia–China, India–US–Russia, India–US–China and India–China–Russia. The configuration of each is sensitive to that of the others, and India would have to play its diplomatic cards skilfully, in tune with its strategic interests.

Conclusion

Over the next decade, India's strategy in Eurasia has to focus on maximizing benefits from the defence, economic and energy links with Russia, consolidating a political and economic presence in Central Asia and Afghanistan, and working to move the Russia–China–India triangle into a more favourable configuration for India, that would enhance New Delhi's options vis-à-vis Beijing in other theatres and issues. It is important to maintain a strategic autonomy that furthers the India–US partnership, prevents a hostile China–Russia axis, and skilfully manages the complex interplay of politics and interests in Central Asia of Russia, China, Iran and Turkey.

The principal thrust in defence cooperation is to ensure continued access to high-technology systems, obtain credible assurance that similar or better technologies are not transferred to India's potential adversaries, and maximize technology transfer and absorption. India should leverage its position as the world's largest arms importer to extract the most advantageous terms for weapons and technologies from suppliers. In this, Russia has hitherto been the most forthcoming. It provides a benchmark that other suppliers should be pressed to match or better. As diversification of acquisition widens, issues of interoperability and confidentiality will need constant attention. The ultimate objective of upgrading technology for indigenous production should always remain in focus.

India's investments in Russia's hydrocarbons sector contribute to energy security, but also meet the geopolitical objective of presence in the Russian Far East and Arctic regions. Investments in the natural resources of the region and their evacuation through the Vladivostok–Chennai route would encourage Russian engagement in the Indo-Pacific. A broad-based partnership with Russia would not only bring economic benefits to India, but would reinforce Russia's incentive to take a more independent stance from China. The Greater Eurasian Partnership, which is now a part of Russia's National Security Strategy, merits support and greater encouragement.

The critical role of connectivity in expanding and consolidating India's presence in the Eurasian region needs recognition. This means not only operationalizing INSTC, but further strengthening it: expanding the capacity of Chabahar port, early completion of the Chabahar–Zahedan rail link and finalizing logistical arrangements with all countries along the corridor in Central Asia, Caucasus, Russia and Europe. It is important to not let the vicissitudes of Russia's and Iran's relations with the West affect the operation of this corridor.

Notes

1. 'Meeting of the Valdai Discussion Club', 22 October 2020, http://en.kremlin.ru/events/president/news/64261, accessed 11 August 2021.
2. Sergey Lavrov, 'Remarks at the General Meeting of the Russian International Affairs Council', 10 December 2020, https://russiancouncil.ru/en/analytics-and-comments/analytics/remarks-at-the-general-meeting-of-the-russian-international-affairs-council/?sphrase_id=72773010, accessed 11 August 2021.
3. SIPRI Fact Sheet, 'Trends in International Arms Transfers, 2021', https://sipri.org/sites/default/files/2022-03/fs_2203_at_2021.pdf, accessed 12 June 2022.
4. Dipanjan Roy Chaudhury, 'India Explores Major Investments in Hydrocarbons & Renewables in Russian Arctic Region', *The Economic Times*, 28 January 2021, https://economictimes.indiatimes.com/industry/energy/oil-gas/india-explores-major-investments-in-hydrocarbons-renewables-in-russian-arctic-region/articleshow/80491769.cms?from=mdr, accessed 11 August 2021.
5. Dipanjan Roy Chaudhury, 'India, Russia Sign Civil Nuclear Action Plan for Second Plant; Third Country Project', *The Economic Times*, 5 October 2018, indiatimes.com, accessed 13 August 2021.
6. See, for example, Kanti Bajpai, *India versus China*, New Delhi: Juggernaut Books, 2021, p. 178, where he describes the India–Russia relationship as 'transactional-commercial'.
7. Condoleezza Rice, *No Higher Honour*, London: Simon & Schuster, 2011, p. 437.
8. 'President Bush Discusses India–Pakistan with President Putin', statement by the White House Press Secretary, 6 June

2002, https://georgewbush-whitehouse.archives.gov/news/releases/2002/06/20020606-3.html, accessed 12 June 2022.
9. Testimony by Dr Christopher Ashley Ford, Assistant Secretary, US State Department, to the US Senate Committee on Banking, Housing and Urban Affairs, 21 August 2018, Implementing CAATSA Section 231 Diplomacy—United States Department of State, accessed on 12 August 2021.
10. Much of the data on Eurasian connectivity is from P. Stobdan, *India and Central Asia: The Strategic Dimension*, New Delhi: KW Publishers Pvt. Ltd, 2020, pp. 317–324.
11. 'Turkmen President Gurbanguly Berdymukhamedov Meets with Wang Yi', press release of the Chinese Embassy in Washington, 13 July 2021, http://sg.china-embassy.gov.cn/eng/jrzg/202107/t20210714_8915363.htm, accessed 13 August 2021.
12. See, for example, Serik Rymbetov, 'Anti-China Sentiment Grows in Kazakhstan as Economic Cooperation Stalls', *Eurasia Daily Monitor*, 26 July 2021, https://jamestown.org/program/anti-china-sentiments-grows-in-kazakhstan-as-economic-cooperation-stalls/, accessed 12 August 2021.
13. The press statements by President Putin and Chinese President Xi Jinping during the latter's visit to Moscow on 4 July 2017 contain a comprehensive listing of Russia–China political and economic cooperation projects, 'Press Statements Following Russian–Chinese Talks', http://en.kremlin.ru/events/president/news/54979, accessed 12 June 2022.
14. A detailed analysis of Russia–China defence cooperation: Ethan Meick, 'China–Russia Military-to-Military Relations: Moving Toward a Higher Level of Cooperation', US–China Economic and Security Review Commission, 20 March 2017, https://www.uscc.gov/sites/default/files/Research/China-Russia%20Mil-Mil%20Relations%20Moving%20Toward%20Higher%20Level%20of%20Cooperation.pdf, accessed on 12 June 2022.
15. 'Joint Statement of the Russian Federation and the People's Republic of China on the Twentieth Anniversary of the Treaty of Good Neighbourliness and Friendly Cooperation between

the Russian Federation and the People's Republic of China', 28 June 2021, http://static.kremlin.ru/media/events/files/en/Bo3RF3JzGDvMAPjHBQAuSemVPWTEvb3c.pdf, accessed 17 June 2022.
16. Kaneshko Sangar, 'Russia and China in the Age of Grand Eurasian Projects: Prospects for Integration between the Silk Road Economic Belt and the Eurasian Economic Union', *Cambridge Journal of Eurasian Studies*, 3 May 2017, pp. 1–15, https://doi.org/10.22261/YDG5KF, accessed 12 June 2022.
17. The tweets in English are from the first author of an article in Russian by Igor Denisov and Aleksander Lukin in *Russia in Global Affairs*, July/August 2021, https://globalaffairs.ru/articles/korrekcziya-i-hedzhirovanie/, accessed 18 August 2021.
18. Sergei Karaganov, Timofei Bordachev, 'Toward the Great Ocean—6: People, History, Ideology, Education. Rediscovering the Identity', 11 September 2018, https://valdaiclub.com/a/reports/report-toward-the-great-ocean-6/, accessed 13 August 2021.
19. 'Remarks by President Biden at Press Conference in Geneva', White House Briefing, 16 June 2021, https://www.whitehouse.gov/briefing-room/speeches-remarks/2022/01/19/remarks-by-president-biden-in-press-conference-6/, accessed 11 August 2021.
20. Charles A. Kupchan, 'The Right Way to Split China and Russia', *Foreign Affairs*, 4 August 2021, https://www.foreignaffairs.com/articles/united-states/2021-08-04/right-way-split-china-and-russia, accessed 12 September 2021.
21. Shivshankar Menon, 'The Fantasy of the Free World', *Foreign Affairs*, 4 April 2022, https://www.foreignaffairs.com/articles/united-states/2022-04-04/fantasy-free-world, accessed on 12 June 2022.
22. 'Who Are Russia's Supporters?', *The Economist*, 4 April 2022, https://www.economist.com/graphic-detail/2022/04/04/who-are-russias-supporters, accessed 12 June 2022.
23. 'Russia's Economy is Back on Its Feet', *The Economist*, 7 May 2022, https://www.economist.com/finance-and-economics/2022/05/07/russias-economy-is-back-on-its-feet, accessed 12 June 2022.

24. Charles R. Kaye and Joseph S. Nye Jr., 'Working With a Rising India A Joint Venture for the New Century', Council on Foreign Relations Independent Task Force Report No. 73, November 2015, https://cfrd8-files.cfr.org/sites/default/files/pdf/2015/11/TFR73_India.pdf, accessed 11 August 2021.
25. For a Russian analysis of how the Russian (and Russians') approach to India needs recalibration, see Dmitri Trenin, 'Russia–India: From Rethink to Adjust to Upgrade', Carnegie Moscow Center, 2 December 2021, https://carnegiemoscow.org/commentary/85903, accessed 1 February 2022.
26. S. Jaishankar, 'Keynote Address by External Affairs Minister at the 13th All India Conference of China Studies', Ministry of External Affairs, 28 January 2021, https://mea.gov.in/Speeches-Statements.htm?dtl/33419/, accessed on 11 August 2021.
27. Joint Statement of the Russian Federation and the People's Republic of China on the International Relations Entering a New Era and the Global Sustainable Development, 4 February 2022, http://en.kremlin.ru/supplement/5770, accessed 17 June 2022.

CHAPTER

5

Old Wars, New Wars: Strategizing for Future Land Warfare

RAKESH SHARMA

हिमालयंसमारभ्ययावत्इंदुसरोवरम् |
तंदेवनिर्मितंदेशंहिंदुस्थानंप्रचक्षते ||

– Barhaspatya Samhita

(Starting from the Himalayas and extending up to the Indian Ocean is the land created by God, which is known as 'Hindustan'.)

The greatest challenge of our times is to be able to make correct and timely assessments of the changes taking place in the world, and the nature and extent of challenges and opportunities they present.[1] India is geographically located in a far-from-benign strategic environment, which justifies the argument for a strong and effective military force capable of defending its territorial integrity and sovereignty from possible threats. Predicting future scenarios, however, is an onerous task. Hans Morgenthau, the eminent German-American political scientist, had prophetically stated that the first lesson a student of international politics must learn and never forget is that the complexities of international affairs make simple solutions and trustworthy prophecies impossible. To consider the environment of the future on which long-term policy decisions invariably have to be based, a distinct rationale is necessary to systemize the perspective. Indeed, one of the most prevalent methods is scenario building, with scenarios being a consistent hypothesis of how the future will unfold—a chain of logic that connects 'drivers' to 'outcomes'.[2] Governments typically focus on the scenario-building approach in long-term planning, as it provides clear-cut alternatives to different situations.

The enunciation of India's short- and long-term security strategies is inevitably based on an appraisal of the prevailing and expected geostrategic environment. Apparently, the situation along the Line of Actual Control (LAC) from 2010 onwards—despite the prolonged standoffs in the Depsang Plains in 2013, Chumar in 2014 and Doklam in 2017—was one of a growing political and economic relationship between China and India. Au contraire, the aggression, intransigence and expansionism shown by the People's Republic of China (PRC) in 2020 in Eastern Ladakh, and the continuing stalemate, has transformed the paradigm. In spite of the reiteration of ceasefire in February 2021, tensions persist across the Line of Control (LOC). Building on such scenarios of distrust, policymaking will suffer from the weakness of postulating the future on current trends.

It can be argued that in addition to domestic politics, bureaucratic politics, organizational inertia, group think, psychological barriers, learning the wrong lessons from history and a failure of security strategies is also due to an inappropriate assessment of the environment.[3] Therefore, in order to contemplate future wars, it is imperative to have holistic visualization of principal regional threats and challenges, along with their collusion, including asymmetric ones, transnational threats and even unanticipated ones. The strategic geography on India's frontiers will change with time, will have clear diktats, and it will lead to a differing strategic context.

The Russo–Ukraine War, 2022, has also clearly indicated that warfare is changing at a dramatic rate and scope, and that historical similarities will not provide any guidance to future ones. The experience of past wars would be divorced from the realities of the twenty-first century and make us infer lessons that may be way off the mark.

Currently, we are seeing a spurt in the growth of military technologies, riding on information warfare (IW) and artificial intelligence (AI). Warfare has expanded beyond the three services—army, navy and air force—with new and modern domains like cyber, space, the electromagnetic spectrum and information having emerged. More fundamentally, the notion of warfare conducted in newer operational domains may simply not require kinetic combat to achieve political ends. The lines between peace and war, currently denoted by a grey zone, already stand subsumed or blurred. Execution of future warfare also has an intrinsic relationship between civil life and the military.

Hence, national strategy and military doctrines would, in the future, envisage the employment of all of a nation's military and civilian capabilities at the highest of levels, along with long-term planning, development and procurement to create the requisite capabilities to assure victory or success. These have to be enunciated by the politico-military establishment in peace; they must be planned, experimented upon and developed, and, in peacetime, forces must be trained for all scenarios. Strategic history is amply populated with cases of soldiers being given impossible tasks by policymakers in the heat of battle and of soldiers being compelled to operate in the absence of clear political guidance.[4]

The central theme of this chapter is that in the coming era of uncertainty and the increased relevance of the globally intertwined geostrategic environment—along with the rising challenger in China and its collusion with Pakistan—India's strategic formulations need to consider the landscape as a systemic one. Many developments in the technological, operational and political domains have converged to create conditions that favour the transition to discriminate force—that is, the use of military power selectively. Future wars can be envisioned as being conducted with the aim of achieving a situation of strategic advantage and not victory. Hence, there is the need to instil a methodical rigour in the discourse for evolving determinants and envision future doctrines for land warfare.

Changing Strategic Geography and Geostrategic Context

South Asia's strategic geography is important as it affects the national security and prosperity of India. This strategic geography is changing dramatically, with demographical changes, the development of nations, their geopolitical ambitions and the strategic relations between them. In the context of South Asia, there have been significant changes that are projected to happen in the next ten years.

India's geographical reality is framed by the Himalayas, the Pamir Knot, Karakoram and Hindu Kush to the north and northwest, the Thar Desert to the west and the mountainous jungles of northeastern India. India is a peninsula—flanked by the Arabian Sea to the west and southwest, and by the Bay of Bengal to the east and southeast—as it extends south into the Indian Ocean. The population of South Asia is nearly 1.9 billion, or about one-fourth of the world's, making it both the most populous and the most densely populated geographical region in the world.

Transition of Strategic Geography

The strategic geography of South Asia is undergoing intense transition due to infrastructural development and demographic changes in Tibet, Xinjiang, Gilgit-Baltistan (GB), Pakistan-occupied Kashmir (PoK) and Pakistan. Added to that are the projects under the Chinese Belt and Road Initiative (BRI), a large number of which should fructify in the current decade. These are trends that must be accepted as inevitable. The national policies of the sovereign countries of the South Asian region and the implementation of these policies have led to differing socio-economic developmental processes.

By studying the changes in strategic geography, we see that there will be five major routes to Tibet—the Sichuan–Tibet highway, the Yunnan–Tibet highway, the Xinjiang–Tibet highway, the Qinghai–Tibet highway, and the Sino–Nepal Friendship highway. It was perceived as immensely difficult, but China has built a highway which includes a 2-km-long mountain tunnel in a remote part of southeastern Tibet, which will end near its border with Arunachal Pradesh. The highway cuts through the world's deepest canyon, the Yarlung Tsangbo Grand Canyon, and its likely terminus is Baibung county (known as Drepung in Tibetan), close to the Indian border village of Bishing in the Upper Siang district of Arunachal Pradesh. Similarly, there is G216, a new highway will connect Urumqi in Xinjiang to Tibet (specifically, Kyirong on the Tibet–Nepal border), over the Kunlun Range, with interconnections with the Western Highway from Xinjiang to Tibet—the G219—that passes through Aksai Chin.

It is significant to note that in Tibet the road network reached a total length of 118,800 km at the end of 2020, up over 50 per cent from the end of 2015. By 2025, the total mileage of highways in Tibet will exceed 120,000 km, and that of expressways will exceed 1,300 km. About 190 billion yuan (USD 29.3 billion) will be channelized into expanding 'transportation infrastructure', into building new expressways and upgrading existing highways, and improving road connectivity in the remote and largely rural areas of Tibet Autonomous Region (TAR)—the longest section of the border with India—over the next five years.[5]

A new railway line will link Lhasa with Nyingchi in eastern Tibet as an important link between central-western Yunnan and southeast Tibet. The Yunnan–Tibet Railway belongs to the 'Five Railways to Tibet' together with the Qinghai–Tibet Railway, Sichuan–Tibet Railway, Xinjiang–Tibet Railway and Gansu–Tibet Railway. In the future, high-speed trains, powered by both electricity and internal combustion, will operate on a 435-km-long rail track to the provincial capital of Lhasa.

There are new attempts to change the demography and create additional infrastructure in Tibet, especially in proximity to the LAC. 'To date, the construction of 965 relocation sites [villages] has been completed and 266,000 people have moved into new houses. The relocation programmes were carried out entirely on a voluntary basis.' It is estimated that some 200 of these xiaokang (moderately well-off) villages are located near the Indian border—from Rutok in Ngari Prefecture in the west to Rima (opposite Kibithu in Arunachal Pradesh) in the Lohit valley in the east. A few model villages have been built on the Chinese side of the LAC in Ladakh, others north of the McMahon Line in the Tsona area. China's border villages pose a threat to India's defences.[6]

With recent evidence of the quick-time construction of the village at Longju, and in Nepal and Bhutan, it is apparent that a very large number of these xiaokang will be along the India–Tibet border—for resettling 'nomads', herders or the Han population, under the control of the Chinese Communist Party (CCP). In time, much of the border region will have substantive populations as permanent inhabitants. China is also commencing development of the 'largest zinc–lead deposit' mine in Huoshaoyun Mountain in Aksai Chin, where it has been stated that the combined recoverable zinc and lead resources stands at 18.87 million tonnes. Again, apparently, this major mining project, probably near the Lakhtang Range in Aksai Chin, will convert the area into a significant permanent habitation.

The BRI is the most significant engine of China's geopolitical ambitions, and South Asia is at the heart of it. While the COVID-19 pandemic has slowed down the initiative, it has not been put on the backburner either. In the coming decade, a number of projects will fructify—though some may get jettisoned for various reasons. In PoK, a long-term project under the China–Pakistan Economic Corridor (CPEC) involves the construction of the 682-km-long Khunjerab railway line between of Havelian and Khunjerab Pass an—with an extension to China's Lanxin Railway (the Southern Xinjiang Railway) in Kashgar—is underway. This railway line will run roughly parallel to the Karakoram Highway, and is expected to be completed by 2030. Between Thakot and Raikot, in Gilgit-Baltistan (GB), plans are underway to construct several hydropower projects, most notably the Diamer-Bhasha Dam and Dasu Dam. Sections of the N-35 around these projects will be completely rebuilt in tandem with the dam construction. A series of energy projects are being planned in PoK, as well. Two Special Economic Zones (SEZ) are planned here. A mixed-industry SEZ is to be established at Mirpur over 1,078 acres. Moqpondass Heavy Industry SEZ in GB is planned, spanning over 35 km in Gilgit and 160 km in Skardu, occupying 500 acres. It is located 200 km from Sust Dry Port enroute to Khunjerab Pass.

The GB region is losing its ethnic identity with planned demographic invasion, and the settling of population from Sindh and Punjab. There is also very large intake of Chinese, from security guards (many of them ex-PLA), to workers, managers and supervisors for every project here. Indeed, the Chinese workers may establish a permanent presence by constructing their own administrative enclaves. This projected makeover of PoK will become too calamitous for India in the next decade or so. The age-old sociocultural character of the region will be largely subsumed by this economic invasion of the area.

The geographic barrier of the Himalayas between Nepal and China, and Pakistan and Nepal, will be changed by railways, roads and tunnels. China will push its technology and deep pockets to ensure that this infrastructure development will make South Asian nations dependent on it for a long period.

It has been often stated that the BRI's flagship project, CPEC, may collapse under its own weight, due to resistance from local populations, financing difficulties (especially the dire straits the Pakistan economy is in currently), the ecological fragility of the region, especially Gilgit-Baltistan, serious vagaries of terrain, altitudes and weather, and the geological apprehension of earthquakes, floods and landslides. Yet, because of the enormous advantages for China— geopolitically, economically and in the prospecting of resources— the plan should succeed in some measure. The Trans-Himalayan economic corridors will come into being, linking Pakistan, Nepal and Myanmar with China's Xinjiang, Tibet, Yunnan, Sichuan and Gansu provinces, and allow intensive trade and interaction.

On the Indian side too, there are major changes afoot, with much better connectivity to Ladakh, Kashmir and Arunachal Pradesh. The current impetus should bear fruit by the end of this decade. The infrastructural changes will also have an effect on the demography and socio-economic state of the border regions. Hence, the changes in strategic geography are laying down the strategic context for the future. China's push at infrastructural construction in South Asia has become extremely significant, in that eminent American geostrategist Robert Kaplan's 'flattening of Himalayas' and the 'defeat of distance' are becoming truer. The strategic geography between India and China has clear diktats. If India wants to be a major geopolitical player in Asia, it needs to leverage its strategic geography to its full advantage. However, the strategic geography and the transition it is undergoing will see several effects on the country.

India's Threats and Challenges

By virtue of its history of antagonist relations with Pakistan and China, India is placed in an adversarial environment. The country has unsettled borders in a rapidly militarizing environment. The omnipotent questions are: will the LAC imbroglio be resolved in the next ten years? Or will it have at least some amicable resolutions that ushers in a relatively long-lasting peace? Will there be a makeover in the Pakistan polity that will settle the LOC and Jammu and Kashmir issues? Will the ensuing decade witness a conventional border war or a non-kinetic/non-contact war? Following current trends, these are problematic issues to forecast.

Assertive, aggressive China

The LAC is the disputed demarcation border line between India and China. The latter occupies Aksai Chin in Ladakh Union Territory, and has claimed territories in the Uttarakhand–Tibet border and Arunachal Pradesh. The LAC had been witnessing transgressions by the PLA in the areas claimed by China, and there have been occasional standoffs. The Indian forces faced scenarios of conflict against the PLA in the Nathu La–Cho La (in Sikkim) skirmish in 1967[7] and in Sumdorong Chu (Arunachal Pradesh) in 1987.[8] These were robustly and successfully handled by the Indian Army. The foundation of the management of eastern Ladakh were the protocols and the confidence-building measures (CBMs) of the LAC, under the four formal agreements of 1993, 1996, 2005 and 2013, which have been pushed to near-oblivion by the incursions of the PLA in 2020 in the region.

China has nearly reached the pinnacle as a superpower with global aspirations and desires to reobtain its primacy of previous times, and is rapidly spreading its wings. In the context of a pending boundary dispute with China, it is mandatory for New Delhi to explore how its relationship with Beijing will unfold. The 2020-21 tensions in eastern Ladakh predict a continuity in aggression and belligerence from China, in pursuance of its geopolitical ambitions. And it will continue to goad its client and rentier state, Pakistan, to keep ratcheting up tensions in Kashmir.

Contemplating China's future behaviour is an onerous task, and may be a frustrating exercise. Chinese military strategy documents highlight the direction for the PLA to be able to fight and win wars, deter potential adversaries, and secure Chinese national interests overseas. There is an increased emphasis on the importance of the maritime and information domains, on offensive air operations, long-distance mobility operations, long-range precision-guided vectors, and space and cyber operations. It is evident that China is sharpening its claws rapidly—from restructuring to exercising the concept of 'informatization' as seen in the PLA writings.

Beijing will have modern military capable of modern war by the time in celebrates the PLA's centenary in 2027, with a focus on 2050—of becoming a great power, by any and all means. In President Xi Jinping's Report to the Party Congress in 2017, China as a 'strong power' or 'great power' was repeated twenty-six times. Chinese actions portray revisionism and expansionism to promote and shape an environment favourable to its ambitions. With increasing strength and global presence, a stronger possibility exists of a threat manifesting from China in the mid and long term.

India, hence, can ill-afford to ignore its neighbour's increasing economic and military might, its assiduous strategic bases in the Indian Ocean region, the deliberate lack of progress in the Sino–Indian border talks, and the country's close economic and military affiliations with Pakistan. The interregnum, up to 2050, with many intermediate milestones, will be an era of major tensions, with India being a major geopolitical competitor in the periphery. This mandates a strong and effective military force, as part of comprehensive national power, to ensure the territorial integrity and sovereignty.

Antagonism of Pakistan

For Pakistan, a nation having taken birth without a clear identity, and with its inability to create and nurture one subsequently, maintaining integrity itself is an onerous task. The country suffers from a crisis of identity, and an omnipresent threat of Balkanization. Animosity with India lends Pakistan some credence of identity, which is crucial to retain itself as a nation state. It is obvious that this attitude is part of the DNA of the Pakistan Army, which virtually controls the polity of the nation. Pakistan defines its security in tangible terms—as a capability to thwart a military threat from India—and this provides legitimacy to its army as the custodian of nationalism. The geostrategic location of the nation, grave asymmetries in development among the provinces and the extraordinary role that the Pakistan Army has played compounds the anxieties of the nation—both at present and in the future. Its current poor economic state (and attempts to seek soft loans) only adds fuel to fire. Hence, any great sociopolitical change in Pakistan that would lead to an attitudinal change may not happen without attendant internal upheavals and instability.

It is important to note that Jammu and Kashmir is an emotive issue, an identity issue for Pakistan, which binds the country. It is a raison d'être for the Pakistan Army to retain its hold on the nation. Pakistan, without crossing established redlines—and exposing itself to the penalties and risks of escalation to conventional war—will attempt to reap success by utilizing proxies.

The country has also greatly enhanced the toolkit of information warfare—from ingenious disinformation and propaganda to taking advantage of social media for faster dissemination, from fanning radicalization to civil unrests. It is typical of Islamabad to be vigorous and aggressive in using strategic communication, and, in doing so, deliberately remains well under the threshold of conventional military conflict.

Suffice it to say, in the foreseeable future, with the state that Pakistan finds itself in politically and economically, it is in no position to initiate an all-out conventional war with India, though its intransigence and proxy fanning of troubles will continue. Pakistan, therefore, will remain an adversary in perpetuity, and does mandate hard power considerations and a war-winning strategy.

'Iron' brothers' collusion

In matters of China–Pakistan collusion, the latter has already upgraded its security calculus with the former through the CPEC. The collusive nuclear-warhead–ballistic-missile–military-hardware nexus between China and Pakistan, described by both as an 'all-weather friendship', has grown to menacing proportions. In a similar context, despite regular interactions at the highest level, little movement is evident on the India–China boundary question. With support from China, Pakistan is also a testing ground for the country's latest technology, in the next conflict or even in peacetime. It would employ a combination of different types of warfare—conventional war, insurgency, terrorism, and information warfare (IW)—a concoction of military and non-military, kinetic and non-kinetic. The burgeoning nexus clearly indicates a unified front of the two adversaries, in the north and west of India.

Grey-Zone Warfare against India

Pakistan's intransigence in supporting terrorist organizations and the proxy war in Jammu and Kashmir are well chronicled. This gives the country distinct advantages against India. However, the breadth of the anti-India grey-zone warfare emanating from Pakistan is fairly large, and is not only related to disinformation and incitement. It remains a low-cost option allowing it to push in fake Indian currency notes, drugs and hawala money, apart from raising varied bogeys at international fora, fanning internal dissent and sponsoring terrorism by using proxies.

Kashmir is but one manifestation of its larger geopolitical rivalry with India. Exploiting social media, technological tools and cyber warfare, the country easily disseminates adverse information, with fakes/deep fakes/the use of the dark web and continuous distortions, without any challenge of accountability. There is a very large strategic canvas created by Pakistan to undermine Indian national security.

This multi-pronged offensive against India is retained below the threshold of conventional war in an ambitious grey-zone campaign. India, by itself, is a large and diverse nation, with a never-ending cacophony of voices and myriad problems, which provide incalculable opportunities that a belligerent and adversarial Pakistan can and does easily take advantage of. Such a war will remain a low-cost option, by an economically and militarily weaker state, as a way to keep in check India's rise as a major power, influencing its neighbours.

China is the master of grey-zone ambiguity. Henry Kissinger had opined that '... whereas Western tradition preferred the decisive clash of force, emphasizing feats of heroism, the Chinese ideal stressed subtlety, indirection and patient accumulation of relative advantage'.[9] Sun Tzu had, centuries ago, prophesized that 'all warfare is based upon deception'. Psychological operations that would end in intellectual confusion for the adversary are part and parcel of the Chinese philosophy. 'Unrestricted warfare'[10] has nullified the boundary between battlespace and non-battlespace, with non-military methods including trade and economic aid, and financial-, ecological-, network- and resource-based warfare and the like being used.

The three-warfare strategy is a form of statecraft that encompasses non-kinetic means to achieve political ends. The first of the three-warfare strategy is psychological, which seeks to influence and/or disrupt opponents' decision-making capability, create doubts, foment anti-leadership sentiment and diminish the will to fight. The second, media warfare, also called public-opinion warfare, is a constant, ongoing activity aimed at the long-term influence of perceptions and attitudes, leveraging all instruments that inform and influence public opinion. And the third, legal warfare, or 'lawfare', exploits the national and international legal system to achieve political and commercial objectives.[11] As one delves into and analyses the three-warfare strategy, it is apparent that though military coercion may be part and parcel of the overall concept, political aims will be achieved largely by manipulation and economics.

Hence, the future security environment of India is one of concern. So, as geostrategic concerns and anxieties remain, they have to be planned for. The Indian Ocean Region (IOR) will be an arena that needs to stand firm under grave provocation. In the Indian context, future warfare seeks readiness to face a focused threat posed by military forces below or above the threshold of open warfare and non-military means across the full range of the threat spectrum. To be prepared for eventualities, it is understandable that future war fighting will be a national endeavour and will encompass national power. Contextually, it is essential to delve into the strategic culture and the civil–military interface in fashioning the national military strategy.

Technology: The Driver of Future Warfare

Warfare has always remained evolutionary, though in the last three decades, there has been a race to create newer technologies. The prospective great transition in warfare can be ascribed to these newer technologies of the information age. This spurt in technologies has been trending decisively in favour of offence. In land warfare of the future, large manoeuvres by heavy formations and deep thrusts, in plains and deserts, will be rendered difficult. It will be an era when combat will, in addition to conventional forces, include an admixture of militias, guerrillas, terror groups, precision projectiles and information warfare.

Technology is thus changing the very way we analysed warfare and fought wars. In future wars, machines will make life-and-death engagement decisions, without relying on human interface. Taking the military technological advancements in China as a cue for futuristic study, the following aspects need to be taken cognizance of in formulating military strategy:

- The PLA is sprinting towards the creation of robotic vehicles, including many that are autonomous, in maritime, aerial or land warfare. In future battlefields, drone swarms of intelligent, autonomous and undercover machines will have a devastating effect on large, expensive and heavily manned systems. There will also be a plethora of sensors of a very wide and sophisticated variety, increasing in coverage and intensity.
- Information warfare constitutes the foundation of the People's Liberation Army's Strategic Support Force (PLASSF) doctrine of winning informationized wars. The PLASSF is responsible for cyber and electronic warfare, and is vital to its capabilities to fight and win. Information warfare (IW) 'relies upon networked information systems and informationized weapons, fighting on air, land, sea, space, and in the electromagnetic spectrum'.[11] In addition, artificial intelligence (AI) and other emerging technologies will change the way wars are fought. While AI will take on myriad forms, it essentially comprises algorithms capable of processing and learning from vast amounts of data, and then taking decisions autonomously or semi-autonomously. Cyber warriors will use AI to process large volumes of data to help detect attacks against critical infrastructures.[12]

- The PLASSF is integrating PLA's IW capabilities, enabling the coordinated pursuit of electronic countermeasures, cyberattack and defence, and psychological warfare missions. The C4ISR (command, control, communications, computers [C4] intelligence, surveillance and reconnaissance [ISR]) capabilities will enable the PLA to effectively conduct joint operations and successfully prosecute 'system vs system' warfare, which will be essential to winning modern wars. China is attempting to utilize AI to direct high-technology-weapons capabilities, especially in the cyber and electronic warfare (EW) domains, and leveraging big data and machine learning for 'cognitive EW'.
- The oncoming fifth generation (5G) of mobile technologies will have potential military applications for autonomous vehicles, command and control (C2), intelligence, surveillance and reconnaissance (ISR) systems—which would each benefit from improved data rates and lower time delays. While each of these applications could increase military effectiveness, there are concerns over data security, particularly passing sensitive information like intelligence or operational requirements over commercial systems.[13]
- A serious oncoming trend is the lethal autonomous weapon systems (LAWS), which are weapon systems that once activated can *select* and *engage* targets without further human intervention. China argues that LAWS are characterized by lethality, autonomy, impossibility to terminate once started, indiscriminate effect in that it will 'execute the task of killing and maiming *regardless of conditions, scenarios and targets*'.[14]
- The increased importance of precision-guided munitions, space warfare, stealth fighters, strategic missiles and rockets are all indications of much increased lethality in warfare. China is moving towards future wars with extreme deadliness, with

loitering munitions, also known as lethal miniature aerial munitions (LMAMs), which will be a form of unmanned aircraft system that incorporate a warhead and can be thought of functionally as an unmanned kamikaze plane. Given their plane-like attributes, LMAMs are able to stay aloft for extended periods—thus 'loitering' over a target area.[15] China's new microwave weapon can disable missiles and paralyse tanks by shutting down electronic systems (even those with traditional shielding against electro-magnetic pulses) by bombarding the target with energy pulses between 300 and 300,000 megahertz. This amount of directed energy interferes with and overloads electronic circuits, causing them to shut down. China is also focusing on the delivery of precision-strike munitions via individual projectiles (such as cruise and ballistic missiles) rather than the platform-based strike forces (such as aircraft, ships and submarines).

- The more that militaries rely on the electromagnetic spectrum for communications and sensing targets, the more vital it will be to win the invisible electronic war of jamming, spoofing and deception fought through the electromagnetic spectrum.
- China currently fields about 1,200 conventionally armed short-range ballistic missiles (SRBMs, 300–1,000 km range), 200 to 300 conventional medium-range ballistic missiles (MRBMs, 1,000–3,000 km range), an indeterminate number of conventional intermediate-range ballistic missiles (IRBMs, 3,000–5,500 km), and 200–300 ground-launched cruise missiles (GLCMs, 1500+ km). An initial wave of ballistic missiles would neutralize air defences and command centres, and crater the runways of military air bases, trapping aircraft on the ground. These initial paralysing ballistic missile salvos could then be followed by waves of cruise missiles targeting

hardened aircraft shelters, aircraft parked in the open, and fuel handling and maintenance facilities.
- Satellites face increasing threats, starting with killer debris in the vast supersonic junkyards circling the earth. Satellites are also vulnerable to a wide array of intentional threats, such as killer satellites. The US Department of Defense, in a report, judged that '... new threats to commercial and military uses of space are emerging, while increasing digital connectivity of all aspects of life, business, government, and military creates significant vulnerabilities. During conflict, attacks against our critical defense, government, and economic infrastructure must be anticipated.'[16] China has proven its kinetic physical counterspace capabilities several times with a range of direct-ascent anti-satellite weapon (ASAT) systems and conventional midcourse missile interceptors that could potentially be used as an ASAT.
- China's military is developing powerful lasers and electromagnetic railguns for use in a future 'light war' involving space-based attacks on satellites. In 2018, the US director of National Intelligence stated that China is making advances in directed-energy technology that can 'blind or damage sensitive space-based optical sensors, such as those used for remote sensing or missile defense'. In 2019, there was a similar claim, stating 'China likely is pursuing laser weapons to disrupt, degrade, or damage satellites and their sensors and possibly already has a limited capability to employ laser systems against satellite sensors.'[17]

There are more significant changes in warfare, brought in by a racing transition in military technology. Writing for Center for a New American Security, scholar Elsa Kania contends that China is starting to catch up in its quest to become a 'science and technology superpower' and that the PLA is pursuing advances in impactful and disruptive military applications of AI. The PLA anticipates that the advent of AI could fundamentally change the character of warfare, resulting in a transformation from today's 'informatized' ways of warfare to future 'intelligentized' warfare, in which AI will be critical to military power. The PLA intends to achieve an advantage through the changing paradigms in warfare with military innovation, thus seizing the 'commanding heights' of future military competition.[18] Obviously, therefore, technology will become the driver of future warfare.

China's leaders continue to emphasize on developing a military that can fight and win. The country's military strategy is to build a strong, combat-effective armed forces capable of winning regional conflicts and employing integrated, real-time command and control networks. The PLA's air force is shifting towards offensive operations, the army is focusing on long-distance mobility operations, and the need for superiority in the information domain, including through space and cyber operations.

The role of non-military means of achieving political and strategic goals is growing, and, in many cases, will exceed the force of weapons and their effectiveness. This implies that wars in the future may remain unannounced, in a non-kinetic format and may even be successful in achieving political goals without transcending to force-on-force wars. This changing paradigm of prospective warfare planned by the PLA dictates fundamental changes in strategizing for future warfare in multi-domains including land.

Strategizing for Future Land Warfare: In the Indian Context

The stark truth here is that the ongoing revolution in military technology, especially in China, demands a revolution in strategic thinking. Five broad strands of future warfare in the Indian context will be relevant for consideration:

- One, warfare can be undertaken, in the modern context, below full conventional warfare. In what is called the grey zone, adversaries aim to achieve geopolitical ambitions without overt military aggression—from routine statecraft, to fuelling insurgencies and terrorism, to limited war and subterfuge. The adversary would attempt to intimidate or coerce India, relying on the threat of future military force to influence decision-making, including the limited use of actual force. Military coercion means the use of armed instruments to alter the opponent's behaviour. The stratagem of the PLA's transgressions in 2020 in eastern Ladakh—undertaken surreptitiously—can be part of that coercive philosophy of China that gains strategic advantages even territorially without escalation into conventional warfare.
- Two, with a disputed LAC and LOC with China and Pakistan respectively remaining hot and tense, escalation into all-out conventional wars is likely. This could involve territorial offence and defence, the use of aerospace and maritime power, along with the newer domains of cyberspace and electromagnetic spectrum. Currently, the dictum is that conventional wars of the territorial kind are passé. This philosophy, in the context of disputed borders, is fraught with generalization and will be detrimental to national security.
- Three, as territorial wars would invariably lead to a large number of physical casualties, adversaries may resort to alternative non-contact warfare using precision-guided munitions (PGMs), space warfare, stealth fighters, strategic missiles, rockets, and robotics and AI. Conventional missile/rocket strikes against important strategic and tactical targets

may become the norm. An equivalent could be the plethora of rockets fired by Hamas from Gaza to Israel in April 2021. An air/missile/PGM campaign will result in the destruction, neutralization or severe damage of:

- command, control and communications capabilities.
- logistical and operational bases for weapons and war-fighting.
- infrastructure such as roads, bridges, railheads, airfields and docks.

- Four, non-kinetic means, which include cyber, social, economic, and psychological strategies, can act as force multipliers by shaping the environment and lowering own will through coercion. Such asymmetric battlefield tactics may not involve physical combat or destruction, or even the armed forces' direct involvement. A case in point could be Mumbai, when on 12 October 2020, trains shut down and the stock market closed because of power outage in a city of 20 million people. Hospitals had to switch to emergency generators to keep ventilators running. A new study lends weight to the idea that those events may well have been connected to a broad Chinese cyber campaign against India's power grid, timed to send a message that if New Delhi pressed its claims too hard, the lights could go out across the country.[19] The authors of the study include transgressions in eastern Ladakh as an event connected with the cyberattack in Mumbai!

- Five, consequent to the Nagorno-Karabkh war, 2020, and the ongoing Russo–Ukrainian war, 2022, many thinkers have spoken about the demise of the tank, or otherwise. Observing the battlespace intently, there is indeed no replacement to boots on the ground or the tank as a platform. However, modern technology with shoulder-fired anti-tank weapons, and irregular warfare practised by the Ukrainian defenders clearly indicate limitations of mechanized warfare, especially in an urban environment. Added to this are the precision-guided munitions, drones and loiter ammunitions, which are increasingly equipped with artificial intelligence and autonomy. There has been conservative use of tactical air force, avoiding low-level operations. Attack helicopters may have limited use in contested airspace. A very large number of ballistic and cruise missiles were fired in the first 24 hours and in the next thirty days of the war in Ukraine. It calls attention to PLA's system-confrontation and system-destruction strategy that has distinctly similar focus. The large Russian tank's destruction must not be pushed under by ascribing it to poor vintage tactics or ill-planned combined arms support. The tank will have to take another avatar, sort out its 'cook off' of ammunition issue, get some directed energy weapons, different metallurgy and active protection to improve its survivability, all without gaining weight.

It is apparent that warfare in any of its different avatars cannot be segregated to land, sea, air or the emerging newer domains. The terminology of jointness has been constantly spoken of in the armed forces, which implies holding integrated military operations with a common strategy, methodology and conduct. A country is said to have attained jointmanship of its armed forces if it institutionalizes the following:

- Joint planning, development of doctrine and policymaking
- Joint operational commands and staff structures
- The evolution of joint-equipment policy and procurement organization

- Integrated preparation of budget and monitoring of expenditure—both capital and revenue
- Joint training[20]

Joint military strategy consists of the establishment of military objectives, the formulation of strategic concepts to accomplish the said objectives, and the creation and use of military resources to implement the concepts. As the Russo–Ukrainian war, 2022, has shown, use of force is a cultural phenomenon, and the politico-military dynamic is most important in constructive and effective formulation of strategy. In this war, there are apparently political constraints in the use of combat force. There were apparently strong political diktats on the use of discriminate fire power, measured response and precision fires, to avoid damage to cities, national infrastructure and the population.

It is also imperative to mention that the 'ends' as contemplated by the political hierarchy will need translation to a military 'end state'—both of which will be different. Contextually, strategy has myriad definitions—its essence being the influencing of the behaviour of the adversary, but the simplest definition being the balance between ends, ways and means. 'Ways' are to employ a 'means' to achieve the 'ends', while recognizing war as a continuation of political objectives.

Successful land strategy-making requires an awareness of combined effects beyond joint and combined arms thinking. Contemporary land strategy needs to be integrated with other instruments of power across all domains—civil and military alike—and present more than a combination of effects. Six issues deserve mention here. First, rightly, in the context of modern wars, doctrine and strategy ought to be joint, and encompass all facets of warfare, as highlighted previously. Future wars will not recognize the land, sea or air environment individually; they would amalgamate all and much more. Diverse and competing doctrines of the three services, and the value each service places on its own individual plans and objectives, will not help in the changing character of the next war.

Second, defence budgets are dwindling in real terms and this status will continue post-pandemic for quite some time. Military technologies, on the contrary, are changing dramatically. With the continued intransigence of India's two adversaries and their collusion, New Delhi faces the dilemma of enunciating a futuristic military strategy, and creating the right future force and capabilities. These need fast experimentation, adoption and adaptation. We really need to think hard, especially now, about what the next wars are going to look like and what we can do to mitigate the dangers. In the twenty-first century, victory is not based on metrics of destruction, of war-waging potential and territory captured, but in achieving the given measure of success and advantage against the adversary.

Third, as is apparent in the Russo–Ukrainian war, 2022, urban warfare is an absolutely different kettle of fish. Recent examples of urban warfare, Grozny (31 December 1994 to 8 February 1995 and 25 December 1999 to 6 February 2000), Fallujah (4 April 2004 to 1 May 2004, 7 November 2004 to 23 December 2004 and 22 May 2016 to 29 June 2016) among others, saw great devastations. A significant case is of Mosul (from 16 October 2016 to 4 January 2017), when US-backed Iraqi security forces conducted a full-scale attack to liberate Mosul from the Islamic State. Urban warfare is a high-cost, high-risk operation, and can have little regard for any humanitarian laws of war, morality or concerns about collateral damage. This brings to fore the immense urbanization (in addition to the water-obstacle-ridden terrain) in the plains of Pakistan and India. The right lessons must be drawn from modern-day urban wars in contemplating military strategies in an urbanized environment. There is a distinct emphasis on morality issues, rules of warfare, human rights of civilians used as human shields, humanitarian corridors for evacuation of civilians from the thick of battle zones, and war crimes investigations.

Fourth, are we still relying on legacy doctrines of the last century? Two of these provide abiding images. One is the linear defence structures, or trench warfare, in multi-tiers, drawn from the philosophy of no loss of territory. Historically, this draws from the French Maginot Line of the Second World War that collapsed in the first six months of the commencement of war. Similar to it was the fate of Bar-Lev Line, along the Suez Canal, in the Yom Kippur war. The second is the method of offensive warfare designed to undertake swift, deep and focused thrusts in the adversary's territory using mobile, manoeuvrable forces and air support—also called blitzkrieg, whose initial proponent was Heinz Guderian of the German Army in the Second World War. The call for indigenization of doctrines may be related to these two that have remained steadfast for over eighty years.

Fifth, is to examine what would constitute capabilities for punitive, credible and dissuasive deterrence, and under what conditions will they work. These terms are loosely used, and lead to tedious questions that mandate the jettisoning of flawed arguments and taking sound decisions. The spectrum of deterrence by denial (dissuasion) describes a nuanced effort to shape the thinking of the adversary, by affecting his psychological state of mind so that he is convinced that his actions are unlikely to succeed, and hence, he seeks alternatives to aggression or belligerence. Deterrence by punishment (punitive action), on the other hand, threatens severe penalties or punishment, even nuclear escalation. In the latter, the adversary has to be convinced that we possess the capabilities and national will to employ them. In our case, deterrence refers largely to military capabilities—a threat of military response. Our deterrence strategies, hence, need to be examined in the context their success or otherwise in the past. With changing warfare, a much broader notion of deterrence that keeps the focus on threats, but expands the scope to non-military capabilities and actions as well is necessary. While all may not be relevant to us, these can be threats of economic decoupling, diplomatic exclusion, information operations, or in the cyber, electromagnetic spectrum and space domains.

Sixth, are the issues that have been constantly debated, of information warfare (IW). It is understandable that virality triumphs veracity, and negativism goes viral in no time. Creation of narratives is a process that mandates specialization and specialists, otherwise social media will become the handmaiden of inimical elements and adversaries. India's military hierarchy needs to get on with creating the strategy, the synergy, structures and specialists for future IW.

Conclusion

The greatest challenge of our times is to be able to make correct and timely assessments of the changes taking place in the strategic environment, the nature and extent of the challenges and threats, and the best methods to combat them. It is obvious that prospective warfare is based on presumptions of the future, which can often go wrong. In war, there is nothing more important than understanding the political objectives of the adversaries involved. States go to war to get something they want, or to preserve what they have. This is the *why* of the war—the reasons why warring states are willing to spill blood and spend large budgets.

Sometimes, the objective is masked in religious or ideological terms—as in Pakistan; sometimes it is obvious, Herculean geopolitical ambitions—as with China. The easiest way out for the Indian military is to remain in status quo, and hence, it is oft-stated that generals have the tendency to 'fight the last war'.

The power of inertia is just too strong. It is critical to obtain a firm analytical foundation—the *why* of prospective war—and to understand the likely political objective or aim, politico-military strategy and the technological changes that have overriding implications for warfare, and create dynamic sectoral profiling on the use of combat force.

This is the time to press pause, contemplate, refashion and reset. Mindful of the ever-ready adversaries, for India the political aim and prognosis of scenarios and the typology of warfare are essential to determine everything—the concepts, doctrines and strategy, and the force capabilities mandatory and organizational structures required. The political objective will lay down military objectives, as also the capabilities and the effort required to achieve them. While it is imperative that the polity formally informs the military leaders what is desired, it is also incumbent on the military leaders to seek clarity of the political objective. This also implies that military leaders should be involved in decision-making that is mandated for national security.

India has unsettled borders and in mid-2021, both the LOC and LAC have seen tensions rise. In sum, what is required is clean drafting pads and a clutch of thought leaders—military and civilian alike—a contemplation afresh of a utilization of national (including military) power optimally, and strategizing twenty-first-century war-fighting concepts. India has to plan capabilities that would be needed till the middle of the century. National military strategy, which will encompass the land strategy, must be both practical and purposeful. The war-fighting strategical transition must precede any force restructuring. A *ways* transition will assuredly lead to serious, well-analysed, credible right-sizing, and internally generate substantial *means* to create a modern, forward-looking force, capable of achieving the *ends*. Such a military war-fighting philosophy will also denote that we have 'arrived', as a force with twenty-first-century credentials.

As the saying goes in Latin: *Si vis pacem, parabellum*. If you want peace, then prepare for war.

Notes

1. Jasjit Singh, 'A Security Strategy for the 21st Century', in Kapil Kak, ed., *Comprehensive Security for an Emerging* India, Centre for Air Power Studies, New Delhi: KW Publishers, 2010, p. 1.
2. S. Bernstein, R.N. Lebow, J.G. Stein and S. Webber, 'God Gave Physics the Easy Problems: Adapting Social Science to an Unpredictable World', *European Journal of International Relations*, vol. 7, no.1, March 2000, pp. 43–76, http://sciencepolicy.colorado.edu/students/envs_5000/bernstein_2000.pdf, accessed 15 February 2005.
3. Shiping Tang, 'A Systemic Theory of the Security Environment', *Journal of Strategic Studies*, vol. 27, no. 1, March 2004, p. 1, accessed 15 February 2005.
4. Colin S. Gray, *War, Peace and International Relations: An Introduction to Strategic History*, Oxon: Rutledge, 2007, p. 7.
5. Sutirtho Patranobis, 'Tibet Infrastructure Plan: China to Invest Nearly $30 Billion in Five Years', *Hindustan Times*, New Delhi, 9 March 2021, https://www.hindustantimes.com/world-news/tibet-infrastructure-plan-china-to-invest-nearly-30-billion-in-five-years-101615293322589.html, accessed 9 March 2021.
6. Claude Arpi, 'China's Border Villages Are a Threat to India's Defences', *The Daily Guardian*, 28 October 2020, https://thedailyguardian.com/chinas-border-villages-are-a-threat-to-indias-defences/, accessed 2 January 2021.
7. Probal Das Gupta, *Watershed 1967: India's Forgotten Victory over China*, New Delhi: Juggernaut Books, 2020, p. 2
8. Mandip Singh, 'Lessons from Somdurong Chu Incident', Manohar Parrikar Institute for Defence Studies and Analyses, New Delhi, 26 April 2013, https://idsa.in/idsacomments/CurrentChineseincursionLessonsfromSomdurongChuIncident_msingh_260413, accessed 15 September 2000.
9. Henry Kissinger, *On China*, London: Penguin Books, 2012, p. 47.

10. Qiao Liang and Wang Xiangsui, 'Unrestricted Warfare', Beijing, 1999, https://www.cryptome.org/ cuw.htm, accessed 15 September 2021.
11. John Chen, 'Choosing the Least Bad Option: Organizational Interests and Change in the PLA Ground Forces', Washington DC: National Defence University Press, 2019, https://ndupress.ndu.edu/Media/News/News-Article-View/Article/1747391/choosing-the-least-bad-option-organizational-interests-and-change-in-the-pla-gr/, accessed 15 November 2021.
12. Debasis Dash, 'Autonomy and Artificial Intelligence: The Future Ingredient of Area Denial Strategy in Land Warfare', Centre for Land Warfare Studies, New Delhi, 2018.
13. P.K. Mallick, '5G, Huawei and India', Vivekananda International Foundation, New Delhi, 2019.
14. Elsa Kania, 'China's Strategic Ambiguity and Shifting Approach to Lethal Autonomous Weapons Systems', Lawfare, 17 April 2018, https://www.lawfareblog.com/chinas-strategic-ambiguity-and-shifting-approach-lethal-autonomous-weapons-systems, accessed 15 November 2021.
15. J. Noel Williams, 'Killing Sanctuary: The Coming Era of Small, Smart, Pervasive Lethality', War on the Rocks, 29 September 2017, http://www.css.ethz.ch/en/services/digital-library/articles/article.html/5097848a-d36d-4918-b62c-aab6c6dee9ea, accessed 15 November 2021.
16. 'Summary of the National Defense Strategy', United States Department of Defense, 2018, https://dod.defense.gov/Portals/1/Documents/pubs/2018-National-Defense-Strategy-Summary.pdf, accessed 15 November 2021.
17. Challenges to Security in Space, Defence Intelligence Agency Report 2019, p. 20, https://aerospace.csis.org/wp-content/uploads/2019/03/20190101_ChallengestoSecurityinSpace_DIA.pdf, accessed 1 June 2021.
18. Elsa Kania, 'Battlefield Singularity: Artificial Intelligence, Military Revolution, and China's Future Military Power', Center for New American Security, 28 November 2017, https://www.cnas.org/publications/reports/battlefield-singularity-artificial-intelligence-

military-revolution-and-chinas-future-military-power, accessed 5 November 2021.
19. David E. Sanger and Emily Schmall, 'China Appears to Warn India: Push Too Hard and the Lights Could Go Out', *The New York Times*, 28 February 2021, https://www.nytimes.com/2021/02/28/us/politics/china-india-hacking-electricity.html, accessed 1 October 2021.
20. Mrinal Suman, 'Jointmanship and Attitudinal Issues', Institute of Defence Studies, *Journal of Defence Studies*, vol. 1, no. 1, New Delhi, 2007, https://idsa.in/system/files/JDS1%281%292007_0.pdf, accessed 2 January 2021.

CHAPTER 6

Aerospace: A Security Perspective

RAGHUNATH NAMBIAR

India, with a population estimated at 1.4 billion, is the second-most populous country in the world. It also is the seventh-largest country by land area, and the most populous democracy in the world. The aerospace sector in the country, given our size and demands, should logically be just as large and must be channelled to become a growth engine for our economy.

India's growth in the civil aerospace sector—at least from the passenger travel data perspective—has been spectacular. In pre-COVID-19 times, it had the world's third-largest civil aviation market, with the number of passengers growing at an average annual rate of 18 per cent between 2000 and 2019. Despite the size of this market, much of the country's aviation potential remains untapped. India does not manufacture any civil aviation aircraft and is fully dependent on imports for satisfying its requirements.

The sector directly supports industries such as research and development (R&D), manufacturing, operations, maintenance, and support for the military and civilian segments. Each of these is, by itself, important for the nation's growth and prosperity, but the military sector is vital for our defence. This chapter focuses primarily on the military aerospace challenges and opportunities that India faces as these have significant security implications.

India's military aerospace sector has closely mirrored the civil aviation sector with a large portion based on imports. It is ironic that while India has one of the largest defence industrial complexes in the developing world—with thirty-nine ordnance factories, nine defence public sector undertakings (DPSUs), and over fifty Defence Research and Development Organisation (DRDO) research laboratories—the country continues to be overwhelmingly dependent on hardware imports, especially in the aerospace sector. We have been able to design and develop a fourth-generation fighter, a nuclear submarine, a main battle tank and an intercontinental ballistic missile, and yes, despite these achievements, we continue to import a substantial portion of our military requirements. This means India spends huge sums of monies each year as one of the world's biggest importers of aerospace products.

The nation is geographically located in a troubled neighbourhood with disputed borders with two of its neighbours—China and Pakistan, both possessing nuclear weapons. The former, which is by far the most serious threat to India, desires to establish global dominance and has, over the past decade, established itself as a major economic power. China's GDP ranks second only to the US. This has enabled its defence budget and military spending, especially in aerospace, to be significantly higher as compared to India.

Pakistan, our neighbour to the west, views itself as ideologically at odds with India and has degenerated over the past decade to the status of a failed economy, with terrorism being routinely employed as part of state policy. Pakistan's economy is in a mess, and this has put serious constraints on its military budget and has diminished its capability. Islamabad has attempted to counter this decline by sponsoring insurgency. While we may be superior in military power to Pakistan today, and in the foreseeable future, the same is not the case with China.

Procurement of advanced aerospace platforms and weapon systems are generally cost prohibitive, and cutting-edge technologies are restricted in the marketplace. Thus, equipping our forces with modern aerospace weapons is a major economic challenge for India. It is presently estimated that about 30 per cent of the government expenditure is towards defence, of which about 60 per cent is for aviation- and air-defence-related equipment. The budget saw severe stress due to the COVID-19 pandemic, but the threat from our neighbours, especially from China, forces India to continue to spend its scarce resources on costly imports.

China has built up considerable conventional forces with the primary purpose of striking at its enemies in what it terms as 'an informatized, no contact battle'.[1] By informatized warfare, what is meant is the use of smart weapons and forces, including battlefield-management systems, precision-strike capabilities, and technology-assisted command and control. The People's Liberation Army (PLA) has had set for itself medium- to long-term objectives of improving and expanding the strength of its ballistic missiles, cruise missiles, submarines, advanced aircraft and other modern systems.

The PLA is working toward these goals by developing and acquiring new weapon systems and military technologies of both foreign and domestic origin. It has also promulgated a new doctrine for modern warfare and reformed its military institutions. As of now, however, China's ability to project its conventional military power beyond its periphery remains limited. It fallaciously claims a policy of 'active defence', which suggests a defensive military strategy and repeatedly stresses that 'China does not initiate wars or fight wars of aggression but engages in war only to defend national sovereignty and territorial integrity and attacks only after being attacked'.[2]

With China, India's only viable option at present, and in the near future, is to deter aggression and prevent it from establishing a hegemony in the region.

Given our long land border with China over some of the most difficult and inaccessible terrain in the world, large armies—no matter how powerful—would necessarily need to establish a substantial advantage in localized strength to deter aggression. In the maritime domain, even with twice the present holdings of naval assets in the Indian Ocean region, India's maritime forces would not be in a position to significantly deter a land battle on our borders, nor significantly influence its outcome. Aerospace power, therefore, remains the most viable and effective option to deter China and Pakistan from both mischief and adventure.

Threat Spectrum in Aerospace

Major challenges impede India's progress in the field of aerospace, both at present and in the foreseeable future. The swift advances in technology in this high-tech field have also resulted in a rapid evolution of the threats we need to counter.

Our nation faces numerous perils and security challenges, especially in the aerospace domain. These range from ballistic missiles fielded by our neighbours at one end of the technology spectrum to attacks by unmanned small-sized drones at the other end. Here, we detail in brief the threats in the region, the possible ways to counter them and the technological advancements we would need to develop.

Ballistic Missiles

China is in the process of building and deploying a sophisticated and modern missile arsenal, and is unwilling to enter any arms control or other transparency agreements. Beijing has focused its missile development for anti-access/area-denial missile systems, which use a combination of ballistic and cruise missiles launched from air, land and sea to target its enemies in the Asia-Pacific theatre. It is also developing a number of advanced capabilities, such as manoeuvrable anti-ship ballistic missiles, multiple independent re-entry vehicles (MIRVs), and hypersonic glide vehicles. The combination of these degrades the survivability of America's aircraft carriers and its forward air bases. China also has a relatively small but developing contingent of nuclear intercontinental ballistic missiles, capable of striking the US homeland, as well as a growing fleet of nuclear ballistic missile submarines.

The People's Liberation Army Rocket Force (PLARF) is the strategic and tactical missile force of China. The PLARF is the fourth branch of the PLA and controls the nation's arsenal of land-based ballistic missiles—both nuclear and conventional. The PLARF was formed in 1966; it comprises approximately 100,000 personnel and six ballistic missile brigades. The six brigades are independently deployed in different military regions throughout the country. China has the largest land-based missile arsenal in the world. This includes 1,200 conventionally armed short-range ballistic missiles, 200 to 300 conventional medium-range ballistic missiles, as well as 200–300 ground-launched cruise missiles.

Over the years, these missiles have increased in accuracy and are now capable of destroying targets even without nuclear warheads. Pakistan too has established a large missile arsenal, which now forms an important part of its defence strategy for offsetting the significant conventional military advantages of India. Pakistan's arsenal consists primarily of mobile short- and medium-range ballistic missiles, but it has also made significant strides in its cruise missile capability. Its missiles now allow it to target almost any point in India. It has also claimed to be working on more advanced technology, such as MIRVs, to complicate the developing Indian missile defence efforts. Pakistan has received significant technical assistance from China in its nuclear and missile programmes, and strong evidence also indicates close cooperation with both North Korea and Iran on the development and proliferation of these systems.

India too has successfully developed a series of strategic missile systems. We have developed, tested, and operationalized a number of missile systems including ICBMs (intercontinental ballistic missiles), ASATs (anti-satellite weapons), SLBMs (submarine-launched ballistic missiles) and hypersonic weapon systems. Threats posed by Chinese and Pakistani missile systems pushed India to pursue a ballistic missile defence programme. The Indian ballistic missile defence (BMD) programme, termed 'Programme AD', aims to develop and deploy a multi-layered ballistic missile defence system to protect the country from ballistic missile attacks. The two-tier system is intended to destroy an incoming missile, at a higher altitude, in the exo-atmosphere (>100 km) and, if that fails, an endo-atmospheric interception will commence. The BMD system consists of separate high- and low-altitude interception missiles. The exo-atmospheric Prithvi Air Defence (PAD) missile interceptors can engage incoming missiles at exo-atmospheric altitudes of 80 km to 150 km, while the Advanced Air Defence (AAD) missiles can engage targets in the endo-atmospheric altitudes of 15 to 30 km.

The first phase of the BMD programme is now complete, and the Indian Air Force (IAF) and DRDO are awaiting governmental approval to install the missile shield for the national capital—about three to four years would be needed after approval to install the shield. In the next ten years, the missile threats from our adversaries are likely to increase and we need to deploy more such systems to counter these threats.

India has also procured five squadrons of S-400 air defence and BMD systems from Russia, and delivery of these were scheduled from October 2021 and would be complete by end-2023. The

S-400 system consists of four types of interceptor missiles, capable of simultaneously engaging all types of airborne threats ranging from low-flying drones to cruise missiles, aircraft and ballistic missiles.

Cruise Missiles

The cruise missile is a guided missile used against surface targets; it remains in the atmosphere and flies most portion of its flight path at a constant speed, approximately, and at low levels to avoid detection. Cruise missiles are designed to deliver a large warhead over long distances with high precision. Modern cruise missiles are capable of travelling at supersonic or high subsonic speeds, are self-navigating, and are able to fly on a non-ballistic, extremely low-altitude trajectory. Recent advances in this field include hypersonic cruise missiles, capable of speeds in excess of Mach 5 (five times the speed of sound). China has developed a family of air-launched and ground-launched cruise missiles and has deployed them. Pakistan currently has four cruise missile systems: the air-launched Ra'ad and the enhanced version Ra'ad II; the ground- and underwater-launched Babur; the ship-launched Harbah missile; and the surface-launched Zarb missile. Both Ra'ad and Babur have been claimed to carry nuclear warheads between 10 and 25 kt and deliver them to targets at a range of 350 and 700 km respectively. Babur has been in service with the Pakistan Army since 2010.

Lack of Fifth-Generation Fighters

These are jet fighter aircraft which employ major technologies developed during the first part of the twenty-first century. As of today, these are the most advanced fighters in operation. The characteristics of a fifth-generation fighter typically include stealth, low-probability-of-intercept radar (LPIR), agile airframes with super cruise performance, advanced avionics features and highly integrated computer systems capable of networking with other elements within the battlespace for situation awareness and control.

China has developed two types of fifth-generation fighters: the J-20 and the J-31. The J-20 made its first flight in January 2011 and entered service in September 2017. The PLA Air Force (PLAAF) has been inducting J-20s into combat units since February 2018 and had even deployed it during the ongoing clash in Ladakh. Another stealth fighter design from China was first seen on the internet in September 2011. This aircraft was named J-31 and made its maiden flight on 31 October 2012. It continues to be under development and has not been reported to be fielded.

India does not have a fifth-generation fighter. It had earlier pulled out of the Indo–Russian FGFA project in 2018. The FGFA was a fifth-generation derivative of the Sukhoi Su-57. The FGFA was to include numerous improvements over the Su-57, including stealth, super cruise, advanced sensors and networking. Unfortunately, the aircraft could not meet IAF requirements for stealth, radars and sensors, and the project was abandoned.

The advanced medium combat aircraft (AMCA) is being developed and designed by the Aeronautical Development Agency, and will be produced by Hindustan Aeronautics Limited (HAL). The AMCA is planned to be a single-seat, twin-engine fifth-generation supermanoeuvrable stealth multirole fighter with internal carriage of weapons. It will have an all-weather swing-role capability with a few 'sixth-generation characteristics'.[3] The AMCA is intended to perform a multitude of missions including air superiority, ground strike, suppression of enemy air defences (SEAD) and electronic warfare (EW) missions, and would be a potent replacement for the Sukhoi Su-30MKI air superiority fighter, which forms the backbone of the IAF fighter fleet today.

The AMCA design is optimized for low-radar cross-section and super-cruise capability. A feasibility study on AMCA and the preliminary design stage are reported to have been completed, and the project entered the detailed design phase in February 2019. The process for obtaining government approval for commencing development of the AMCA has been in progress for over three years. The first flight is expected to be within five years of government sanction and serial production might begin in ten years.

Drone Warfare

Unmanned aerial vehicles, or UAVs, as they have sometimes been referred to, have only been in service for the last sixty years. Modern UAVs have come a long way since the unmanned drones used by the US Air Force (USAF) in the 1940s. These drones were built for intelligence gathering and reconnaissance, but were not very efficient. Over the years, UAVs have been developed into the highly sophisticated machines in use today. Modern UAVs are used for many important applications, including coast watch, news broadcasting and the most common application, defence.

The employment of drones in combat commenced in the mid-1970s in Israel for what were termed as 'dull, dangerous and dirty', or D3, missions. Drones were a defining weapon in the War on Terror in Afghanistan and Iraq, especially during the Barack Obama administration (2009–2017). Drones were first inducted in the IAF in the 1990s, initially for intelligence, surveillance and reconnaissance (ISR) tasks. In the 2000s, IAF imported drones for attack missions from Israel. Today, nearly 100 countries have acquired drones, with Iran, Turkey and China having built for themselves large arsenals.

Drone warfare, like guerrilla warfare, has humbled even the mightiest of powers, from the US to Russia and Saudi Arabia. In September 2019, a drone swarm evaded air defences to attack two of Saudi Arabia's major oil fields. Yemen's Houthi rebels claimed responsibility, and apparently were helped by Iranian technology. Drones have also fought each other in Syria, as Turkey attacked the

Russia-backed forces. Insurgents, militants and terrorists see drones as a means to employ air power at relatively low cost. They often buy off-the-shelf quadcopters and modify them for attack missions. ISIS, Hezbollah and Boko Haram all have drones, as do some militant groups in the Ukraine and Philippines.

Simple drones can be neutralized by blocking their satellite navigation signals, or by jamming their control networks. But, if they have autonomous guidance, or their own optical system or artificial intelligence, they have to be destroyed with directed energy weapons, like lasers, or kinetically struck by missiles/guns. In 2018, China made a dramatic revelation of its capabilities, with a swarm of drones flying in formation in a stunning light show. China has been exporting combat drones to nearly twenty countries. Drones will, doubtless, play a role in any future global confrontation—so we do need to develop them and their countersystem.

The threat spectrum described above are not all-encompassing or complete. The air medium offers a multitude of opportunities for exploitation from the military perspective, be it for logistical support or for offensive action. Each of these facets must be factored in for our benefit and, at the same time, be countered and neutralized to resist their employment by those inimical to our interests. The challenge for us lies in anticipating future technologies and employing them to establish a strong deterrence against a formidable enemy like China, which has vast resources at its command.

The Triple Challenge in Aerospace

India's aerospace challenges could be loosely grouped into three categories, which are somewhat interlinked to each other. The first and foremost is the lack of sufficient technology. India's research into basic science has been inadequate and this has resulted in the lack of a knowledge base, which is extremely relevant, especially in the field of aerospace. This sector requires some unique, cutting-edge technologies which have traditionally been denied to us by more advanced nations. These nations would prefer to sell us aerospace products, but are not willing to share technologies for commercial and political reasons. Those technologies that are shared are primarily second-rung and related to production rather than the critical 'know-how and know-why' necessary for developing new-generation indigenous products. Serious effort to overcome these handicaps have been funded by the government only in the public sector, and has been plagued by serious time and cost overruns.

The second challenge in aerospace is from the fiscal angle. Acquisition of aerospace systems is extremely cost-intensive and research in this field even more so. India, being a developing nation, could ill afford the large outlay in monies required. Furthermore, being in a troubled neighbourhood and facing two nuclear-armed nations, has resulted in our scarce resources being spent on immediate operational exigencies, rather than on long-term solutions which would synergize and self-sustain our military and economic growth.

The third challenge to progress in aerospace has been managerial. India has long suffered from serious issues on project management. Even simple programmes, which are not impeded by either technical or fiscal challenges, are invariably stretched over many years. This has been the bane of this country in all sectors—even more so in the aerospace field. The rapid technical advancements in this field mean that delays in development and deployment of products would lead to obsolescence and prohibitive cost overruns.

Aerospace Opportunities

In addition to the national security aspects associated with it, the defence and aerospace sector is also at the forefront in most developed countries due to its impact on the overall economic growth, in terms of foreign direct investment (FDI) inflows, outflows, fiscal deficit, growth in gross domestic product, job creation and per capita income. Although defence and aerospace as a sector has been identified as a major thrust area by our government, its role in the overall growth of the economy is yet to fully evolve.

Until the economic reforms of 1991, private players were not allowed to operate in the aircraft industry in India. In 2001, the government allowed 100 per cent domestic private investment in the defence sector upon obtaining an industrial licence (IL) and FDI of up to 26 per cent with conditions. This has started to attract a number of Indian companies into the sector. A few big businesses have made small forays in this field, as a part of the offset trade arrangements in defence procurement. Some of the private sector groups, such as Tata, Larsen and Toubro, Mahindra & Mahindra, Kirloskar and a large number of smaller companies, have been supplying limited parts and equipment to the armed forces and PSUs.

The introduction of the defence offset policy in 2006 and significant liberalization in 2008 have provided additional incentives for Indian companies entering the sector. New players are coming into the industry and are aggressively building capabilities to make them attractive partners for the primes and Tier-1 suppliers. Foreign companies are also showing interest in establishing their presence in India, but we have a long way to go and lots of catching up to do.

To address the imbalance between the import of defence equipment and indigenous manufacture, the Indian government launched an ambitious 'Make in India' initiative in 2014, which aims to encourage companies to manufacture in India and attract inward investment. Under this, several reforms have been undertaken to revitalize and promote an indigenous defence industry. These reforms include raising the FDI cap, simplification and streamlining of the defence industrial licensing, the articulation of a first-ever defence exports strategy, the rationalization of taxes and, most importantly, an ongoing attempt to simplify the procurement procedure.

India's new defence acquisition procedure (DAP) was released in September 2020. These new regulations attempt to further strengthen the defence ecosystem in the country. Defence and aerospace remain a critical sector for India—and for the success of Make in India. A flourishing defence sector requires increased foreign technology transfer and foreign investment, which will ultimately lead to the co-development and co-creation of capabilities that can meet not just the needs of India but also be exported to third countries.

The Centre's repeated attempts towards creating an enabling framework of laws and regulations governing the defence sector have been somewhat slow in alleviating some of the concerns aired by the industry. The ecosystem is still evolving, and certain initiatives are anticipated to considerably reduce the headwinds facing the industry. Some of these initiatives are listed below.

India announced a Strategic Partnership (SP) Policy in 2016. This envisages the selection of a private industry strategic partner, which would team up with a foreign OEM (original equipment manufacturer) to produce in India the necessary equipment and systems to satisfy our aerospace requirements. Similar to India's 'MAKE' procedure (which was introduced to encourage the development of indigenous products), the SP policy is directed to further the self-reliance agenda. Even if this policy is spun into quick action, it would still take anywhere between four and seven years before any actual order would be placed to the strategic partner. If one were to go by the track record of such programmes actually taking off, the MAKE programmes are a good example. The 'MAKE' category was introduced in 2006. Even sixteen years later, the two major MAKE programmes, which have down-selected vendors, still haven't seen the light of the day in terms of actual prototype development.

Both the strategic partnership as well as the MAKE categories (Make I and Make II) were no doubt started in the right spirit; however, the implementation has been sluggish. If the SP policy is implemented properly, it can actually transform India into an export-oriented defence economy. Another important aspect the Centre would have to bear in mind would be to look at each programme not just through the lens of public probity, but also from the viewpoint of commercial viability. Rules framed for defence acquisition have attempted to address this issue from time to time at the procedure level, but what India now needs is seamless and committed implementation of these processes. The government would need to expedite decision-making on such matters without succumbing to red tape. This might have some impact on cost, but that would seem an acceptable price to pay for achieving a sustainable level of self-reliance within a reasonable time frame.

Fundamental strength in the Indian industry already exists, in the form of a large number of small and medium-sized enterprises (SMEs), which, in the past, have been suppliers at the subcomponent and component level for aerospace DPSUs, such as HAL, DRDO, ISRO, etc. These companies are gradually transforming themselves into major players in this sector, modernizing with cutting-edge technologies to become suppliers for global aerospace companies vying to outsource products and components from India. The domestic capability is being significantly enhanced through extensive tie-ups, joint ventures and technology transfers, as the industry has set itself on a firm path towards a transformational change.

The Indian aerospace industry, both military and civil, stands uniquely poised today, on the threshold of catapulting itself into the global arena. The need of the hour is the full support and involvement of the government in generating the demand and supply for defence and civil aerospace products. The process of transformation appears to have begun and there are encouraging signs that the industry is emerging as a major factor in our increasing self-reliance, and may develop into an export-oriented sector, with the potential and capacity to provide world-class opportunities for established firms in the global market.

The Way Forward

We have to address the entire spectrum of threats we face from aerospace—from ballistic missiles to low-cost drones. We need to leverage the advantages aerospace offers to our military and industries to our benefit. There is a need to take a holistic view of the techno-economic dilemma we face today and respond to these challenges appropriately.

We need to improve our capabilities to develop and manufacture aircraft, be they fighters or civil. It is a known fact that aircraft design, development and production are expensive. The fixed costs involved in the design and manufacture of new fighter aircraft are estimated at upwards of USD 10 billion today. These costs are a critical entry barrier to private industry participation in the aviation sector. The so-called Ambassador and Fiat model of progress, which plagued the automobile sector in India for over forty years, continues to dominate the aviation sector as well.

The Indian aircraft industry is dominated by one big public sector player—Hindustan Aeronautics Limited—which is involved in both designing and manufacturing aircraft. Alongside HAL, DRDO is responsible for research and development. A few more government-owned and -run organizations also exist, such as the National Aerospace Laboratories (NAL) and the Aircraft Development Agency (ADA). Being government-owned, they suffer from the typical ills of bureaucracy, and rely upon the government for funds and clearances for R&D. Moreover, projects are mostly undertaken only when a specific requirement is projected by the user to the government. This situation leads to difficulties in retention of expertise and a lack of regular R&D in cutting-edge technologies.

These challenges are also an opportunity for private industry to step in. The Centre is the only buyer in the defence sector and can play a major role in facilitating growth in the civil aerospace sector as well.

Both HAL and DRDO have had some success in the design and manufacture of the Tejas LCA airframe and avionics, but have failed to develop a number of niche technologies that make up to two-thirds the cost of a fighter aircraft. These largely consist of a number of subassemblies and components like electrical alternators, fuel pumps, radar, hydraulic pumps and actuators, APU (auxiliary power unit), avionics, jet engines, etc. These are developed and produced by other specialist OEMs for earlier programmes, either as a commodity-of-the-shelf (COTS), or developed based on specific requirements from the aircraft OEM, where the items are to be integrated. Jet engines today remain the most challenging and complex technologies to master. Only a few Western nations have mastered this unique capability. India is thus forced to import fighter engines or licence-manufacture them.

In capital-intensive sectors like aerospace and defence, the government plays a crucial role in supporting the industry and encouraging the development of a critical mass of capabilities, technologies and suppliers, as it is the only buyer till exports kick in. The Indian government has embarked upon several measures to develop and promote the aerospace sector. But there are areas, such as licensing and special economic zone (SEZ) policies, where greater clarity in policy as well as easing and rationalizing some procedures are necessary.

India is poised to become a large commercial and defence aircraft market. With rising passenger traffic, and increasing military and defence expenditures, the demand for aircraft is expected to increase.

A demand of between 900 to 1,000 commercial aircraft worth USD 100 billion approximately is expected in the next twenty years. What is now needed is a formal civil offset policy. This would logically result in a significant spurt of business opportunity, due to the associated offsets. The total spending in the next five years is expected to be between USD 25 billion for commercial aircraft and USD 100 billion as defence expenditure.

Out of the defence expenditure, approximately 15–20 per cent (USD 15–20 billion) is expected to be spent on military aircraft. Assuming an offset of 30 per cent for the civil sector too, the total offset opportunity for the aerospace sector is valued to be at least USD 10–15 billion. This would be a significant boost to our aerospace industries.

Notes

1. Edmund J. Burke, Kristen Gunness, Cortez A. Cooper III, and Mark Cozad, *People's Liberation Army Operational Concepts*, Santa Monica: RAND Corporation, 2020, https://www.rand.org/pubs/research_reports/RRA394-1.html, accessed 21 June 2022.
2. J.L. Babbin, E. Timperlake, *Showdown: Why China Wants War with the United States*, Houston: Regnery Pub., Inc., 2006.
3. Nader Elhefnawy, 'A Sixth-Generation Fighter? An Overview of the Essential Background', SSRN, 18 July 2018, https://ssrn.com/abstract=3215780 or http://dx.doi.org/10.2139/ssrn.3215780

CHAPTER

7

Trajectory of India's Maritime Security Challenges

SHEKHAR SINHA

The Mughal invasion into India and successive invasions across the Hindu Kush mountain range have had a near-permanent impact on the psyche of rulers, who began to believe that the threat to India was from the land borders to the north. Therefore, the Mughal rulers maintained large armies for protecting their extensive land borders. The country's geography in the northwest extended up to what is now Pakistan and parts of Afghanistan. The Mughals administered the country from the northern states while they made peace with princely states in the south. Across the northern borders, they also smoked the peace pipe with the rulers of Tibet and Central Asia. Therefore, it was assumed that the great Himalayas would provide a natural barrier against any invader from the north.

Even after five centuries of Mughal rule followed by 250 years of British colonization, Indian politicians continued to remain sea-blind, perceiving external threats only across land borders. A large part of peninsular India had remained under the purview of regional rulers in the south during the Mughal period—thus, maritime knowledge was marginal for Mughal rulers. Maritime defence hardly featured in their discourse, though occasionally some rulers did raise a naval combat force only to be beaten by battle-hardened navies of coastal states. On the other hand, rulers of peninsular India, particularly of the Chola empire and the Kalinga region, had exercised their maritime prowess and prospered. Their trade influence extended across the seas in the east right up to Southeast Asia and the South China Sea kingdoms, and in the west up to the Arabian Gulf much before the Europeans started extending their maritime trade influence across oceans. Western countries categorized their new destinations as 'discoveries' (by Columbus, Vasco da Gama et al.), ignorant of the progress that was made by these Asian countries during their civilizational history.

The Dutch, Spaniards, Portuguese and British travelled across hostile oceans and occupied/colonized territories the world over. The British had used sea routes to establish their business in India and then went on to rule the country for approximately 250 years. It was period of British colonization in the world; it was said that the sun never set in the British Empire—so vast was their control across the world. One of the strategies the British pursued was to keep the thinking of the Indian political class centred on the security of its land borders to the north. The attention to maritime India never seemed to have permeated into Delhi's ruling elite. This explains India's sea-blindness and land-fixated security strategy which, to some extent, exist even today

However, the twenty-seventh viceroy to India, Lord Curzon, had identified three tenets relevant for the country as it found itself confronted by an aggressive China. This has been reflected by Wess Mitchell, former US assistant secretary of state, describing them in an opinion piece published in *Hindustan Times* on 12 June 2021:

> First, Curzon recognised that India's security depended upon its ability to exercise influence over a defined geopolitical space beyond

India's own shores. He identified this space as extending from the Gulf of Aden in the West to [the] Straits of Malacca in the East. To the contrary, the Mughals tended to see India as an extension of the geopolitics of Central Asia. Curzon understood that India's security and greatness were intimately tied to the maritime routes and choke points connecting it to Europe and the Far East. Lose control of these, and India would be hostage to its strongest landward neighbour (meaning China).

He goes on to write: 'Second, Curzon recognised that India's main landward attention must be directed to its frontiers—namely, to the task of maintaining viable buffer states in the adjacent regions. For Curzon, the frontier was 'the razor's edge on which hang suspended the modern issues of war and peace'.

Wess leads on to the third tenet: 'Curzon understood that building influence in these neighbouring spaces required India to offer an attractive commercial and strategic alternative to the charm of its rivals … This required an active rather than passive policy aimed at the integration of neighbouring states into the Indian economy and infrastructure.'

Curzon always believed such a day would come when a confident, self-governing India would become a major source of stability in its own region and the wider world. How right he was! But it was not till 2014 that Prime Minister Modi expounded 'Security and Growth for All in the Region (SAGAR)', 'Act East' and 'Neighbourhood First' policies. Since then, the maritime domain has become central to India's foreign policy.

Fast Forward

The record must be set right immediately. Has India's sea-blindness been cured? Well, in the present political class, the answer is a resounding yes. A report on the evolving strategic environment of the Indian Ocean by the International Institute for Strategic Studies (IISS), London, summarizes that international recognition of the economic and political importance of the increasingly globalized wider Indo-Pacific region has resulted in shared interest in the stability and security of the Indian Ocean. The report says that this frame of reference for governments is related to India's own rise as a regional and economic power, as it chiefly projects its strategic ambitions into the Indian Ocean.

From 2014, since the time the Narendra Modi-led government came into power, the maritime domain has seen significant influence on the foreign policy of India. According to the IISS report, under Modi, India has begun to treat the Indian Ocean as a priority, and as a critical element of India's grand strategy to outgrow South Asia.

During his keynote address at the Shangri La Dialogue in 2018, Prime Minister Modi stated that the Indian Ocean was both the heart and the beginning of India's Indo-Pacific vision. The nation's strategic reach in the wider region will depend on its ability to exercise predominant influence in the Indian Ocean. The sentiment has been well reflected in the Indian Navy's Maritime Security Strategy, which was sanguine about this fact and identified the entire Indian Ocean region (IOR) as within its primary and secondary areas of responsibility.

The navy's maritime capability-development plans have factored these responsibilities in the entire IOR since the 1960s, when it first projected the need for three aircraft carriers—one each for the eastern and western seaboard, and one in routine maintenance—giving it the ability to project power and deliver ordnance at the place and time of the government's choosing in the event of war. Its peacetime role was envisaged as supporting HADR (Human Assistance and Disaster Relief) and security to the littorals. This has acted as a deterrence to date.

Possibly, Modi's acquaintance with maritime trade is to do with his being a native of a coastal state—Gujarat—and having served as chief minister there for over a decade. Also, he has recognized that India's continental strategy, fixated on land borders for over six decades, has resulted in defensive outcomes, and hardly added any significant advantage to trade and commerce, which is the single most important factor for the prosperity of India's citizens. Our neighbours in the region have always hedged between India and China. India has been in territorial dispute with China since Independence, with China gradually biting into Indian territory in what has come to be known as their salami-slicing strategy. The government has understood that India's globalized economy is increasingly reliant on maritime commerce and its ports, which handle 95 per cent of the trade by volume and 70 per cent of the country's external trade. This too has made maritime issues an important foreign policy priority. The maritime domain offers India space to expand and explore without getting boxed in the south of the Himalayas. Additionally, the country's initiative of looking east, acting east and thinking west provides appropriate impetus for maritime orientation to the foreign policy.

With further growth, India is likely to become the world's third-largest economy, behind China and the USA. This necessitates outreach and cooperation with Indian Ocean littorals and beyond, which fits into Curzonian tenets squarely.

Is that the only reason driving India's urgency to enter into collaborative arrangements with other powers of the world? Not really.

Geopolitical Landscape

The single biggest geopolitical change being witnessed by the world today is the 'painful' and aggressive rise of China. It is 'painful' for the world for it has nearly upset the existing rules-based international order. After the end of the Cold War, the US has been the economic and military leader of the free world. No other country has come even a distant second. But this is rapidly changing. While the US was engaged deeply in West Asian politics of oil and Islam—and later in the Afghanistan–Pakistan region, fighting the global War on Terror, China made rapid economic progress and also built up its military–technology complex.

As was witnessed prior to both the world wars, assimilation of economic and military power in the hands of authoritarian regimes was extremely troubling for the world, particularly weaker neighbours. Now, we are witnessing an increasingly aggressive Beijing in the South China Sea, East China Sea and on India's Himalayan land borders, alarming the world. China claims sovereignty over nearly 80 per cent of the South China Sea based on some fictitious historical claims of the so-called 'nine-dash line'. It has occupied a number of islands, shoals, reefs and rocks in the Paracel and Spratly group of islands, which fall within the Exclusive Economic Zone (EEZ) of five other claimants in the region. China has gone ahead and reclaimed many more acres around some of these features, and converted them into advanced military outposts.

Scarborough Shoal, belonging to the Philippines, has been occupied by China. The Philippines placed the matter before the International Court of Justice at The Hague. The Permanent Court of Arbitration ruled that China didn't have any basis for historical claim and it couldn't deprive countries of their genuine maritime claims. To the horror of the world, however, China rejected the judgment and defied the international rule of law (the United Nations Convention on the Laws of the Seas) to which it is a signatory. On the other hand, a few months earlier, India had given up its claim on some parts of its EEZ to Bangladesh post an ICJ judgment. Also, India had settled its maritime borders with Myanmar and Indonesia bilaterally. It was all in the spirit of ensuring stability in the IOR as also magnanimity of a larger nation towards not so-large-ones.

China's assertive behaviour has become much in variance with its earlier motto of 'hide your capabilities and bide your time' coined by Deng Xiaoping. China has entered into the Xi Jinping–era with 'Chinese characteristics'. It is the belief of the general secretary of the Chinese Communist Party (CCP) that China's moment to be the leader of the world has arrived by displacing the US—initially from the South China Sea (the first island chain) and then from its unipolarity of the world altogether. While China would replace the US as the largest economy of the world in the near future, it is quite some distance away from being the leader of military–technological complexes anytime soon. And that causes turmoil, when, for the first time, the world is likely to witness two different nations in the leadership position of the two most important pillars of statecraft, namely economic and military at the same time. China has systematically curtailed US influence in the world by economic coercion over countries with weaker economies but of strategic importance to itself.

In its Military Strategy Paper of 2015, China has officially stated that its prosperity lies over the sea and therefore the overemphasis on superiority over land should be abandoned. Beijing would build very strong PLA Navy (PLAN) which will be deployed wherever it has economic interests across the globe. The CCP has placed PLAN in the category of strategic command along with nuclear, space and cyber forces. Since then, its navy has been adding to its capacity at a very rapid pace and has overtaken the ship/submarine numbers of the US Navy.

China's dual-purpose strategic agenda is visible across the globe; on the face of it, a project appears to be purely economic in nature, intended to be beneficial to itself and the recipient country. However, it is associated with infrastructure development built with loans provided, which have opaque terms and conditions which often sinks the economically weaker countries into a debt trap, recovery from which is only by compromising their sovereignty. There are many examples: Sri Lanka's economic crisis, Pakistan sinking economically, a few African countries on the brink where nearly forty-six port upgrades are in progress, approximately fifty port projects across Europe and Southeast Asia, and the near-trap situation of Myanmar, Maldives and now the Pacific islands. China has concluded an agreement with the Solomon Islands under which the Chinese police force and military could operate under the guise of training and security.

China's Belt Road Initiative (BRI) and Maritime Silk Road, though classified as bringing prosperity to citizens worldwide, only helps China spread its economic influence, kills local industries and compels participating counties to permit PLAN units to utilize those ports. Claiming a historical right over nearly 80 per cent of the SCS, it hinders free and open sea passage of merchant marine traffic by making it mandatory for them to seek prior approval. China has also declared an Air Defence Identification Zone in the air space above the South China Sea, which necessitates prior intimation for aircraft overflights. The PLA has frequently intercepted aircraft of different nationalities and endangered their safety. In a recent incident, a PLA fighter flew dangerously close to an Australian Maritime Patrol Aircraft P8A and released chaff and flares ahead on its flight path. This could have been ingested by the engines leading to permanent damage to the engines. Similar nonprofessional incidents have been reported in the recent past, of which one lead to a collision.

China's aggressive behaviour across the Taiwan Strait, threat of invading Taiwan (possibly also encouraged by the Russian invasion of Ukraine), threat of taking over Senkaku island belonging to Japan, forcibly implementing PRC laws in Hongkong, extreme violation of human rights in Xinjiang, attempts to change the status quo on the

Tibet–Ladakh border and now its attempt to militarize the Pacific Islands are extremely worrying trends for the world and tend to disturb the existing rules-based international order.

Challenges for India

These geopolitical changes have also impacted India's security significantly. Sensing its economic and military power on world stage, China has begun opening a number of fronts to prove itself a superpower. Its threat to militarily change the status quo of Indian borders is one such concern.

1. China has made incursions into Indian territory on the unresolved land borders in the north and east. However, on two occasions, its moves into Doklam and the Ladakh–Tibet border were firmly pushed back by the Indian Army, with both sides losing a few lives. China had thus far been bullying its weaker neighbours, but has not succeeded against India in 2017 and 2020. As of now, the agreed withdrawal of troops hasn't been completed by China on India's northern borders for full disengagement to take place. The Indian stand has been firm—in that, peace and tranquillity on the border would be a prerequisite to any future bilateral trade dialogue. The Indian government has also banned Chinese apps and imposed tariffs on imports from China. Dependence on Chinese trade is being reduced gradually.
2. China has used economic coercion on India's neighbours and pushed them into a debt trap. When they fail to repay the loan to Beijing, the nations are compelled to transfer strategically important locations to China, thus multiplying India's immediate security concerns. The ongoing bankruptcy of Sri Lanka, and the long-term leasing of Hambantota port and Colombo South terminals are the latest examples

in a long list. The Kyaukphyu port in Myanmar too is under Chinese operational control. The Maldives is under tremendous debt stress from China, created during President Abdulla Yameen's regime. There are attempts being made in Seychelles, Mauritius and Madagascar too, which have traditionally been India's partners.

3. The most significant development has been China's deep engagement with Pakistan. Despite enough evidence of Pakistan funding terror groups worldwide, Beijing has scuttled all attempts by New Delhi to bring up the issue at the UN Security Council. Blacklisting of Pakistan by the Financial Action Task Force (FATF) too has been stalled by China. It is also arming Pakistan to the teeth. Apart from nuclear proliferation, China is supplying eight diesel submarines and three modern frigates to the country. Most of the land-based weapons and ammunition held by the Pakistani armed forces are supplied by China to Pakistan, and will most likely be used against India. This has upset the power balance in the region to some extent.

4. China has also built the China–Pakistan Economic Corridor (CPEC) from Kashgar to Gwadar under its Belt and Road Initiative. The CPEC passes through Gilgit-Baltistan, which is Pakistan-occupied Indian territory. Pakistan has also handed over Gwadar port on the Makran coast to China, boosting its surveillance and ability to interdict shipping at the mouth of the Straits of Hormuz, an important choke point connecting the Arabian Sea to the Persian Gulf. In the Bay of Bengal, China is firmly established in Myanmar with operational control on a deep water port. Having supplied weapons and platforms including a submarine to the Myanmar armed forces, it is actively training their personnel. Access to ports and naval installations provides

China strategic influence in the Bay of Bengal, wider Indian Ocean and Southeast Asia. It has developed a deep water port in Kyaukpyu which can be used for Chinese submarines. As per some media reports, China has also built an 85 metre jetty, naval installations and electronic intelligence systems on Great Coco Islands, which are just around 30 km from Andaman and Nicobar Islands. If true, it could give China the ability to monitor India's missile test progress. China has done partial development of Sittwe naval base. Sittwe and Yangoon are being connected by a Chinese-constructed road giving shortest access from Southern China to the Bay of Bengal in the Indian Ocean. Though Myanmar has deeper relations with the Chinese polity, India has increased its developmental activity along with diplomatic and military cooperation with Myanmar. Over a period of time, India may mitigate Chinese influence. However, China has already arrived in the Bay of Bengal, which has increased India's concerns and surveillance operations in an otherwise peaceful maritime environment. So far, the Bay of Bengal was a peaceful sector in the Indian Ocean Region but this is changing rapidly. In future, Chinese pressure on our eastern land borders could be accompanied with turbulence in the Bay of Bengal. India needs to be prepared for this eventuality.

5. India's geographical advantage has gradually been mitigated by China at three strategic choke points in the IOR. Beijing now controls operations of the Malacca port right in the middle of Malacca Straits, Gwadar on the mouth of the Straits of Hormuz and Djibouti in the Gulf of Aden, which joins the Arabian Sea to the Mediterranean through the Red Sea on the way to Europe (and the Atlantic). These are all in preparation to its larger and stronger emergence in the Indian Ocean.

Chinese ships and submarines (around six or seven) are present in the Indian Ocean on a near regular basis on the pretext of anti-piracy patrols. The naval base in Djibouti has approximately 3,000 marines positioned, along with long-range artillery guns, which gives China the ability to interdict shipping across the Gulf of Aden. As mentioned earlier, China's influence on India's immediate neighbours gives it the strategic maritime reach which has the potential of misuse given the adversarial relations and near war situation on our northern borders.

China's future behaviour in the Indian Ocean must be seen through the prism of its arrogance in the South China Sea and East China Sea. It has been threatening the forceful takeover of Taiwan, as well. Speaking at the Shangri La Dialogue as recently as 12 June 2022, the Chinese defence minister General Wei Fenghe spoke of war if Taiwan declared independence. There is large-scale aerial incursion into Taiwanese air space on a daily basis. Its ships, including its lone aircraft carrier, Liaoning, has been exercising frequently on the fringes of Taiwan's EEZ, which it claims to be its own. The US too has maintained a threatening posture by deploying its nuclear-powered aircraft carriers in the SCS to prevent China from taking any offensive action.

China is also making claims on Senkaku island that belongs to Japan. Chinese ships have frequently made threatening postures in the vicinity of the island. Given the historical friction between Japan and China, any Chinese offensive on Senkaku could flare into a bigger confrontation. In the recently concluded Shangri La Dialogue, Prime Minister Kishida of Japan stated that Japan would strengthen its defence and has allocated a huge amount in their budget. Overall, the maritime security scenario in the SCS remains explosive with all indications of it spilling over into the IOR and the Pacific. The peace and stability in the Indian Ocean Region remain uneasy.

ASEAN has been negotiating a code of conduct with China for over two years, but talks have remained inconclusive. China has been coercing the member nations to agree to terms beneficial to itself. If accepted in their present form, there could be restrictions on non-resident navies conducting bilateral or multilateral exercises, as well as restrictions on exploration activities in the SCS.

China's ingress into the IOR for securing its sources of energy will be in contest with India—both countries have economies that are rising simultaneously. Writing in his famous book *Monsoon*, American writer Robert D. Kaplan has mentioned, '… The Greater Indian Ocean, stretching eastward from the Horn of Africa past the Arabian Peninsula, the Iranian plateau, and the Indian Subcontinent, all the way to the Indonesian archipelago and beyond, may comprise a map as iconic to the new century as Europe was to the last one.' Kaplan goes on to say, 'In this rimland of the medieval Muslim world that was never far from China's gaze, we can locate the tense dialogue between Western and Islamic civilisations, the ganglia of global energy routes, and the quiet, seemingly inexorable rise of India and China over land and sea. For the sum total effect of US preoccupation with Iraq and Afghanistan has been to fast forward the arrival of the Asian century, not only in the economic terms that we all know about, but in military terms as well.'

He wrote this in 2011—and how prescient his words were!

What we are witnessing now is a rapidly changing geopolitical environment in the world, post the Taliban's assumption of power in Afghanistan. With Pakistan's proximity to the Taliban and Pakistan's proxy Haqqani group gaining an important position in governance, China is gradually moving towards Afghanistan to realize its continental strategy dream by operationalizing its Belt and Road Initiative—ignoring the impact of terrorism it would have in its neighbourhood. It may be recalled that al Qaeda's arrival in Afghanistan in the past and its close association with the Taliban, saw terrorism spilling over the adjoining oceans and moving right through the Indian subcontinent to Southeast Asia. The role of the Indian Navy is going to be most challenging in the coming decade. India and China will compete with one another for protection of their sea lanes of communication (SLOCS) carrying trade and commerce, invariably bringing them on a path of contestation—which may turn into confrontation, or worse, even a conflict. Warships of two adversarial nations being in close vicinity of each other is potentially explosive.

China's ability to wage a war is compounding by leaps and bounds. The compressed timeframes in which they are building warships, submarines and aircraft carriers is alarming; that too when China has no real threat in sight. China has overtaken the US Navy in capacity, i.e., the number of ships and submarines. It should not surprise the world if China commissions its Indian Ocean fleet in Gwadar or Djibouti or another African port in near future. It has enlarged its autocratic space in the countries which are financially parasites on China. For rest of the world China's ability to start a war may still be matter of debate since the US defence budget and quality of weapon systems is much ahead of China; but for India, the Chinese economy is five times larger and so is the navy. In the circumstances that we are in on our northern and eastern borders, the developments in the maritime domain point at all-out skirmish/conflict wherein it will have Pakistan playing a supporting role. The interoperability of systems between China and Pakistan are nearly 100 per cent, the two armed forces headquarters are connected with a fibre optic network which assists the two countries to be associated in joint planning. Nearly all weapon platforms are common and can be operated by each other's personnel. For India, the threat of aggression by the China–Pakistan duo is real. Encirclement of India around land borders and around India in the Indian ocean seems to be the larger strategy of China.

Confrontations Likely to Occur

The Indian Navy has a defined role of security of SLOCs (sea lanes of communication) through which our trade flows in the Indian Ocean and beyond. With growing seaborne trade, there has also been a phenomenal rise in dealing with non-traditional threats, apart from human assistance and disaster relief (HADR) which is frequent in the IOR. Piracy, thefts, drug and human trafficking, terrorism and IUU (irregular unreported fishing) are some of the serious challenges the navy faces on a daily basis. However, the real emerging threat is economic contestation and frictions for geopolitical supremacy, which has resulted from rapidly rising China and its opacity in international relations. Its intention of leadership of the world is also associated with pushing India away from Asian leadership.

Beijing's assertive behaviour and disregard of United Nation's Convention on the Law of the Sea, the world is preparing to face a country whose rapidly rising military power is becoming a threat to peace and stability. Democratic countries see this as risk from an authoritarian regime which is challenging the existing rules-based order by threatening use of its military. Examples are raising naval bases in Djibouti and possibly in many other countries. As a precaution, the US has rechristened its Pacific Command as 'Indo-Pacific Command', acknowledging the importance of the Indian Ocean in the changing geopolitical landscape. China's claim of sovereignty on nearly all of the SCS is associated with restrictions it imposes on the flow of trade and commerce over the seas. Four democracies of the Indo-Pacific—Australia, India, Japan and the United States—have come together in a quadrilateral maritime security partnership—known as the Quad—to support free and open seas.

India, on its part, has deployed its navy at the choke points of the Indian Ocean. These spaces are patrolled by its ships, submarines, aircraft, satellites and human intelligence. While this is just one part of operational necessity, the capabilities and capacities of the Indian Navy need to be enhanced manifold to deter China from repeating a South China Sea-like incursion in the IOR and colluding with Pakistan to stress the IOR while slicing land borders simultaneously. This calls for examining the naval power balance in the Indian Ocean. Yet, it will be naïve to compare the military power of China with India's. The fact remains that China is the largest trading partner of over 120 countries; it is likely to replace the US to become the world's largest economy, its navy and military are many times bigger than the US's. And therefore, the formulation of long- and short-term strategies by like-minded democracies, who have come together to prevent the Chinese ideology of autocratic governance gobbling up weaker nations, is necessary.

Writing in the 'Global Strategy 2021: An Allied Strategy for China', a document published by the Atlantic Council, there are a few important points that are relevant for India. Under long-term strategy, it recommends a stable relationship with China that avoids permanent confrontation, and enables cooperation on issues of mutual interest and concern. These strategies are expected to turn China into a responsible member of a revised and adapted rules-based system of the world, which respects individual rights and China's legitimate interests. However, it is extensively believed that under President Xi and the current generation of piggyback CCP leadership, Beijing will continue its path of confrontation.

The document also recommends short-term strategies for like-minded democracies. These measures must prevent China from continuing to threaten their interests in the economic, diplomatic, governance, security and public health domains. This strategy, therefore, seeks to prevent, deter, defend against and impose costs on Chinese actions that violate widely held international rules and norms. These actions must make Beijing realize that challenging like-minded partners would be difficult and costly. At the same time, these partners must keep lines of communication open, find areas of mutual cooperation, and work to convince the Chinese leadership that their interests are better served by playing within the revitalized and adapted rules-based system rather than by challenging it.

What should India and the Indian Navy be doing to achieve these objectives? Since China's economy is five times larger and their navy twice as big, our strategy must be such that it deters China in the maritime domain in the IOR. The strategy should have three major elements: strengthen, defend and engage

As a combat force, the navy needs to identify areas of Chinese vulnerability in the Indian Ocean and strengthen/increase capacities to exploit those. China must be reminded to resist from expansionism both on land and sea. We need an all-of-nation approach. Tomorrow's war may not be a battle at sea alone—it may just begin with a cyberattack on our critical infrastructure, which may disable our command-and-control systems that make our navy move. It may just begin with China launching hundreds of underwater unmanned vehicles capable of causing damage to underwater hulls or the components which reduce the fighting capabilities of our ships. It may just deploy maritime militia in the guise of fishing vessels which restrict the movement of our fleets. Maybe these remotely controlled or autonomous vessels will collide with warships and damage them extensively—as was done to *USS Cole* in the port of Aden. These are all disruptive technologies which keep the tempo just below full-fledged war levels.

China's dependence on the Indian Ocean is very important for the import of its energy and food for survival. The country imports over 80 per cent of fossil fuels from the Gulf region whereas 40 per cent of balance trade (other than oil) traverses on the Indian Ocean. The crude carriers travel past choke points. Therefore, these are vulnerable to interdiction while slowing down to negotiate narrow passages.

Secondly, China feeds 20 per cent of world's population, but has only 11 per cent of world's arable land. It is the largest importer of energy and food. This worries CCP no end. Even if China builds transit routes of fossil fuel through land routes, it is estimated that till the year 2050, it will still have to depend on the sea for approximately 53 per cent of its fuel requirements. China has made a base at Djibouti and is making one at Gwadar. Earlier reports indicated China's interest in Tanzania but latest reports suggest a bilateral agreement with Comoros, located closer to Madagascar. These will help China mitigate some of its security challenges in the Indian Ocean, but it will also expose these land-based assets to overt and covert threats.

China has few true friends. Strategically, it is aligned to Russia and Iran, but the longevity of partnerships between autocracies is not known to be prolonged. These countries may not be deep and trusting allies.

Other vulnerabilities include a top-down command and control structure of PLAN, which limits opportunities for individual initiatives and, therefore, it is ill-prepared to handle messy battle-space realities where situations develop quickly and leave little opportunity for delays caused by tight command and control systems. Additionally, China's logistics support system at sea in a long-distance conflict remains untested. Theaterization of Commands has not been of much relief.

Lastly, China has fears of internal instability. Though this has little impact on maritime security, it definitely could affect matters if instability occurs on the mainland while the combatants are deployed at sea.

Post-pandemic economic recovery has given China an opportunity to strengthen its abilities to build disruptive technologies—for instance, in artificial intelligence, robotics and automation. It has also made rapid advancements in space technologies. The latest demonstration was the launch of a hypersonic missile from a satellite and its control in glide phase. However, the recurrence of COVID-19 and the total lockdown of the port city of Shanghai has hit the economy and much research work. Some districts of Beijing too had been affected.

Power Projection in PLAN

China's economy is four or five times larger than India's; therefore, its navy is much larger. The force was built around ensuring energy and food security, which is essential for China's prosperity and also internal stability. Additionally, PLAN has enlarged its capability to push the US Navy out of the South China Sea and break free from the second island chain. Thus, India need not match ship to ship, submarine to submarine or aircraft to aircraft with China. Its attention and deployment on a large scale in the IOR is still a few years away. Retaking Taiwan is its maritime priority right now.

Maritime power of a country is not only its navy's combat power, but needs to be seen in the overall maritime matrix. The number of ports to support trade, hinterland road and rail connectivity, ability to absorb scientific advancements—such as nuclear technology, quantum technology, underwater unmanned vehicles capable of hydrological surveys, and construction ability to build ships, submarines and submarine communication cables—these add to the robustness of the overall maritime power of a country. China leads the world in these technologies by virtue of its leadership in artificial intelligence systems. It has also used its fishing vessels as maritime militia to keep the tensions up, particularly in grey zones, forcing the opposition to make tactical errors. This enables the Chinese to put the blame on the opposition for any retribution that it might mete out to them. Chinese vessels are engaged in unauthorized seabed mining, fishing and hydrological surveys. These vessels are surreptitiously engaged in the surveillance of assets of adversaries, and have military applications.

An US intelligence report in 2015 assessed that PLAN considers the eastern Indian Ocean as strategic, since it lies just beyond China's defensive perimeter from the mainland. The Indian Ocean remains an area of secondary national security interest for Beijing. However, since it began counter piracy operations in the western Indian Ocean, China has insisted that her maritime trade routes must be secured in order to sustain prosperity as a global trading nation. Speaking at the 2018 IISS Shangri La Dialogue (as a co-panel with this author), PLA Military Science Academy's senior colonel, Zhao Xiaozhuo, said that the Indian Ocean had become 'increasingly more important to China'. He provided a rare public assessment of China's specific strategic interests in the Indian Ocean, Zhao highlighted the importance of resource security, particularly in relation to oil from the Gulf, and also security of trading routes: 80 per cent of total oil transported to China, and 40 per cent of China's total trade were conveyed across the Indian Ocean. He also argued that the security of China's western borders was at stake; moreover, there was concern about the safety of its nationals in the region, more than one million of whom reside in and around the Indian Ocean.

Zhao went on to cite the Indian Ocean as an important region because it is crossed by China's twenty-first-century maritime Silk Road. In 2017, China's 'Vision of Maritime Cooperation', under the BRI, identified a corridor running through the Indian Ocean to Africa and the Mediterranean. BRI has also involved significant investment in the economies of Indian Ocean island states: the Maldives, Mauritius, Seychelles and Sri Lanka. Possibly, China would have done the assessment of the Indian Navy's deployment patterns and its cooperation with IOR littorals, and concluded raising the level of strategic importance of the Indian Ocean in its calculus. With Gwadar and Djibouti ports under its belt and few more in the pipeline, China seems to have encircled India in the Indian Ocean (with its String of Pearls).

These threat perceptions at sea are significant for India, since it is here that New Delhi has leverage to deter China from an expansionist approach on land borders. This leverage remains an important reason for capacity building of the Indian Navy. Gwadar and CPEC alone are very unlikely to allow China to overcome its 'Malacca dilemma'. Its seaborne trade and energy supply will remain vulnerable to interdiction by the US and its partners. One of the reasons why China has positioned 3,000 marines each at Djibouti and Gwadar underlines the importance of the ports to Beijing.

China's naval exercises are limited to Pakistan and Bangladesh at present. There are ongoing defence equipment sales to these two countries and to Djibouti, Tanzania and Myanmar. China is also involved in military education and capacity building efforts in these regional states. The restricted activities are largely due to the difficulties inherent in supporting deployments over long distances from the homeland. China is also facing stiff resistance from IOR nations due to their awareness of cyberattacks, the debt traps it lays out and other covert activities. It is for this reason that China's foreign ministry has emphasized that it wants the Indian Ocean to serve as a stage for 'win–win' cooperation, rather than 'geopolitical competition or confrontation'. It is on this basis that Xi agreed to the 'China–India plus one' or 'China–India plus X' framework for cooperation framework for cooperation, which included Afghanistan and Rwanda. The Chinese military hierarchy have emphasized on the relevance of a code for unplanned encounters at sea (CUES) and the importance of avoiding unintended incidents in the region as areas for bilateral cooperation. However, the key issue is its vulnerabilities in the IOR and its expanding global footprint passing through India's backyard.

These strategic concerns of China have taken a further nosedive after the Galwan clashes and India's assertion that no bilateral dialogue can progress without peace and stability on the land borders. India must ensure that any maritime cooperation in the IOR with China is conditional to a final land border settlement in the north.

PLAN POWER

Submarines		Surface Combatants		Naval Aviation	
Strategic: SSBNs	6	Aircraft carriers	CV 3 (18–24 aircraft, 17 Ka28 H)	Bombers	2 Regiments
Tactical: SSNs	6+3 (Reserve)	Cruisers	1	Fighter Ground Attack (FGA)	4 Brigades + 1 Regiment
SSK	46	Destroyers	31	Ground Attack	1 Brigade
		Frigates	46	Anti-Submarine Warfare	2 Regiments
		Corvettes	55	Electronics Intelligence (ELINT)	1 Regiment
		Mine Countermeasures Ships (MCMs)	56	AEW & Control	3 Regiments
		Amphibious:			
		LPDs	6	Transport	1 Regiments
		LSTs	28	Training	8 Regiments
		LSMs	21	Helicopters	3 Regiments
		LCUs	11	Air Defence	2 SAM Brigades
		LCMs	30		
		LCACs	14		
		Logistics and Support	154		

In addition to these assets, China has an unspecified number of maritime militias—though their entry in the IOR is seldom. China's cyber, space and underwater unmanned vehicles will pose a serious challenge to India.

The Quad

The formation of the Quad as a subset of the Indo-Pacific strategy has been hastened by China's presumed indulgence in the spread of COVID-19 and its subsequent inability to maintain supply chains, particularly that of vaccines. Four countries, Australia, India, Japan and the United States, are working together to overcome the challenges encountered during the COVID-19 episode. Quad has come about to ensure maritime security in the Indo-Pacific, though the working groups for maritime security have been formalized. It is believed that adequate interoperability and standardization has been achieved amongst these four navies in the Malabar series of exercises; therefore, should the need to resist China's assertiveness at sea arise, the Quad could 'plug and play' the Malabar naval armada which would be more than capable.

Simultaneously, India should maintain the capability to deter PLAN in the IOR with its strong naval fleet. It is expected that intelligence on the movements of PLAN ships, submarines and aircraft will be shared by Quad partners and France with whom India also has a 2+2 agreement. In the foreseeable future, till around 2030, it is unlikely that PLAN aircraft carriers will achieve operational standards to operate fighter aircraft by day and night without a diversionary airfield. This may restrain them from operating in the IOR. It is expected that thereafter, they may use diversionary airfields (to support recovery of aircraft in any emergency which prohibits their return to the carrier) in Sri Lanka, Myanmar, Malaysia, Gwadar, Djibouti, etc., for aircraft-carrier operations in the IOR.

This development needs to be watched and remedial preparation must be put in place.

During the second in-person Quad summit in Tokyo on 19 May 2022, very significant and far-reaching decisions have been taken as far as maritime issues are concerned. There is integration of all Maritime Domain Awareness centres in the Indo Pacific (IPMDA) and provides the centres satellite linkage to present data of all vessels in the entire region. At present the centres are operational in standalone mode at Gurugram (Indian Ocean), Singapore (SCS and West Pacific), and Solomon Islands managed by Australia for Pacific Islands. These will get linked and provide a near real-time picture of all vessels, including dark shipping, in the vast region. Commitment has been made to invest USD 50 billion for achieving this target within the next five years. Though it has been stated that it will monitor illegal fishing in the region, this could become the backbone for any future Quad security architecture. Surveillance is the prelude to enforcement. Having located the areas of illegal infringement, Quad must have the capability to reach the location and evict the vessels engaged in illegal activities. This should not be a difficult proposition since the four countries have their navies operating together in the Malabar series exercise wherein complex maritime combat exercises are practiced and full interoperability of platforms has been achieved.

Another area of major concern is that China had deployed a fleet of twelve underwater drones in the IOR, according to Chinese government sources. These Sea Wing gliders were launched by the specialist survey ship *Xiang Yang Hong 06* in December 2019 and recovered in February 2020. In this period, it made over 3,400 hydrological observations before recovery and return of the ship to Rizhao. The mission has been described as a winter survey for the joint ocean and ecology research project run by the Ministry of Natural Resources. It can be assumed that China will have the capability to conduct underwater interdictions on Indian naval vessels in the event of a contest at sea. Chinese maritime threats must be seen as collusive operations by PLAN and the Pakistan Navy, which is being prepared for such an event. China's joint construction with Pakistan will witness eight submarines (possibly Ming class), at least three frigates and an unspecified number of AWACS (airborne warning and control system) and maritime patrol aircraft in support of any operation.

AUKUS (Australia, United Kingdom and United States)

This an alliance which has been formed recently amongst Australia, UK and the USA. At present Australia does not have nuclear-powered attack submarines, which limits its ability to support maritime operations in the Pacific and the South China Sea. Under the provisions of this alliance, the USA and the UK will provide nuclear propulsion technology and training to the Australian Navy. The ecosystem for building these submarines will also be created in Australia for manufacturing and supporting submarine operations. These will have conventional weapon systems but will be capable of sustained high speeds underwater. It must be noted that with the increase in the number of China's combat ships, and the US commitment to protect its allies—Japan, South Korea and Taiwan—against PRC attack, quick-reaction combat capability in and from the Pacific has become necessary. Australia's nuclear submarines (SSN) could fill in those blanks to fulfil those commitments. Presence of these submarines will deter China from aggression in the South China Sea or from deploying its submarines in the Pacific at will.

Prescription

Given the vast asymmetry in economies and maritime power, India must sharpen its disruptive combat power. Mission-based deployment is a good beginning by the Indian Navy, and now the assets must be increased to sustain this effort. The number of surface ships, maritime-patrol aircraft and carrier-borne fighters, and submarines at the choke points must go up to make the maritime domain awareness network very robust. Intelligence on PLAN units must be sharpened using intelligence-sharing mechanisms with the Quad and other friendly countries—for instance, France, Indonesia, Philippines, Vietnam and possibly Taiwan. The Eastern and Western Naval Commands must increase the duration of their routine exercises and deploy over a much larger area, and so should the navies engaged in Malabar.

India must upgrade its maritime security cooperation with Indonesia. There is a need to activate Sabang port and airfield. Agreements should be reached for the installation of sound-operated underwater surveillance systems at all choke points through the straits of Indonesia to keep track of submarines attempting to navigate towards the Indian Ocean Region. These will also be useful in detecting underwater unmanned vehicles/gliders. Prior notice by Maritime Domain Awareness (MDA) and Underwater Domain Awareness (UDA) would improve the navy's prosecution ability. There is urgent need to utilize Andaman and Nicobar Islands as an important base to support anti-submarine assets to deny access to Chinese submarines in the Indian Ocean.

Very close monitoring of so-called 'ocean-research vessels' and fishing vessels of China—which are also tasked with acting as a satellite link for nuclear submarines as also controlling underwater unmanned vessels—must be undertaken.

Our agreements on maritime security with Mauritius, Seychelles, Madagascar, Sri Lanka and Maldives need to be operationalized expeditiously. The Colombo Security Conclave and BIMSTEC security should be encouraged to form integrated Indian Ocean

Regional Security architecture within the larger Quad in the Indo-Pacific.

Our inventory of submarines, anti-submarine helicopters (such as the MH R-60) and maritime patrol aircraft needs to be increased as per threat perception by the navy. These assets would play a decisive role in surveillance, detection and destruction of PLAN assets, should there be a conflict at sea.

In order to meet the commitment of IOR littorals, the force level of two carrier battle groups is near mandatory. While submarines are invisible assets which deny the use of sea space to the adversary, a carrier battle group is a visible offensive weapon system that deters the adversary from misusing areas of our own national interest. It is also a major platform for meeting challenges of non-traditional peacetime threats as well. The advanced missile and decoy systems in and around a carrier battle group make an adversary's task of targeting near impossible. Practically, satellite tracking of carrier battle groups is continuous and targeting is near impossible. Carrier groups have the ability to move over 900 km in a day, which makes weapon launch more difficult. The Indian Navy should not allow its carrier battle group assets to fall below two at any given point in time.

Start-up companies must become part of the design development and induction chain, consisting of the navy, the Indian Institutes of Technology and the Defence Research and Development Organization for the development of disruptive systems, such as underwater unmanned vehicles, drones, cyber offensive assets, laser cannons, rail guns, etc.

Our country has many domestic developmental challenges and therefore, funding will remain inadequate in the foreseeable future. The Quad mechanism would be useful to fill some of the gaps; so will the start-ups. As the economy grows, given our pursuit for self-reliance, or Atmanirbharta, so will the allocation for defence and research and development. In the interim, the navy needs to deny the PLAN (People's Liberation Army Navy) and PN (Pakistan Navy) use of sea space from where our interests can be threatened. India is geographically blessed, and that gives the navy the option to not only to harass the shipping critical to the adversary's energy and food security, but also interdict long unprotected sea lanes and choke points (ensuring that global commons do not get impacted). It is time to convert China's 'Malacca Dilemma' to 'China's Indian Ocean Dilemma'.

CHAPTER

8

Emerging and Disruptive Technologies

PRABHAT RANJAN

Security is basic for survival not only for individuals but for a society or a nation, at large. At the individual level, this relates to food, health and physical security. At the societal/national level, the definition of security becomes enhanced, and technology plays a big role in it. Technology has been used to protect nations from enemies and also to improve quality of life.

Disruptive technologies are those that build upon an established base of technologies and are either revolutionizing warfare already or will do so in a short time span (five–ten years). Emergent technologies are those that explore brand new fields of study, but their use is currently very limited and their larger, disruptive effects are expected to be felt only over a longer time frame (ten–twenty years). However, frequently, we have noticed that technology is evolving faster than expected and thus, some of the technologies in this latter group can grow in a much shorter time span and we need to keep a watch. This chapter focuses on those technologies that are called 'weak signals'—they are hardly discernible at this stage, but may emerge as a very important trend in the coming years. Most of these emerge from other fields and experts tend to miss them.

One of the ways that technology has advanced and become disruptive over the last few decades has been through digitization. According to well-known futurist Peter Diamandis, the growth cycle of digital technologies takes place in six key steps (referred to as the 'Six Ds of Exponentials'): digitization, deception, disruption, demonetization, dematerialization and democratization.[1] The last one means it becomes available on a very large scale and is typically driven by mass-market requirements rather than the specific needs of strategic sectors. Thus, digital technology is mostly driven by civilian needs, and the differentiation between military and civilian technology blurs. Recognition of this has led to many countries adjusting their military–technology development policies—China, for instance, initiated the Military–Civil Fusion (MCF) Development Strategy.[2]

Based on the digital revolution taking place, we are on the cusp of a seventh revolution:[3] the autonomous revolution. By combining machines and computers in ways thus far envisioned mostly through science fiction, this era will merge the changes generated by the Industrial Revolution and the Information Age with potentially significant alterations in how war is conducted. Of particular salience in this new era are developments in artificial intelligence—especially machine learning and deep-learning AI, combined with unmanned systems. These developments are the underlying breakthroughs that make self-driving cars and operational robots possible, with greater functionality and self-learning.[4] The seventh revolution would be characterized by autonomy and speed.

Stage	Military Revolution	Implications
First Revolution	Westphalian System	Revenue generation, banking and taxes for financing wars, and the rise of a professional military
Second Revolution	French Revolution	National mobilization, levies en masse and large-scale armies with conscription
Third Revolution	Industrial Revolution	Mass production, standardization and large-scale economic exploitation
Fourth Revolution	First and Second World Wars	Combined arms, armoured blitzkrieg, carriers, bombers and jets
Fifth Revolution	Nuclear Revolution and Missiles	Development of nuclear weapons and intercontinental ballistic missiles
Sixth Revolution	Information Revolution	Command and control, connectivity and instant global reach, imagery, and cyber levy en masse by violent extremists
Seventh Revolution	Autonomous Revolution	Autonomous weapons, swarms of robotic vehicles in multiple domains, self-organizing defensive systems, automated weapons, big data analytics, and machine and deep-learning programmes

Digital technologies depend on developments in four key areas: sensing (bridging the physical world with the digital world), processing (making sense of digital data and taking decisions), actuating (acting on decisions taken in an either purely digital way or connecting back to the physical world), and communication (connecting these components). Three of these are covered in the next three sections. Following this, we dive into artificial intelligence—that is, the algorithm driving the processors. The next section focuses on projectiles, propulsion and platforms. And the last section covers the other technologies available to us. I have intentionally left out our cybersecurity as this is well recognized as a threat now and the changes take place very rapidly in this field. However, I have covered cyberbiosecurity, which is not well understood.

Sensing

Sensors play a very critical role in the collection of information for the decision-making process. Based on the sensing range, these can be used in a variety of ways—from sensing by contact to remote sensing from space. Miniaturization of sensors (for instance, micro electro-mechanical system [MEMS] sensors), driven by their large-scale commercial use in smartphones, etc., has also had an impact on defence and homeland security. Here, we highlight some of the developments in sensor technology that can have an impact in our area of interest.

By Type	By Platform	By Application
• Imaging sensors	• Airborne	• Intelligence, surveillance and reconnaissance (ISR)
• Seismic sensors	• Land	
• Acoustic sensors	• Naval	• Communication and navigation
• Magnetic sensors	• Satellite	
• Pressure sensors	• Munitions	• Combat system
• Temperature sensors		• Electronic warfare
		• Target recognition systems
		• Command and control

By Type	By Platform	By Application
• Torque sensors		• Weapon and fire control systems
• Speed sensors		
• Level sensors		• Wearables
• Flow sensors		• Cybersecurity
• Force sensors		• Simulation and training
• Angle of attack (AOA) sensors		• Engine and operations systems
• Altimeter sensors		
• Position or displacement sensors		
• Accelerometers		
• Gyroscopes		
• Global positioning system sensors		
• Proximity sensors		

An increasing demand for battle-space awareness among defence forces, ongoing advancements in MEMS technology, an increasing use of unmanned aerial vehicles (UAVs) in modern warfare and an increasing focus on weapon-system reliability are fuelling the development of military technology. Requirements of mass market products—for instance, smartphones—are leading to the development of miniaturized sensors. In the 'Technology Vision 2020' document, prepared by Technology Information, Forecasting and Assessment Council (TIFAC) and released in 1996, a separate roadmap for advanced sensors was prepared for India to leapfrog into this sector. However, we have hardly made any progress and are totally dependent on imports. As sensors are playing a critical role in precision-guided munition, the country would continue to be dependent on imports of such weapons. This, combined with various delivery platforms, such as drones and their countermeasures, are going to be crucial for India in the coming years.

Satellite-based navigation, using systems such as GPS, have become a necessary part of both civilian and military applications. India's own indigenous navigation system, NavIC, is now in league with the US, China and Russia as a recognized component of the World-Wide Radio Navigation System (WWRNS). It covers India and nearby regions, extending up to 1,500 km, and consists of seven active satellites. Three of these seven satellites are located in the geostationary orbit (GEO) and four in the inclined geosynchronous orbit (IGSO).

China has completed its BeiDou navigation and positioning system, consisting of twenty-seven satellites in the medium Earth orbit, five in the geostationary orbit, and three more in the inclined geosynchronous orbits. This has given it the ability to be independent in this area and provides it more accuracy in the Asia-Pacific region. BeiDou is of immense strategic value to China, with the capability of carrying out cyber espionage and tactical manoeuvres.

The proliferation of chemical, biological, radiological and nuclear (CBRN) weapons, as well as their means of delivery, greatly complicate the ability of a country to manage international affairs, and protect its national and collective interests. These weapons provide the conventional military and non-state armed actors with tactical advantages on the battlefield. They put various aspects of human life or the economy at serious risk. Furthermore, they hinder the effectiveness of military operations by degrading the physical readiness of military personnel.

Unlike chemical weapons, biological warfare agents are yet to be deployed in real, large-scale combats—the threats posed by it in armed engagements and terrorist attacks are well recognized. They have the potential to contaminate areas and facilities, leading to sickness, injuries and even deaths among troops. Their impact is only visible after an incubation period, and thus require early detection and warning mechanisms to minimize disruptions to planned or ongoing military operations.

The emergence of biosensors has led to powerful and innovative analytical devices with wide-ranging applications in the civil and defence sectors. Combining a physical sensor with a biochemical-recognition component, these serve as innovative countermeasures against harmful biological agents. They enable higher sensitivity, selectivity and specificity in the detection of targeted molecules. Integrating multiple technologies—for instance, electrochemical sensors in combination with nanomaterials—these have the potential to enhance the accuracy of physiological monitoring and improve the quality of emergency responses to soldiers.

To ensure soldiers' safety against potential chemical attacks, one can incorporate the naturally flexible Nafion membrane into a soldier's clothes to detect chemical agents in the air while preventing them from interacting with the skin.[5]

Processing

In 1965, Gordon Moore made a prediction that would set the pace for our modern digital revolution. From careful observation of an emerging trend, Moore extrapolated that computing would dramatically increase in power, and decrease in relative cost, at an exponential pace. The insight, known as Moore's Law, became the golden rule for the electronics industry, and a springboard for innovation.[6]

While Moore's Law was mainly based on progress in semiconductor technology, it is expected that in the next few years, we would hit a dead end based on this. However, many new possibilities have now emerged that can influence the progress of processing technology. These include:[7] neuromorphic; neurological; spintronics; quantum; DNA; optical; chemical; amorphous; peptide; membrane; and fluidic technologies.

While it is not possible to go into the technical details of each of these, we will take examples of a few to show the possibilities from security point of view.

Neuromorphic Computing

Neuromorphic computing mimics the human brain to some extent and gains capabilities in those areas where the human brain still seems to be much better than traditional computers—for instance, with lower power consumption or fault tolerance. It would give computers eyes and ears like a human being! From a military and security point of view, drones equipped with such chips would be able to learn to recognize sites and objects previously visited, and detect subsequent changes in the environment. Robots embedded with neuromorphic chips could be left to act and decide their course of action independently in combat zones. The aerospace, military and defence sectors are expected to make maximum use of neuromorphic computing.

Neuromorphic computing has the capability to improve communication or risk analysis. It could also give distinct advantage to some countries, which will benefit from more sophisticated intelligence than others and gain an upper hand in international diplomacy. Effectively, it would give us a large number of 'human brains' without the cost of humans!

Quantum Technology[8]

Discovery of quantum phenomena is at least a century old and, quantum technology translates the principles of quantum physics into technological applications. Though it is still in its infancy, it is progressing fast towards usability. From the sensing, encryption and communications point of view. it could hold significant implications for the future of the military.

The development of lasers, semiconductors and other related technologies has used quantum phenomena since the 1950s and has resulted in the development of modern computers using information in the form of classical bits of 0 and 1. Quantum phenomena can be used to make devices as well as store, process and analyse new types of information.

Quantum applications rely on a number of key concepts, including superposition, quantum bits (qubits) and entanglement. Superposition refers to the ability of quantum systems to exist in two or more states simultaneously. A qubit is a computing unit that leverages the principle of superposition to encode information. Unlike the classical computer, quantum computer encodes information in qubits, each of which can represent 0, 1, or a combination of 0 and 1 at the same time. Thus, the power of a quantum computer increases exponentially with the addition of each qubit.

Entanglement underpins a number of potential military applications of quantum technology. Both superposition and entanglement are, however, difficult to sustain due to the fragility of quantum states, which are very sensitive to movements, temperatures and other environmental factors. Recent progress in Japan in achieving triple entanglement in silicon may be a major quantum computer breakthrough.[9]

A Chinese research team has successfully designed a 62-qubit programmable superconducting quantum processor containing the largest number of superconducting qubits so far in the world, but has been superseded by IBM announcing a 127-qubit computer in November 2021. IBM is planning to build intermediate-size machines of 433 qubits in 2022 and follow it up with a 1,000-qubit machine in 2023. Furthermore, they are targeting a one-million-qubit machine in the near future. Google is also planning a similar machine in ten years' time.

One year ago, Google grabbed headlines when the company announced its researchers had used their 53-qubit quantum computer to solve a particular abstract problem that they claimed would overwhelm any conventional computer—reaching a milestone known as 'quantum supremacy'. A significant obstacle preventing a future in quantum supremacy is the error-prone nature of the current class of quantum computers. Google's recent experimental demonstration of how to correct this problem and scale it up for much larger devices is a big step in this direction.[10] With a million-qubit machine, it is expected that one can break current internet encryption schemes.

Quantum information technologies could touch everything from extremely secure communications to faster codebreaking to better detection of aircraft and submarines, resulting in a major impact on national security.

Advanced quantum information technologies afford the possibility of affecting some of the most important national security tools and tasks—such as intelligence collection, solution optimization, encryption, stealth technology, computer processing and communications. While it can help us improve our security, it can also lead to a loss of security if we are not careful and prepared.

Communication

Communication links sensors/actuators with processors. The outcome of processing can result in changes in the digital world or, with the help of actuators, in the physical world. Since its discovery more than a century ago, radio communication has played a major role in the defence sector. This communication can be one-way (e.g., broadcasting services) or two-way (e.g., telephony). Progress in digital cellular telephony has revolutionized the way man-to-man, man-to-machine or machine-to-machine communication takes place. In this, we have moved slowly from 2G to 3G to 4G, and now 5G technology is in progress across the globe.

Radio Communications

5G is the fifth generation of cellular technology, which would provide a more rapid, stable and secure connection. The data transfer rates in 5G are expected to be 100 times faster while the network latency will be significantly reduced to 1–10 milliseconds (ms). It would further boost advancements in the fields of the internet of things (IoT), artificial intelligence (AI) and augmented reality (AR). Worldwide use of 5G technology for mobile communication is growing. In India too trials are being conducted and commercial launch has been delayed till mid-2022.

5G will operate on three segments of the electromagnetic spectrum:

- Low band, which operates at frequencies lower than 1 GHz;
- Mid band, which operates at frequencies between 1 GHz and 6 GHz; and
- High band, or millimetre wave, which operates at frequencies between 24 and 300 GHz.

The high band has much higher bandwidth and is of great interest to the military. However, it has a very short range of communication, and implementing it in the frontline of a battlefield may not be easy, where intentional radio frequency (RF) jamming or other kinds of interference from enemies is likely.

5G would enable soldiers, vehicles, command posts, ships, satellites and planes to connect with information almost in real time along with maps, photos and other information about the operation under way. If we couple 5G networking with AI and machine learning, the potential for new applications start to expand exponentially.

China has launched a communications satellite in November 2020 to study 6G physics in the environment of space with terahertz electronics. Terahertz waves would boost transmission speeds many times faster than 5G, when engineers and researchers develop effective technology and take the bandwidth into the tbps domain. it is expected that 6G technology may start to happen around 2030 onwards with 1,000 times more bandwidth and latency as low as 1 ms. All this would mean massive data fusion across systems and much more interactivity.

Satellite Constellation-based Internet

Skylink, launched by Elon Musk, is targeting LEO (low earth orbit, flying at a height of less than 1,200 miles) satellite constellations due to the fact that launching costs are lower and signal transmission times (and hence, latency) is less. However, as the satellites are not geostationary, to provide coverage at a location, one needs to have a large number of satellites. Skylink is not the only one in this segment—multiple companies are targeting satellite-constellation-based internet service, some in LEO and others in higher orbits.

Skylink is providing low latency, high bandwidth (up to 300 Mbps) internet connectivity across the globe. It has already started providing beta test capabilities to different parts of Earth. Realizing its military significance, Defense Advanced Research Projects Agency (DARPA) has planned on sending the first satellite of its Blackjack network into orbit later this year. Blackjack is intended to eventually offer the US military a persistent global communications network by blanketing the globe with low-Earth orbit, low-cost small satellites that can quickly transmit data to one another using optical lasers.

Defence experts believe that LEO constellations would provide a host of services to fighters in the conflict zones—both as alternatives to positioning, navigation and timing (PNT) systems and as something that would be difficult to track and destroy.

This has become very important in view of anti-satellite weapons (ASAT), which are space weapons designed to damage or destroy satellites for strategic or tactical purposes. Several nations possess operational ASAT systems. Although no such system has yet been utilized in warfare, a few countries (such as the United States, Russia, China and India) have successfully shot down their own satellites to demonstrate their capabilities.

Free-space Optical/Laser Communication

While optical communication has been used for passing information/signals since time immemorial, its use in data transmission for terrestrial applications in recent days has been limited. With the advent of lasers in 1960s, it generated a lot of interest among military organizations. Growth of optical fibre-based data transmission both on the ground and through the seabed reduced this interest. However, free space, optical point-to-point communication can be established using infrared lasers. On Earth, communication up to 2–3 km at 10 Gbit/s has been demonstrated, but it gets seriously impacted by weather conditions.

When we go into space, though, laser communication becomes very useful. In applications like Skylink, communication between several hundred to thousand satellites is done using lasers—this is done by effectively creating a space-based optical mesh network. Satellites that use lasers to exchange data promise to make military communications faster and harder to intercept—if the technical problems plaguing them can be resolved. Space-based laser communication is only possible with a very narrow beam, making it much harder than radio-frequency communication, but also much more difficult to jam or interfere with.

Artificial Intelligence

The seventh revolution would be driven by AI. As computers started to develop, efforts to bridge the gap between the way computers work and the way the human brain works began. While neuromorphic computing is trying to do this at the hardware level, AI is trying to do this at the software level. For the purposes of this document, we will use the US Defense Science Board's definition of AI: 'The capability of computer systems to perform tasks that normally require human intelligence'.[11]

If the task is perfectly scripted with a set of specified and known rules, then it is considered to have 'low autonomy' and is described as 'automated'. If the entity performing the task is empowered to proceed without rules or boundaries, it is described as fully 'autonomous'. Nearly all tasks that machines perform fall somewhere between these two extremes, so it makes sense to discuss the applications of AI in terms of degrees or levels of autonomy.

Autonomy-at-rest describes systems that operate in software, or in the virtual world, whereas autonomy-in-motion describes systems that interact largely with the physical world. In such cases, a human might execute the strikes, but an AI system could play a substantial role in informing decision makers whether to attack and what targets to strike.

Early approaches to AI involved developing automated systems with the ability to perform scripted tasks according to sets of specified rules. With AI encompassing so many kinds of systems and levels of autonomy, it is helpful to classify these technologies in a graphic taxonomy, illustrating the relationships between them.

Recent Progress in AI Driving Military Applications

While many technological developments came about because of military requirements—including technology like the ethernet—the progress in the development of AI is being driven largely by commercial interests. Thus, it is reasonable to expect that most future military applications will be adaptations of technologies developed in the commercial sector. I have briefly outlined a few of the most important areas of progress in AI that have potential military applications. We give below a broader distribution of some of these.[12]

Big data: Internet of things (IoT)

Logistics: Block chain, IoT, reinforcement learning, k-nearest neighbours, naive bayes, logistic regression, random forest, deep neural networks

Objects location: Fuzzy ARTMAP, rules-based methods of AI, Gaussian mixture model, generative adversarial network, fuzzy c-means clustering

Underwater mines location: Convolutional neural network, fully convolutional network, dead recognition (DR) navigation methods based on neural networks, Markov random fields

Cyber security: Support vector machine, deep neural networks, decision tree, random forest, k-nearest neighbours

Bio-inspired robots: Swarm AI, deep neural networks

- Image recognition

Image recognition is a task that is easy for people but hard for computers. But this is an exception, as many tasks are very hard for human beings but very easy for computers. Deep neural networks are changing this, and companies like Facebook (Meta) are doing a good job on this. The progress extends to both facial recognition and more subtle aspects of facial expression, making technology for biometric identification through facial features and even emotional analysis viable. Neuromorphic computing and imaging in non-optical wavelengths are helping it further.

An ability to detect objects and recognize images, and especially recognize faces and perform emotional analysis, has clear military applications.

- **Text analysis**

Natural language processing had made rapid progress with the help of deep neural networks' application to the vast quantities of digitally written data, thanks to the internet. Although human-level performance is far away, it has already become useful as seen in various devices such as Google Home, Amazon's Alexa, etc. Substantial advances in summarization and sentiment analysis, not to mention search engines, has also been made.

We could leverage voice translation techniques to help soldiers communicate with locals and support medics while they're treating foreign patients. Hands-free translators for tactical and emergency situations have also been developed.

- **Self-driving cars**

Significant progress has been made in the development of self-driving cars in recent years and we are close to developing fully autonomous vehicles. Currently, these systems require humans to be available to intervene, much the way pilots are required when aircraft are on autopilot; using the terminology of weapon systems, we would refer to them as 'supervised autonomous systems'. However, for military applications, they can be used easily in unpopulated areas. Development in image recognition and sensor technology has played a key role in this.

- **Game-playing**

Another common benchmark for measuring progress in AI throughout its history has been its ability to play games. It made big news in 1997, when AI systems beat human chess players and, more recently, AlphaGo players. However, these are still structured games with full information about the state of game available. A greater challenge is presented in games such as poker, where players have only partial information and bluffing is involved, but AI systems have recently beaten professional poker players as well. And now an effort is underway to develop AI that can play even tougher games, such as StarCraft. These game-playing AI systems tend to rely on an approach called reinforcement learning. A similar approach can be applied to robot motion too. Despite these advances, applying game-playing AI to abstract military strategy or war gaming is still a bit futuristic.

Benefits of Artificial Intelligence in Warfare

Based on expert opinions, we try to identify application areas of AI, where it may be beneficial to the military. But we must remember that sometimes these benefits may be harmful too.

- **Speed of decision-making**

Speed of decision-making is often referred to with respect to the time taken to go through the OODA (observe, orient, decide, act) loop—a four-step approach to decision-making. The idea being to see if it is possible to cycle through the OODA loop faster than one's adversaries to take counteractions. However, this would be only advantageous if timelines are dominated by the decision-making process and not by the time it takes to perform counteractions—moving equipment, for instance.

- **Use of big data**

Big data refers to data that is too large to be stored on a computer's memory or is generated too quickly to be managed by a single computer, or is data that takes on many different forms or formats. It is challenging for humans to make sense of the information contained in this data, but machines and AI tend to perform better here. The sheer volume of information being collected by various sensors often requires use of big data techniques.

- **Improved targeting and vision**

With ever-increasing resolution and the number of cameras collecting images and videos, the amount of data to be handled keeps skyrocketing. AI automatically emerges as a winner for automation in the process of analysing incoming video and imagery. Improvements in this sector are definitely a major plus point for the military or counterterrorism applications. Identifying terrorists or known combatants (even with masks on, etc.) is going to be very helpful. Further, facial-expression analysis could help alert soldiers and other security personnel to risky situations or better manage social interactions while building peace. There are efforts going on to beat AI in face recognition by various face-camouflaging techniques too.

- **Decision support systems**

Even if these technologies are not appropriate for use in making combat suggestions or decisions, experts anticipate that they could be used to provide a wider range of possible adversary actions in war gaming and red-teaming events (such as testing messages, actions, or strategies on exercise participants who have studied a potential adversary's typical behaviour in an effort to anticipate their reactions in the real world), or to provide blunder-detection assistance.

Driven largely by the progress observed in gaming systems and personal assistant technology, AI is anticipated to be able to recommend options to decision makers more quickly, and sometimes superior to what human beings could suggest. A familiar example is routing technology, such as Google Maps, that can ingest complete maps and real-time or projected traffic information in ways that humans would not be able to. Blunder avoidance is one of the benefits of using computer teammates in chess, because as circumstances grow complex, it is easy for humans to forget about some aspects of the problem or the implications of their actions.

- **Mitigation of manpower issues**

The military has a variety of unmet needs for tasks such as image analysis and foreign language translation. These are the types of tasks that arise from the rapid growth in the volume of data available for processing. Fortunately, they are also the types of tasks for which AI is becoming well positioned to assist humans. AI is also key to providing robotic assistance on the battlefield, which will enable forces to maintain or expand their war-fighting capacity without increasing manpower.

- **Improvements in cyber defence**

With cyber warfare as a present and growing military concern—and one that originates in the same digital world as AI—it is natural to expect intersections between the two. These intersections have already begun to manifest as antivirus companies push forward in the cat-and-mouse game between attackers and defenders. Historically, one of the ways that antivirus systems have identified malware has been to watch for tell-tale static tags, fixed invisible images that indicate whether the code is illegitimate. However, it is no longer sufficient to simply use static tags to identify malware, because attackers have discovered ways to generate malware with fewer tags.

In response, antivirus companies have looked into their large data sets of malware behaviour to create AI that can observe software on a system and flag actions that are identified as suspicious. As illustrated by DARPA's Cyber Grand Challenge, there is also growing interest in the potential for machines that can find and patch vulnerabilities in friendly systems or find and attack vulnerabilities in enemy systems—but these applications still cannot perform these tasks at the level of experienced humans.

- **Improvements in accuracy and precision**

Machines, in general, can have greater accuracy and precision than humans. For example, it is possible to use machines to fabricate electronic transistors that make up computers, despite those transistors being only nanometres in length. Machine precision also extends to AI, which can have floating-point precision, easily incorporating 32 or 64 bits per number being represented, whereas humans tend to think in rough estimates or round numbers. Machines can also be more accurate than humans due to certain inherent properties, such as uniformity from machine to machine and uniformity over time, whereas people have more individual differences and get tired or bored.

- **Labour and cost reduction**

As is happening throughout the economy, tasks that once required a dedicated person to perform are now progressively being performed by AI or robots. This trend allows a single person to perform quantities of work that would previously have required several people or, for some jobs, to be automated altogether. The military, a large employer, is no exception and may find ways to reduce staffing levels without sacrificing the services being offered.

Additionally, AI has demonstrated the ability to improve or optimize processes of many different types, which, in turn, leads to cost reductions. With the large number of complex and expensive processes employed by the US Department of Defense, from logistics to heating and cooling to recruiting, there are plenty of opportunities for AI to improve efficiencies and effect cost savings

- **Improvements in intelligence, surveillance, and reconnaissance (ISR)**

The trend to invest in the use of AI for ISR by military is going to continue. The ability to autonomously collect data from sensors deployed on ground, in air and under water and in cyberspace is continuously increasing volume, velocity and variety of data. Before being transmitted from the field, some of these need to be locally analysed to reduce the data volume, velocity and variety to save on bandwidth of transmission. This is likely to get a big boost with the help of neuromorphic computing. The next level of analysis will be done in intelligence processing centres, where use of AI would further improve the quality of intelligence.

Using ISR would also help in operating in those regions that are too lethal for human operators, platforms and bases. ISR, along with autonomous systems, would reduce the numbers of human operators at risk in these environments. They would potentially be more combat capable than inhabited weapons platforms as they can be smaller, faster and more agile.

- **Improvements in deception and information operations**

Capability to generate text snippets or carry out short conversations by a large number of autonomous agents may allow one to persuade a target audience to believe a particular narrative of geopolitical or military significance. By harvesting social media data, it is already possible for AI to analyse the large amounts of information that people reveal about themselves online, and an improved understanding of how to tailor specific messages to increase the likelihood of influencing them can be developed. With technologies like Deepfake, it is even becoming possible for AI to create false but realistic images, videos and audios of people for such purposes.

Risks of Artificial Intelligence in Warfare

Although the military applications of AI are expected to yield a good range of advantages, they also present significant risks. There are concerns that decisions could be taken too quickly without the ability to adapt to the inevitable complexities of war. AI-based systems may make errors while distinguishing between combatants and non-combatants, or threats and system anomalies. Lack of adequate testing in the realistic environment or success of adversaries in spoofing or hacking the systems could lead to such situations.

AI and autonomous systems could lower the price of war in terms of human casualties. This could encourage commanders to take greater risks and act more aggressively, which could fuel an arms race or escalate it. Military operators and leaders might also put too much trust in their AI systems and may exhibit an 'automation bias', relying on the outputs of these AI systems even when they do not seem to make sense. This tendency can lead to wrong actions and an initiation of conflict where there was none.

Projectiles, Propulsion and Platforms

If we lump together major vehicles, ships, aircraft, rockets, missiles and the various engines and fuels that propel these large platforms, changes are not likely to be disruptive. This is due to the long time required to design, test, build and field major weapons platforms. However, there are areas that are emerging and we will focus on those in this section. We start with robotics and autonomous systems.[13]

Robotics

Military robots have moved out of science-fiction novels and movies to battlefields and streets. Autonomous aerial robots—or drones—are already being deployed for many purposes, including attacks, and have already caused several thousands of casualties. Many debates have started, covering the legal and ethical aspects of this new military technology.

Boston Dynamics is a world leader in bio-inspired robots with the goal of protecting the health and lives of soldiers. Their robots can move independently, detect and avoid obstacles, follow a predetermined route, as well as recognize and respond to voice messages coming from the environment. One of their robots, Spot, is a nimble quadruped that can move over almost any terrain. These are likely to become the new standard of warfare in a short time. They are resistant to extreme weather conditions and fatigue, and do not require food and water. However, they can easily be disturbed by hackers and that weakness needs to be addressed. Swarm robotics can allow cooperation among humanoid robots and yield better results on the battlefield as well. Wireless sensor networks (WSNs) consisting of small (almost invisible) nodes are similar, without the mobility aspects and can be very useful for gathering information from adversary regions.

Drones

Drones or UAVs have been in use for nearly two decades now. Slowly, their size, weight and cost has come down. Civilian applications have grown tremendously—recently, India has made drone rules even more liberal to promote drone and drone-based industry. As this is now a well-understood technology among experts, we will focus more on counter-drone technologies. These fall into two categories: monitoring equipment and countermeasures.[14]

- **Drone-monitoring equipment**

Drone-monitoring equipment can be passive (they simply look or listen) or active (by sending a signal out and analysing what comes back), and can perform several functions, including detection, classification or identification, locating/tracking and alerting.

Detection usually is not enough and classifying it is important to separate drones from other types of objects. Some equipment can identify a particular model of drone, or even identify the drone's or controller's digital fingerprint, like a media access control (MAC) address, for example. Being aware of a drone present somewhere in the vicinity is useful, but the ability to deploy countermeasures is greatly enhanced if we know the drone's (and/or the controller's) exact location and are able to track them real time.

There are four main types of drone monitoring equipment:

1. Radio frequency (RF) analysers: They work by trying to detect radio communication between a drone and its controller. However, they would not be useful for autonomous drones.
2. Acoustic sensors (microphones): They pick up sound using a microphone (individual or array) and can be useful in quiet environments, but are not very helpful in noisy surroundings. With multiple sets, they can be used to locate the position, in addition to the presence itself.
3. Optical sensors (cameras): Video cameras (specially with automated real-time analysis) are useful if a drone is in sight, but may need to use infrared or thermal imaging techniques for detection in the night.
4. Radar: Millimetre wave radar can detect drones of smaller sizes. Nano drones (with a radar backscatter cross-section of less than 0.01 m^2) may be missed out, but they are not considered a significant threat. A high-precision analysis of the doppler spectrum also allows a distinction to be made

with regard to the number of rotors and the rotor type, thus facilitating the determination of the drone class.[15]

• **Drone countermeasures equipment**

These include either physically destroying the drone, neutralizing the drone, or taking control of it.

1. RF jammers: An RF jammer is a static, mobile or handheld device, which transmits a large amount of RF energy towards the drone, masking the controller signal. This results in one of four scenarios, depending on the drone: controlled landing in its current position; it returns to the user-set home location; it falls, uncontrolled, to the ground; or it flies off in a random uncontrolled direction. These are useful over a short range, but can affect other radio communications and can also result in unpredictable drone behaviour.
2. GPS spoofers: A GPS spoofer sends a new signal to the drone, replacing the communication with GPS satellites and affecting its coordinates measurements in real time. This way, it can be directed to a 'safe zone'. This also works over a short range, and can affect other radio communications and GPS-based systems.
3. High-power microwave (HPM) devices: An HPM device generates an electromagnetic pulse (EMP) capable of disrupting electronic devices. The EMP interferes with radio links and disrupts, or even destroys, the electronic circuitry in drones due to the damaging voltage and currents it creates. With an antenna to focus the EMP in a certain direction, one can reduce potential collateral damage.
4. Nets and net guns: Firing a net at a drone, or otherwise bringing a net into contact with a drone, stops it by prohibiting the rotor blades. There are a different variety of

these, depending on how they are fired or carried to the target drone. It can physically capture a target with less chance of collateral damage.
5. High-energy lasers: A high-energy laser is a high-powered optical device which produces an extremely focused beam of light, or a laser beam. The laser defeats the drone by destroying the structure and/or the electronics. It is a high-cost system with a risk of collateral damage.
6. Birds of prey: Eagles have been trained to capture certain types of drones. This requires a lot of manpower for training and for maintaining the birds of prey.

Hypersonic Vehicles

Progress in missiles is ongoing. Today's air-to-air missiles, for example, can now range over 320 km and reach speeds of Mach 6, in some cases. The most interesting developments in the coming years are likely to be in the realm of hypersonic vehicles (those whose speeds exceed Mach 5), which may become capable of longer-range or even global strike operations over the time frame of interest in this paper. That could put any target on Earth within reach in less than an hour of decision and launch.

Hypersonic flights are not new. It is the capability to have controlled flight that is attracting attention to these, rather than their speeds. These new systems have two subvarieties: hypersonic cruise missiles (HCMs) and hypersonic glide vehicles (HGVs). Glide vehicles are lofted on high-velocity boosters and separated. Then they use their momentum and control surfaces to skip and glide through the upper atmosphere before crashing onto their targets. For powered flight, the cruise missiles use an advanced propulsion system (a scramjet). While the descriptions are straightforward, the engineering needed to accomplish the guidance and manoeuvring (not to mention, the survivability) of these weapons is far from clear.

For the utilization of hypersonic missiles, including those bearing nuclear warheads, 5G communication would be essential. It is necessary to collect, elaborate and transmit enormous quantities of data over a very short time, in order to guide them on variable trajectories. The same thing is required to activate defences just in case of an attack with this sort of weapon—since there's not enough time to take such decisions, the only possibility is to believe that 5G automatic systems are the way forward. Russia, China and the USA have developed good capabilities, and India is also working on it. In the recent Russia–Ukraine conflict hypersonic missiles have been used.[16]

If we consider ground vehicles and several key trends in their underlying technologies, the changes are going to be significant but not revolutionary. As for armour for heavy combat vehicles, most of the main innovations in widespread use today—depleted uranium armours, explosive-reactive armours, ceramic materials, etc.—were developed in the late twentieth century. Today's newer concepts involve ideas such as laser defences, perhaps more than armour itself. Progress will also occur by adopting recent innovations in armour more broadly and widely across key military vehicles. This pace of innovation may, however, be roughly matched by progress in ordnance used to attack armour, including the wider introduction of nanomaterials into explosives as well as the expanded use of explosively formed penetrators (which focus their power in a given direction for greater effect).

If we consider large rockets, change has been slow. Economic efficiency has not improved by a big margin. Reusable rockets show promise through private efforts, such as those of SpaceX. These promise to cut costs by 50 per cent or more. There has been significant progress in making the payloads themselves smaller through the use of miniaturization. This is leading to satellite constellations-based applications such as SkyLink.

Missile defences are also gradually improving—for instance, longer-range systems are getting better—but less dramatically. Further progress is expected. With expected improvements to the kill vehicle, and to sensor networks, including the sea-based X-band radar and long-range discrimination radar, mid-course missile defence seems likely to achieve reasonably good performance capabilities against simple threats in the coming decade. However, decoys need not be particularly complicated to fool even advanced sensors.

There are three more categories in platform-related technology: surface ships, submarines and aircraft stealth. With regard to basic ship technology, only evolutionary changes are expected. Submarine quieting continues to advance, through the classic methods of isolating machinery within a submarine, using anechoic materials on its surface and further extending 'snorkelling time' through air-independent propulsion and related methods. New ideas in submarine quieting involve using low-magnetism steels in the hull, to reduce detectability by magnetic detectors, or placing new coatings on submarines that could absorb or redirect sonar in order to reduce detectability. If the Seawolf class of submarines really offered the potential for quieting that was sometimes purported in its unclassified literature—approaching a tenfold improvement in quietness—it seems plausible that such technologies could be engineered to be more economical in the coming years, and thus be used on more vessels.

Regarding aircraft stealth, some important new concepts and approaches are in the works. The designs of key parts of aircraft, such as intakes to engines and exhaust vents, continue to be refined. Materials that can attenuate returns from lower-frequency radars are being investigated. These include so-called 'metamaterials'—composite artificial materials assembled from various types of constituent elements like metals and plastics. Electronic countermeasures that can cancel out radar returns from stealth aircraft are also evolving and improving. Materials that are less inclined to degradation or to heating (which produces a potentially detectable infrared signature) are being researched too. In the competition between submarines and anti-submarine warfare, as well as the net trend in the stealth–counterstealth competition, not much is expected to change fast. In many water conditions and locations, the submarine is likely to enjoy a certain basic advantage over sensors. Quantum computing, though, seems to offer the potential to find a submarine's wake through sustained monitoring and analysis of ocean surface conditions by picking signals in very noisy data.

Other Weapons and Key Technologies

Finally, there is a category of miscellaneous technologies that deserves mention. They range from non-lethal weapons of various kinds to biological pathogens and other weapons of mass destruction, to lasers and particle beams, to rail guns and long-range kinetic strike systems, to enabling technologies such as nanomaterials and additive printing or 3D manufacturing.

Among the directed energy weapons, high-energy laser (HEL) weapon systems have made rapid progress. Current HEL weapon systems primarily consist of continuous wave (CW) laser sources with output powers in the kilowatts. These kilowatt-class CW laser systems predominantly engage targets via the absorption of light. This can cause the target to burn and melt or overwhelm its optical sensors with high intensities. Emergence of diode and fibre laser technology has made these systems ruggedized to the point that they have been integrated onto platforms ranging from ground to sea.

Soon, mobile lasers may be able to incapacitate a given individual in a flock, disperse crowds or disable a vehicle, without a high risk of fatalities. Lasers may soon damage or destroy many threatening systems on the tactical battlefield. However, some of the most promising applications may be in maritime domains, for the short-range defence of ships. Aircraft may also use them for protection against threatening missiles.

There is also an effort to develop an ultrashort pulse laser (USPL) system. While most CW lasers simply melt targets, USPL systems are able to neutralize threats via three distinct mechanisms: ablation of material from the target, the blinding of sensors and the generation of a localized electronic interference to overload a threat's internal electronics.[17]

Consider several more technologies. The field of rail guns is making considerable strides. They may soon replace traditional guns on some major ships. For example, they could extend direct-fire ranges of ship-borne weapons to 160 km or more, with round velocities at least twice that of traditional chemical-propelled ordnance. High-powered microwaves have some promise, as well. However, uncertainties about whether they have successfully destroyed the electronics of a given enemy system, combined with their inherently limited range (given that their power falls off inversely with the square of the distance from the weapon to its target), may limit their future roles, unless the terminal defences protecting a given asset can be reliably penetrated.

Among the next weapons of mass destruction, most chemical and nuclear weapons technologies are fairly mature and evolving only modestly. The main exception to this assertion may be in the new category of drugs, including opioids, fentanyl and carfentanyl, which behave in many ways like advanced chemical weapons, and could be employed that way in war.

The Nuclear Test Ban Treaty, though never ratified, has nonetheless been respected by major nuclear powers since the 1990s and thereby impeded fundamental new work on nuclear explosives.

Cyberbiosecurity

The COVID-19 pandemic has renewed interest in biological weapons. While there is fairly good understanding of biological weapons, its combination of information technology and biology needs attention. The information technology revolution has not left any area of study untouched, and the field of biology is no exception. So, work on biological systems depends now greatly on IT tools. While this has made development in biological sciences much faster, including drug discovery, etc., it also brings with it the possibilities for new, combined threats, previously unanticipated vulnerabilities and unintended consequences along with it. It is in this context that a new term, 'cyberbiosecurity', has emerged,[18] which is defined as 'understanding the vulnerabilities to unwanted surveillance, intrusions, and malicious and harmful activities which can occur within or at the interfaces of comingled life and medical sciences, cyber, cyber-physical, supply chain and infrastructure systems, and developing and instituting measures to prevent, protect against, mitigate, investigate, and attribute such threats as it pertains to security, competitiveness, and resilience'.[19] Cyberbiosecurity systems need very good understanding of both biological and cyber systems, as well as their interaction.

Food production, such as the manufacturing of packaged meals for soldiers, also need cyberbiosecurity. It is important to note that attackers can simply get access to control systems and play around with the temperature settings, etc., to affect the food quality. The incorporation of IT tools, starting from agricultural production to the end users, as well as marketing, etc., and use of cloud-based storage of large data sets, increases opportunities for hacking. Similarly, within research laboratories, the use of biological and genetic analytical technologies is widespread for the evaluation of food quality. They are also used to identify zoonotic disease as well as monitor animal and plant health. Additionally, the rate of development of new products and crops is getting enhanced through the use of bioinformatics and genetic technologies.

While both cybersecurity and biosecurity efforts are underway independently, there is an obvious gap when it comes to cyberbiosecurity. Even this term is not known to most policymakers. COVID-19 should make us aware of the importance of cyberbiosecurity and an integrated approach must be initiated in India.

This needs a programme to identify and assess cyberbiological risk. At a minimum, such a programme should identify new cyberbiological threats, vulnerabilities and consequences (for instance, those associated with pathogens and biomanufacturing data systems, dual-use synthetic biology, biological intellectual property and bioeconomy). This programme should result from a public–private partnership among all government agencies, apart from academic institutions and other non-governmental organizations.

Synthetic Biology

Another technological development related to biology is the area of 'synthetic biology', which could be defined as 'the design and construction of new biological parts, devices and systems or the redesign of existing natural biological systems for useful purposes'.[20] In some sense, synthetic biology aims to make biology easier to engineer. A plethora of enabling tools has made synthetic biology different from previous iterations of bioengineering. These include the relatively well-known CRISPR/Cas9, but perhaps the most important enabler has been the steady increase in computational power that makes it more possible than ever to develop powerful tools. Even more worrying is the fact that these tools have become easy to access—they can even be ordered online—and can be used by non-state actors too.[21]

Artemisinin (used in antimalarial drugs) has been manufactured using synthetic biology. High-value chemicals dependent on labour-intensive and single-crop agriculture are already being replaced by synthetic versions. Some of these processes may disrupt the Indian economy, as well as reduce its soft power. An example is that of guar gum—India produces nearly 80 per cent of global production, but China produced a synthetic substitute and impacted Indian industry as well as a large number of farmers and others dependent on this for their livelihood.

Synthetic biology has tremendous potential for crime as well as large-scale bioweapons. Eight potential crime types have been identified:[22] bio-discrimination, cyber-biocrime, bio-malware, biohacking, at-home drug manufacturing, illegal gene editing, genetic blackmail and neuro-hacking. The ongoing challenge of the COVID-19 pandemic reveals weaknesses in our healthcare system, our biosecurity protocols and our preparedness to act. In the medical sciences and healthcare sector roadmap for Technology Vision 2035,[23] details related to the control of infectious diseases have been provided in a full chapter and may serve as a good resource to prepare India for any such possibilities, either natural or manmade.

Synthetic biotechnology may help the military develop next-generation, living camouflage and other never-seen-before organisms and materials. In the next ten years, we may see the impact of this technology.

Bio and Human Enhancement Technologies (BHET)

Human-performance enhancements of various types are sure to improve by 2040. Various types of exoskeletons show the ability to increase the power of limbs or joints, or reduce the metabolic energy consumption required to create a certain amount of force or torque—by 25 per cent or more. Relatively safe medications like modafinil can keep people awake and at a high level of performance for up to two days; even more powerful and relatively safe medications seem likely to emerge over the next two decades. These kinds of changes seem likely to happen in the competitive domain of warfare, whatever reservations a country like the United States may have had about them in the abstract. That said, it remains unclear how much difference they will really make if combatants on all sides of a given conflict have access to comparable performance enhancers.

Biotechnologists use, manipulate or create living material by intervening in its normal function or by genetic engineering to perform a number of different tasks. Examples range from the creation of novel pathogens or cloning to nano-scale engineering using viruses. A BHET is a technology to improve the human body and mind beyond their normal limits—for instance, implants, exoskeletons, biosensors or drugs. Due to better pharmaceutics and better monitoring through biosensors, combatants in the field will be more efficient, while, behind the scenes, exoskeletons will make logistical operations far easier.

Advancement in brain–computer interfaces (both invasive and non-invasive) are going to make a major impact in this area by improving memory, reducing training time by knowledge transfer, as well as developing capabilities like the quick learning of a language. Technologies like Neuralink (by Elon Musk) are also going to be game changers in this field.

Another group of human enhancement technologies on the horizon is portable personal air mobility systems. DARPA wants these to be capable of low- to medium-altitude flight and have a range of five kilometres. It requires systems to fit in one bag or box and be ready to go after just ten minutes of assembly. Jetpacks, powered gliders, powered wingsuits and powered parafoils are some of the examples of such technologies which could leverage emerging electric propulsion technologies, hydrogen fuel cells or conventional heavy fuel propulsion systems. They can help during military missions, enabling cost-effective mission utility and agility in areas like urban augmented combat, personnel logistics, combat search and rescue, maritime interdiction and special operations forces (infiltration/exfiltration).

Similarly, the US is reaching out to industries to find companies that can develop exoskeleton technologies to improve soldier performance during repetitive tasks on the battlefield or in moving cargo.[24] Exoskeletons can improve soldier strength, endurance and ergonomics safely and reduce the danger of physical injury while lifting heavy loads, traversing challenging terrains and completing repetitive motion. These also have civilian usage.

In India, the Defence Research and Development Organisation (DRDO) has also been working on exoskeletons for several years now, but it is not yet field ready. China has come out with military-grade exoskeleton suits, which are powered and used for carrying ammunition. In late 2020, Chinese border defence troops used non-powered exoskeletons for supporting operations like supply delivery, patrol, etc.[25]

Meanwhile, a robot has been developed which will mimic a chameleon's colour-changing abilities and movement. Researchers stacked several layers of nanowire heaters underneath the crystal layer to make different patterns, starting from dots to grids. Selectively heating layers creates colourful patterns allowing the bot to mimic its surrounding environments.[26]

Russia has developed a technology to camouflage its troops and armoured vehicles in plain sight. It is a unique coating that can change its colour depending on the surrounding environment. It can even replicate complex graphics like the movement of leaves in the wind as the whole thing is electrically operated. This would not only give soldiers an element of stealth but can also be used to cover equipment, weapons, outfits or even armoured vehicles.[27]

Additive Manufacturing

Additive manufacturing (AM) is a broad term to describe digitally driven manufacturing. It's popularly known as '3D printing'. Traditional manufacturing is now also referred to as subtractive manufacturing. A system using both these in combination is called 'hybrid manufacturing'. AM is going to have such a revolutionary impact on defence preparedness that one could devote a whole book to it. The US Department of Defense, as well as other countries, are aware of this and have prepared their own national strategies.

India's Ministry of Electronics and Information Technology released a national strategy for additive manufacturing in December 2020.[28] According to this, 'Additive manufacturing (AM) is the digital revolution of industrial production that embraces innovation in digital processes, communications, imaging, architecture and engineering to provide digital flexibility and efficiency to manufacturing operations. The computer-aided design (CAD) software data is used directly to the hardware under this technology to deposit material layer upon layer in precise geometric shapes.'

In the aerospace and defence sector, AM has been identified as useful for landing gears, thrust reverser doors, surveillance drones, gimbal eyes, grenade launchers, complex brackets, and jet engine components. In addition, it has also been mentioned for the repair of turbine blades and high-value components.

Defence maintenance requirements are huge, with machinery across generations requiring different types of spare parts as well as consumables. Operations require high levels of customization and the production of parts in remote locations in low volumes and on tight timelines, which imposes high entry barriers for suppliers of traditionally manufactured parts. This results in long lead times, higher transportation costs, lower operational readiness and sortie rates, and considerable excess inventory and waste. Often, it has been noticed that suppliers raise the price of spare parts to a very high value over years.

AM makes it possible to produce replacement parts on site in near real time. Manufacturers can deliver systems faster, sometimes with improved design. Fleets of ships, aircraft and vehicles can extend their range and payload capabilities with these improvements too. Submarines and spaceships can produce spare parts on demand so that the requirement of stocking up on spare parts reduces.

AM also represents a security threat in many ways, which requires completely new thinking both in terms of policies and monitoring. Some of the security implications are not difficult to imagine. As it becomes easier and cheaper to print weapons, the threat of violent attacks can grow significantly. The assassin of Shinzo Abe is reported to have used a gun that he may have printed with AM technology.[29] Through the internet, terrorists and extremists can readily procure printable designs of dangerous weapons. It will also make it easier for them to print weapons quickly in locations where it would be difficult to track them, such as schools.

Combinations of AM and cyber create other security threats that are more diffuse and could be more difficult to monitor or effectively counter. Cyberattacks were by themselves mostly limited to accessing sensitive information or disabling computer systems. With AM, hackers may not stop at just stealing personal or financial information, but go on to gain access to designs for sensitive technologies, allowing them to commit cyber sabotage. They can introduce design flaws into critical parts (such as in an autonomous vehicle or in an airplane's fuselage) by infiltrating a printer or corrupting digital designs. These attacks will begin to have real-world consequences beyond the digital space.

In addition, AM has the potential to disrupt economies and the prevailing world economic order just like what happened in the

Industrial Revolution. It could upend traditional economies of scale while making highly customizable and complex products widely available to consumers. It also might allow non-state actors to develop items that previously required expertise and industrial capabilities exclusive to more advanced states. While it is still not clear how many and which types of products will be additively manufactured in the future, the proliferation of AM machines, ready access to raw materials and the free flow of digital plans—coupled with automation and AI—could profoundly alter the global economy, international security and the organization of society.[30]

By decentralizing manufacturing, individuals and firms might choose to produce locally, completely upsetting the current manufacturing systems that connect disparate parts of the globe through complex, multicountry supply chains. It could displace traditional manufacturing and cheap labour-based economies. It could result in an increasing importance of digital technologies, service-based industries and intellectual property (IP) resources. Many experts believe that these forces will cause profound disruptions to the current economic order and may result in an increased security threat.

Novel Materials

In concluding this section, we will take a look at some new materials and processes that can go into the construction of various weapons platforms. The two broad categories are: nanomaterials and 'bespoke' materials. The so-called bespoke materials, exquisitely designed to have very specific chemical and atomic structures and compositions, are probably not on the horizon as major components of key military systems in a big way before 2030. So, we will briefly cover nanomaterials, nanotechnology and 2D materials in this section.

Nanomaterials

Nanomaterials are those with dimensions in the order of one-billionth of a metre. They are already in use in some applications and they are further growing. They are likely to have a major impact in improving the power of explosives, the strength of materials and the storage capacity of batteries. Nanorobotics techniques may be useful in manufacturing compounds at the molecular level. Large-scale manufacturing issues and cost may constrain their applications. However, they are expected to improve the performance of explosives, body armour and high-performance batteries. Lithium-ion batteries and other forms of energy storage are likely to make rapid strides as a result of the availability of such materials.

Nanotechnology

Nanotechnology is a branch of nanoscience in which molecular systems are designed, produced and created in the nanoscale (1–100 nm). It unites a variety of scientific fields, including physics, material science, chemistry, biology and engineering. Advancements in this area have led to the categorized development of nanoweapons with classifications varying from small robotic machines to soldier battle suits, hyper-reactive explosives, communication devices, mini-nukes and electromagnetic supermaterials that can have a major impact on warfare and defence. USA and China are both leading in this segment.

2D Materials

2D materials (for example, graphene) and heterostructured 2D materials can be used to develop energy storage devices, sensors, electronic devices, weapon systems, etc., that have great potential for military applications. To obtain correct data required for planning, optimization and decision-making, advanced 2D material–based sensors and detectors provide a high awareness and significant opportunities. These play a very important role in the command-and-control processes in military operations. 2D materials such as graphene, hexagonal boron nitride (hBN) and their combination to obtain heterostructures can be used to develop high-capacity sensors and detectors or energy-storage devices.[31]

For devices that are used in weapon systems, chemical–biological warfare sensors and detection systems, 2D materials have been used to develop phototransistors, flexible thin-film transistors, IR detectors, electrodes for batteries, organic photovoltaic cells and organic light-emitting diodes. These materials will play a very important role in the future of advanced sensors, weapon systems and energy-storage devices for military applications.

Concluding Remarks and Lessons for India

As mentioned in the introductory section, we are on the cusp of the seventh revolution that will be characterized by autonomy and speed. In this phase, borders and distances are not going to be important in defence, as has been the case so far. Threats can come from anywhere, and not only neighbours. Cyberspace threats had already broken this barrier. The COVID-19 pandemic has exposed us to the dangers of biological weapons, which can impact us in ways we could not imagine earlier. Hypersonic vehicles can bring any target on Earth within one hour of strike capability. Precision strike capabilities can target individuals in any part of the world without significant collateral damage—for instance, the killing of Qasem Soleimani, an Iranian major general on 3 January 2020, via a drone strike.

These developments have huge implications for India's security challenge in the next decade or so. There needs to be a fundamental change in defence strategy. We need to quickly bridge the gap in the way we treat military technologies vs civilian technologies. In India, military technological developments have been mostly carried out under government-funded and controlled organizations, while civilian technologies have been developed or acquired by the industry. The contribution of the academic community in all of this has been minimal. Most of the projects have missed their deadlines by more than one or two decades and with major cost overruns.

Notes

1. Pater H. Diamandis, 'The Six D's', https://www.diamandis.com/blog/the-6ds, accessed on 15 June 2022.
2. 'Military and Security Developments Involving the People's Republic of China 2020', Annual Report to Congress, Office of the Secretary of Defense, USA, 2020, p. 18.
3. F.G. Hoffman, 'Will War's Nature Change in the Seventh Military Revolution?', *Parameters*, vol. 47, no. 4, 2017.
4. David Schatsky, Craig Muraskin and Ragu Gurumurthy, 'Demystifying Artificial Intelligence: What Business Leaders Need to Know about Cognitive Technologies,' Deloitte Insights, 4 November 2014.
5. 'Color-Changing Fabric Warns Military about Chemical Agents', University of Cincinnati, https://www.eurekalert.org/news-releases/708741, accessed 15 September 2021.
6. Gordon Moore, https://www.intel.com/content/www/us/en/history/museum-gordon-moore-law.html, accessed 15 June 2022.
7. William Gasarch Nathan Hayes, Emily Kaplitz, William Regli, 'Alternative Paradigms of Computation', 2021, CoRR abs/2111.08916
8. Scott Buchholz, Joe Mariani and Adam Routh, 'The Realist's Guide to Quantum Technology and National Security', The Deloitte Center for Government Insights, 2020.
9. Michael Irving, 'Triple Entanglement in Silicon Marks Major Quantum Computer Breakthrough', New Atlas, 12 September 2021, https://newatlas.com/physics/quantum-computer-triple-entanglement-silicon/, accessed 15 September 2021.
10. Peter H. Diamandis, 'Google Gets Us Closer to Error-Corrected Quantum Computing', https://www.diamandis.com/blog/google-gets-us-closer-to-error-corrected-quantum-computing, accessed 15 September 2021.
11. 'Autonomy', Report of the Defense Science Board Summer Study, USA, 2016, p. 5.

12. M. Bistron and Z. Piotrowski, 'Artificial Intelligence Applications in Military Systems and Their Influence on Sense of Security of Citizens', *Electronics*, vol. 10, no. 7, 2021, p. 871, https://doi.org/10.3390/electronics10070871
13. Michael E. O'Hanlon, 'Forecasting Change in Military Technology, 2020–2040', Brookings Institution, 2018.
14. '10 Counter-Drone Technologies to Detect and Stop Drones Today', Robin Radar Systems, https://www.robinradar.com/press/blog/9-counter-drone-technologies-to-detect-and-stop-drones-today, accessed 15 September 2021.
15. 'Detection of Small Drones with Millimeter Wave Radar', Fraunhofer Institute for High Frequency Physics and Radar Techniques FHR, https://www.fhr.fraunhofer.de/en/businessunits/security/Detection-of-small-drones-with-millimeter-wave-radar.html, accessed 15 September 2021.
16. Brad Lendon, 'What to Know about Hypersonic Missiles Fired by Russia at Ukraine', CNN, https:// edition.cnn.com/2022/03/22/europe/biden-russia-hypersonic-missiles-explainer-intl-hnk/index.html, accessed 15 June 2022.
17. 'Tactical Ultrashort Pulsed Laser for Army Platforms', SBIR STTR, https://www.sbir.gov/node/1654485, accessed 15 September 2021.
18. S.E. Duncan, Reinhard, R., Williams, R.C., Ramsey, F., 'Cyberbiosecurity: A New Perspective on Protecting U.S. Food and Agricultural System', *Frontiers in Bioengineering and Biotechnology*, vol. 7, 2019, https://doi.org/10.3389/fbioe.2019.00063
19. R.S. Murch, So, W.K., Raman, S., 'Cyberbiosecurity: An Emerging New Discipline to Help Safeguard the Bioeconomy', *Frontiers in Bioengineering and Biotechnology*, vol. 6, 2018, https://doi.org/10.3389/FBIOE.2018.00039
20. M.A. Cunningham and J.P. Geis II, 'A National Strategy for Synthetic Biology', *Strategic Studies Quarterly*, vol. 14, no. 3, 2020, https://www.jstor.org/stable/10.2307/26937411, accessed 15 September 2021.
21. Annie Sneed, 'Mail-Order CRISPR Kits Allow Absolutely Anyone to Hack DNA', *Scientific American*, 2 November 2017, https://www.scientificamerican.com/article/mail-order-crispr-kits-allow-absolutely-anyone-to-hack-dna/, accessed 15 September 2021.

22. M. Elgabry, D. Nesbeth and S.D. Johnson, 'A Systematic Review of the Criminogenic Potential of Synthetic Biology and Routes to Future Crime Prevention', *Frontiers in Bioengineering and Biotechnology*, vol. 8, 2020, https://www.frontiersin.org/articles/10.3389/fbioe.2020.571672/full, accessed 15 September 2021.
23. 'Medical Sciences and Healthcare Roadmap, Technology Vision 2035', published by Technology Information, Forecasting and Assessment Council (TIFAC), Government of India, 2016.
24. John Keller, 'Army Experts Reach Out to Industry for Exoskeleton Technologies to Boost Endurance and Help Lift Heavy Loads', Military+Aerospace Electronics, 10 February 2021, https://www.militaryaerospace.com/unmanned/article/14197174/exoskeleton-endurance-heavy-loads, accessed 15 September 2021.
25. Arfa Javaid, 'Exoskeleton Suit for Indian Army by DRDO: Here's All You Need to Know', Jagran Josh, 8 June 2021, https://www.jagranjosh.com/general-knowledge/exoskeleton-suit-for-indian-army-by-drdo-1623137006-1, accessed on 15 September 2021.
26. Meagan Cantwell, 'Watch This Chameleon Robot Blend In with Its Surroundings', Science, 10 August 2021, https://www.sciencemag.org/news/2021/08/watch-chameleon-robot-blend-its-surroundings, accessed on 15 September 2021.
27. Shubham Sharma, 'Russia's Color-Changing "Stealth Camouflage" Could Hide Military Troops, Vehicles In Plain Sight', *International Business Times*, 22 August 2018, https://www.ibtimes.com/russias-color-changing-stealth-camouflage-could-hide-military-troops-vehicles-plain-2710603, accessed 15 September 2021.
28. 'National Policy on Electronics (NPE 2019)', Ministry of Electronics and Information Technology, Government of India, 2019.
29. 'Did Japan Ex PM Shooter Use 3D Printed Gun?', NDTV, 8 July 2022, https://www.ndtv.com/world-news/japan-ex-pm-shinzo-abes-shooter-used-home-made-gun-reports-say-it-was-3-d-printed-3140082, accessed 10 July 2022.
30. T.A. Campbell and O.S. Ivanova, '3D Printing of Multifunctional Nanocomposites', *Nano Today*, vol. 8, no. 2, 2013, pp. 119–20.
31. Özkan, D., Özekinci, M., Öztürk, Z., & Sulukan, E., 'Two Dimensional Materials for Military Applications', *Defence Science Journal*, vol. 70, no. 6, 12 October 2020, pp. 672–681.

CHAPTER

9

China–India Riparian Relations: Upstream–Downstream Dynamics

UTTAM KUMAR SINHA

It is now a common national security refrain that a stable supply of fresh water is paramount to a country's political, economic and social stability. Rivers—the great carriers of fresh water, and often described as the 'unsurpassed carvers' of Earth—are complex natural realities. At one level, particularly when they criss-cross political boundaries that are intensely competitive, they lead to contestations and unwanted outcomes and, at another, they create cooperative pathways of water sharing and benefits with a possibility of larger political goodwill. Without emphasizing on 'water wars' or overstressing the norms and principles of 'equitable utilization', the 'no-harm rule' and 'restricted sovereignty', there are several riparian hotspots like the Nile, Jordan, Euphrates–Tigris and the Indus basins that can set up an inherently combative relationship. The Yarlung Tsangbo/Brahmaputra basin, shared between India and China, can potentially fall in this category.

From time to time, water emerges as a contentious issue between the two countries. As riparian neighbours, the two are part hydrological owners and part technical users of the Yarlung Tsangbo/Brahmaputra basin. No international river basin can match such a powerful interface of two dominant global actors who compete, contest and, at times, cooperate. While China is in a unique position, given its upstream geographical location, to unilaterally secure its water supplies, India, as the downstream partner, is strategically hindered, if not completely impeded by Chinese upstream water development projects. Moreover, as the Brahmaputra meanders into Bangladesh and becomes the Jamuna before draining into the Bay of Bengal, India carries an added responsibility of ensuring Bangladesh is not disadvantaged.

The middle riparian position in which India finds itself on the Brahmaputra presents a unique challenge to its regional diplomacy. Further, the Yarlung Tsangbo/Brahmaputra, despite its massive basin expanse and as the fifth-largest river in terms of volume, remains ungoverned, with no permanent agreement or treaty. There, however, exists a non-permanent mechanism for hydrological data sharing that is contractual, limited in scope and non-binding.

To recall, in 2002, India had entered into a memorandum of understanding (MoU), for a period of five years, with China on the provision of hydrological information on the Brahmaputra during flood season. The information related to the water level, discharge and rainfall at three specified stations—Nugesha, Yangcun and Nuxia—from 1 June to 15 October every year, is utilized in the formulation of flood forecasts by the Central Water Commission. This arrangement ended in 2007. A new MoU with the same provisions and with a validity of another five years was signed in 2008. Meanwhile, in April 2005, another memorandum was signed for the supply of hydrological information with respect to the Sutlej (Langquin Zangbu) in flood season for a period of five years and was subsequently renewed in 2010 and again in 2016.[1] Clearly, and as can be observed, China does not want a permanent mechanism on water sharing with India. By reviewing and renewing the MoUs on the Brahmaputra and the Sutlej, Beijing dictates the proceedings as an upper riparian.

Further, in November 2006, during the visit of President Hu Jintao to India, it was agreed to set up an expert-level mechanism (ELM) to discuss wider cooperation beyond flood season hydrological data to emergency management. Subsequently, a joint ELM was constituted at the joint-secretary level.[2] The ELM meets once a year, alternately in Beijing and New Delhi, and essentially focuses on the exchange of hydrological information and for the smooth transmission of flood season hydrological data. Though, again limited in scope, it can form the base on which future water cooperation can be developed. This remains a long shot given the current political climate, however.

One can also recall that during the visit of Chinese Premier Li Keqiang to India in May 2013, serious time was spent discussing water issues. India's proposal of a joint mechanism for better transparency on the dams being constructed on the Yarlung Tsangbo failed to elicit a clear commitment from China, but it extended the MoU for another five years stating, 'China will provide to India twice a day [earlier it was not specified] the hydrological data of the Brahmaputra River in the flood season between June and October.'[3] The scope of cooperation was expanded by signing a new MoU in 'ensuring water-efficient irrigation'.[4]

Later, in October 2013, when Indian Prime Minister Manmohan Singh visited Beijing, an MoU on 'Strengthening Cooperation on Trans-Border Rivers' was signed. It laid out the specificity of hydrological sharing. 'Hydrological information of above-mentioned stations [Nugesha, Yangcun and Nuxia] will be provided to India within 30 minutes after 08.00 hrs and 20.00 hrs in Beijing Time

(05.30 hrs to 17.30 hrs in Indian Standard Time) from 15 May to 15 October each year [earlier it was from 1 June to 15 October]. The Chinese side also agrees to provide hydrological information if water levels of above-mentioned stations are close to or reach warning water levels in non-flood season.'[5]

Interestingly, the Chinese gave a breakdown of the costs for the hydrological information for the flood season that India received. 'The Indian side will transfer payments to the Chinese side amounting to RMB 850,000 by US dollar (convert RMB Yuan into US dollar according to exchange rate of pay-day) at the end of every April within the period of validity of the present Implementation Plan.'[6]

These mechanisms apart, any hydro-relations with China cannot ignore the border stand-offs. Beijing is notoriously known to mix 'compliance' with 'intimidation'—what Antonio Gramsci termed 'a mix of force and consent'.[7] Amid the Doklam stand-off in 2017, China had withheld data on the Brahmaputra and Sutlej. The spokesperson of the Ministry of External Affairs had observed then: 'At periodic levels, China is expected to share [the hydrological] data with us. As per my knowledge, this year there has been no data shared by China.'[8] The spokesperson, however, did qualify this by saying that it would be 'premature' to link Doklam with the failure of China to share the hydrological information.

That said, military face-offs and political tensions with India can allow China to turn a blind eye to the existing water mechanisms or even disband them altogether. The riparian relations between the two countries will increasingly be influenced by the prevailing political dynamics and strategic considerations or what analysts describe as a 'hydro-political security complex'. In this complex, factors like availability, distribution, quality and competing uses will not only contribute to regional water insecurity but also influence peace and stability in Asia.[9] It is also becoming clear that water cannot be understood in isolation from a variety of broader contextual issues—particularly food and energy security, as also wealth generation. The internal water challenges that both India and China face will also greatly impact the transboundary water relations.

Yarlung Tsangbo/Brahmaputra Profile

Blessed with enormous glaciers and alpine lakes, the Qinghai-Tibetan Plateau, the 'rooftop of the world', is the location of the Yarlung Tsangbo/Brahmaputra river basin. The meandering river, traversing a large geomorphological territory links China (Yarlung Tsangbo), India (Brahmaputra and Siang), Bhutan (through tributaries) and Bangladesh (Jamuna), eventually drains into the Bay of Bengal. The river carries around 138 million litres, or 364 million gallons, of water during flood season, which is more than one-and-a-half times that of the Amazon river.[10] With varied territories, differing perspectives and an estimated 625 million people living in its basin, the Yarlung Tsangbo/Brahmaputra acquires a set of challenging approaches and multiple pressures to manage it. Climate change evidence suggests that in the next thirty years, the river's ability to support the basin-dependent population will drop by 30–40 million people, even as the population of the area is expected to nearly double.[11] And, as earlier mentioned, the absence of a bilateral or multilateral water management accord raises serious concerns for regional stability and only serves to increase the potential for tension over water resources.[12]

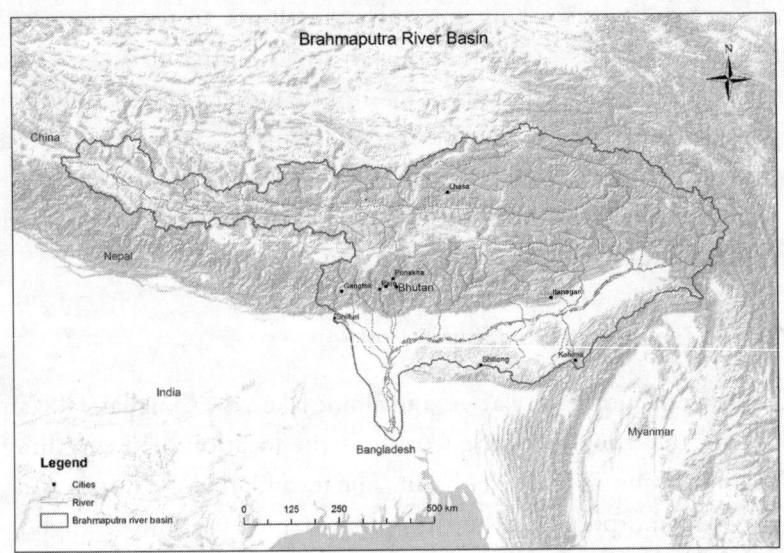

Source: International Centre for Integrated Mountain Development, Kathmandu

Facts indicate that China's hydrological position is one of upper-riparian supremacy. According to the Ministry of Water Resources, China shares more than fifty major international watercourses with its downstream riparian neighbours, which include thirteen directly bordering countries and three closely neighboured countries.[13] It is interesting to note that approximately less than 1 per cent of water comes from outside China's territory, while the volume of surface water flowing out of China is about 730 bcm (billion cubic meters) annually.[14] India alone receives nearly half of all river waters that leave China, or 48.33 per cent. This translates to about 354 bcm of water flows into India from Tibet, of which the annual average flow in the Brahmaputra is 78.10 bcm.

Often less emphasized is the fact that India is a multi-river-dependent country with the Brahmaputra on the east, and the Indus and the Sutlej on the west—and thus, the country's riparian relations with China are exceptional and critical. The Ganga, which originates in India, has nine tributaries joining it from Nepal, three of which—Karnali, Gandaki and Kosi—arise in Tibet. India's lower-riparian position increases its dependency on the headwaters of the rivers such as the Indus, Sutlej and Brahmaputra, which originate in the Tibetan plateau.

While China has no water sharing treaties/agreements on its transboundary rivers, India, on the other hand, has entered into water-sharing treaties with its own lower-riparian countries—Pakistan (Indus Waters Treaty of 1960) and Bangladesh (Ganga Treaty of 1996). China's per capita water resources in 2013 were just over 2,000 cubic metres with an overall water availability at nearly 2.8 trillion cubic metres.[15] The average annual per capita availability of water in India as per the 2011 census was 1,545 cubic metres, with utilizable water resources of only 1,123 bcm.[16] While both China and India are currently in high water stress category, it is projected that by 2040 both will be in the top fifty water-scarce countries.[17]

Currently, both countries face wide-ranging challenges, including deteriorating water quality, uneven distribution of water resources in space and time, and inefficient utilization. The critical difference between the two is that China is far more water secure, while India receives a large portion of its water from outside its territory and is, hence, water dependent. The hydrological equation gives China a huge strategic advantage that can be translated into political leverage and bargaining with India.

China's Legacy of Hydrocontrol

Rivers are not only territorial, but symbolize political supremacy. The history of the Chinese civilization is, in many ways, a history of hydrological engineering, canal-building and water conservation. Mao Zedong, one of the most enigmatic personalities of the twentieth century, established the People's Republic of China in 1949 and transformed it into a modern, industrialized, socialist state. In 1950, Mao issued a directive that 'the Huai River must be harnessed'. That entailed constructing a new route for the river to the sea in order to mitigate flooding. It was an audacious plan, but for Mao it was a 'triumph of political mobilisation over seemingly overwhelming obstacles',[18] or, as he would often state, 'nature is an enemy that had to be beaten' and that 'man must conquer nature'. Systematically, since 1950, Mao's leadership created a hydrological society, with control of water supply for irrigation as the basis of the Chinese mode of production and of a powerful, exploitative bureaucracy.[19]

Some historical narratives suggest that Mao had first come to Tibet in the 1930s as part of the Long March of the communist revolutionaries, who were on the run from the advancing Kuomintang troops. And as the narrative goes, Mao and his companions returned to China wearing 'Tibetan clothing and disguised as Khampa traders'.[20] In 1949, after a string of military victories against Chiang Kai-shek's nationalist party, Mao proclaimed the establishment of the People's Republic of China. In 1950, the communist regime 'invaded' Tibet with its natural resources and strategically important border with India. The Chinese communists, projecting themselves as modernizers, sold to the pre-industrialized Tibetan society scientific and technological progress, while intimidating them with military might. Of course, the official Chinese historiography describes the resolution of the 'Tibetan question' as a 'peaceful liberation'.

Having established authority over Tibet, what Mao referred to as a 'British colony', he soon started admiring his new territorial acquisition and gloated over the mighty rivers flowing from the landscape. In 1952, Mao made a seemingly innocent but purposeful remark: '… the south has a lot of water, the north little … If possible, it is okay to lend a little water'.[21] Since then, the Chinese establishment has unveiled major water development projects to establish control and authority over the Tibetan watersheds. It spawned a whole breed of Chinese leadership who think hydrologically and understand the strategic value of the rivers flowing from Tibet.

In contrast, India never weighed the significance of Tibet's water and when, in 1954, the then prime minister, Jawaharlal Nehru, signed the Panchsheel (Five Principles) Treaty forfeiting all the British-inherited extraterritorial rights and privileges, Chinese control of Tibet became unhindered.[22] Nehru failed to understand the outcome of his actions and his famous statement in Calcutta after his return from Beijing in October 1954 that 'the people of China do not want war' was proven gravely wrong. Mao created a cult of personality to legitimize his rule and quickly realized that without the control of the Tibet massif, China's unity and power would be overturned—and had it not been for Tibet, China would not have been the world's most independent riparian country. In fact, Beijing's total control over Tibet in effect is its 'total' control over the water resources.

Tibet: A Water Tower

The Tibet landscape, which forms part of the Hindu Kush Himalaya (HKH) region, is a storehouse of fresh water and contains the headwaters for many of Asia's mighty rivers including the Huang He and Yangtze (in mainland China), and the Mekong, Brahmaputra, Salween, Indus and Sutlej (transboundary) rivers. Tibet's water resources, as explained earlier, have become a crucial strategic, political and cultural element for Chinese authorities. Marking seventy years of Tibet, China brought out a white paper in May 2021, titled 'Tibet Since 1951: Liberation, Development and Prosperity'. While claiming to be a 'balanced account of the enormous transformation that has taken place in Tibet',[23] in reality, it is a statement and a counter to 'Tibet independence as a product of imperialist aggression against China in modern times.'[24]

Interestingly, the paper describes the Qinghai-Tibet Plateau as the 'water tower of Asia', probably recalling Mao enviously eyeing Tibet's water-richness, and states: 'A holistic approach to conserving mountains, rivers, forests, farmlands, lakes, and grasslands has been adopted. The Plan for Protecting and Improving the Ecological Safety Barriers in Tibet (2008–2030) and the afforestation project in the watersheds of the Yarlung Zangbo River, Nujiang River, Lhasa River, Nianchu River, Yalong River, and Shiquan River have been implemented.'[25] There is no mention of the huge dams that China intends to build on the Yarlung and other transboundary rivers in Tibet; rather, the whole document is promoted as a 'green development model' that '… from 2015 to the end of 2020, 6.5 billion kwh of clean-energy-generated electricity was transmitted, which greatly reduced carbon dioxide emissions.'[26]

The rivers in the Hindu Kush Himalayan (HKH)–Tibetan region are among the most meltwater dependent in the world. But there are large variations in terms of glacial and snow melt contribution to the rivers. While the upper Indus basin has about 41 per cent glacial melt and 22 per cent snow melt, the upper Yarlung Tsangbo/Brahmaputra runoff is dominated by 59 per cent rainfall while meltwater contributes only 25 per cent.[27] On the western front, the Indus flow change will be far more vulnerable to climate change and receding glaciers, whereas because of predominant precipitation contribution, the Yarlung Tsangbo/Brahmaputra and Mekong would be relatively less vulnerable to glacial melt. It is not surprising that the Chinese will pitch for greater dam constructions on these rivers and maximize electricity generation.

With extensive river development projects being planned in Tibet by China, the scale of environmental destruction has been unprecedented in the last six decades. Evidence suggests that lithium and copper mining activities by Chinese state-owned companies in Tibet have led to a high level of pollution in the rivers.[28] Likewise, excessive logging and dam-building activities along the rivers have resulted in the destruction of forests, leading to frequent landslides and mudslides in the region, which can have a serious impact on a downstream country like India. Caught up in making Tibet the world's largest hydropower generator, the Chinese leadership is brazenly ignoring their own law on National Regional Autonomy that 'gives priority to the rational exploitation and utilisation of the natural resources that the local authorities are entitled to develop'.[29]

China's Dams and Diversions

In the search for renewable electricity power, China has been constructing dams in a way that has been unprecedented in human history. As Chinese engineers build reservoir upon reservoir that turn the turbines and accelerate the promotion of a low-carbon economy, the negative downstream effects are ignored. Since the 1950s, China has built over 22,000 dams of more than 15 metres height. China's promotion of large-scale water projects with classic slogans like 'big diversions, big irrigation' continues. Unrelenting in its efforts to harness rivers and become carbon-neutral by 2060, China, in March 2021, announced its plan to build the world's largest hydroelectricity dam on the Yarlung Tsangbo. The project conceives of eleven hydropower stations generating a capacity of 60 gigawatts of power—three times more than the Three Gorges.

It is interesting to observe President Xi Jinping's speech in the Boao Forum in April 2013. He asserted that '… while pursuing its own interests, a country should accommodate the legitimate concerns of others … [w]e need to work vigorously to create more cooperation opportunities, upgrade cooperation, and deliver more development dividends to our people and contribute more to global growth'.[30] It was a well-calibrated political messaging, emphasizing on China as a benign power and respecting peaceful co-existence. In reality, however, its emphasis on sovereignty and territorial integrity is far more pronounced than on mutual benefit in managing its transboundary waters. It is a conundrum that will define how China balances its domestic water needs with its 'good neighbour' policy.

As Xi made his softening-of-China speech, a few months earlier, the energy sector blueprint (2011–2015) was released in January 2013. Far from restraining itself, Beijing outlined the need to construct more hydroelectricity dams on the Nu (Salween), Lancang (Mekong) and Yarlung river basins.[31] Many of these projects are in ecologically and seismically sensitive areas. The blueprint was a reassertion of an aggressive 'supply-side hydraulic' approach of increasing storage capacity, making water transfers, and prospecting and extracting groundwater. This approach was the result of a combination of factors that includes food and energy needs, plans to meet the low-carbon-intensity goals of the 12th Five-Year Plan (2011–2015), and the intensive lobbying of the dam builders and electricity companies.

In March 2021, China adopted the 14th Five-Year Plan (2021–2025). According to the plan, China's energy consumption per unit of GDP and carbon dioxide emissions per unit of GDP will be reduced by 13.5 per cent and 18 per cent respectively, between 2021 and 2025. It also aims to increase the share of non-fossil energy in total energy consumption to around 20 per cent. To achieve its 'climate pledge for 2030' and 'carbon neutrality for 2060', emphasis on hydropower projects will continue. The 14th Plan explicitly mentions, '… hydropower development on the lower reaches of the Yarlung Tsangpo river',[32] but also states the aim is 'systematic governance of mountains, rivers, forests, farmland, lakes and grasslands, and [to] build a natural protected areas system …' and 'strengthen ecological protection management for large rivers and important lakes and wetlands …'[33]

The Yarlung is the only transboundary river mentioned in the plan and, in the same paragraph, it observes that there are 'major water diversion and transfer efforts' for promoting 'construction of major projects that have strong foundations.'[34] Water in China is unequally distributed, leading the planners to push ahead with invasive water-diversion plans going back to the idea of shou-tian, or 'reverse flow', of the Tibetan rivers that was espoused in 1988. Chinese engineers, who are a leading voice in decision-making, firmly believe that the diversion of rivers into the water-scarce northern and western regions is crucial for growth and stability.

An example of China's capital-intensive water projects is the South-to-North Water Transfer Project from Tibet, which got under way in 2002, and is expected to take more than fifty years to complete—making it the world's largest transfer scheme ever. The project involves drawing 44.8 bcm of water from the southern rivers in Tibet and linking it to mainland China's four main rivers—Yangtze, Huang He, Huaihe and Haihe—through three diversion routes: the eastern, central and western.[35] The eastern and central routes are now functioning and the rivers that have been linked are within the territory of China, but the western route, which factors diverting the transboundary rivers including the Yarlung Tsangbo/Brahmaputra at the 'Great Bend' is controversial and of direct concern to India.

There are questions related to the technical, economic and seismic feasibility of the project, but it has not been shelved either. In fact, in May 2021, President Xi convened a symposium on the follow-up development of the South–North Water Transfer Project in Nanyang and articulated that 'strong support of water resources is needed in the country's efforts to shape a nationwide unified market, boost smooth domestic circulation, and promote the coordinated development of the southern and northern regions'.[36] He underlined that 'the South-to-North Water Diversion Project is a backbone project for the allocation of the resources across different river basins and regions'.[37]

Given China's uneven water distribution, its energy needs and its food requirements, it is difficult for the country's planners not to consider water diversion as an option. Upstream diversion of water is hugely scary for downstream riparian states and is regarded as a malignant act. Along with a series of dam constructions, the possible diversion of the Yarlung would be a double whammy for India. However, in the more immediate term, concerns over the dams and storage projects that China is pushing forward vigorously are greater.

About a decade ago, as part of China's 12th Five-Year Plan, a cascade of dams was proposed on the upper and middle reaches of the Yarlung, including a 640 MW dam in Dagu, a 510 MW dam in Zangmu, a 320 MW dam at Jiacha, and a dam at Jiexu. Only the Zangmu has since been operationalized, while the other three are in various stages of development.

With the 14th Five-Year Plan, which gives greater emphasis to water development projects on the Yarlung, reports suggest that the state-owned hydropower company, PowerChina, has signed a strategic cooperation agreement with the government of Tibet Autonomous Region to implement hydropower exploitation in the downstream of the Yarlung Tsangbo river.[38] It will be for the first time that the downstream section of the Yarlung in Tibet will be tapped, with Chinese engineers claiming it to be a 'historic opportunity'. On the other hand, the leadership in Beijing is quite gung-ho over the prospects of dam building, and projecting it to enhance China's efforts in dealing with climate change and reducing its reliance on coal.

For the Chinese, who are used to water projects on a gigantic scale, the capacity of the planned dams on the Yarlung is relatively 'small'. From an Indian perspective, however, these projects are sufficiently large to be storage dams, especially if the purpose is for flood control, as is the Yarlung.[39] Run-of-river (ROR) projects, as the Chinese planners officially describe them, can be misleading. The basic principle of the ROR dams is to return the waters to the river after it passes through the turbines. But what if they are not returned? There is no mechanism to verify that they will be.

Given the political equation between the two countries, China could well maximize its upper riparian position. It suits Beijing to be ambiguous and not show enthusiasm towards formal arrangements on sharing design-related information. Chinese hydrologists explain that 'the Brahmaputra has plenty of water; it won't make any difference to India'.[40] Even the Indian Water Resource Ministry has stated, to allay unnecessary fears, that the Yarlung enters India (as the Siang in Arunachal) with 78 bcm of water and is then 629 bcm when it enters Bangladesh.[41]

On the question of the Yarlung diversion, the Central Water Commission has suggested 'a 50 per cent reduction of the 31.25 bcm currently available in the non-monsoon season and a reduction of 50 per cent in power generation in the Upper Siang project'.[42] The figures suggest that India's concerns are both about non-monsoonal, or dry season, flow as opposed to flood water release in the monsoon. The solutions for Indian planners are essentially two-fold: build storage dams at various locations and effectively put in place flood mitigation programmes.

India Needs to be Proactive not Reactive

The geographical reality of China cannot be changed, but India's lower riparian position does not necessarily mean an acute disadvantage. For China, water is immensely strategic. Its internal stability depends a lot on a steady water supply and it is unlikely that Beijing will compromise on this aspect. Given this reality, India has to view its downstream status rationally. Hydrological facts and objective data-based analysis will be important in its calculation, and not a generalized fear hypothesis. Informed science is a good starting point for India to build its capability and capacity on the Brahmaputra, and in the process, it can de-emphasize China as a hydro-hegemon. The reasons are explained below.

The Yarlung Tsangbo/Brahmaputra originates from the Angsi glacier in the Burang county of Tibet. The total length of the river, from the source to the mouth, is 2,880 km, of which 1,625 km flows through Tibet, 918 km traverses India and the rest, 337 km, is in Bangladesh. On the face of it, since 56 per cent of the river flows in the Chinese territory it can be easily mistaken that China controls the larger share of the water. However, and this is an important fact, the volumetric flow of the Yarlung Tsangbo/Brahmaputra is not proportional to its length inside a country. The Yarlung is a trans-Himalayan river where the annual precipitation averages about 300 mm. Once it crosses the Himalayan crest line, the annual precipitation reaches about 2,000 mm.[43] Translated, this means that the Yarlung, when it reaches India's territory and becomes the Brahmaputra, swells and becomes mightier because of the heavy monsoon rain, spring water and also the contribution of the fast-flowing tributaries—the Lohit, Dibang and Siang/Dihang. Peer-reviewed data clearly suggest that during both the lean and the peak flow, the total annual outflow of the Yarlung from China is significantly less than the Brahmaputra. This means that India has ample water on its side to develop and harness.

The country needs to have more water development footprints in Arunachal Pradesh to enhance economic growth in the region, particularly by building more water storage dams to mitigate dry season flow and thereby exert down-riparian prior appropriation rights. It must not be forgotten that China's claim to the Arunachal territory is also a claim to the vast amount of water flowing in the area. Greater economic integration in the border region is an effective way to neutralize Beijing's claim. Of course, the hydro projects in Arunachal, apart from being scientifically sound and technologically robust, need to be framed in a cooperative and consultative manner with wider stakeholder and inter-provincial participation in the northeast of India, particularly with Assam, which is downstream to Arunachal. It will be counterproductive for India to create upstream and downstream acrimony within its own territory.

In probably the most authentic physical account of the Indian frontier, the *Imperial Gazetteer of India* (1909) described the Brahmaputra basin as the 'great highway' of the Himalayas. Inland navigation is an important entry point to bolster basin-level cooperation and to harness the potential of the Brahmaputra basin. This could possibly lead to major dividends, including economic growth, increasing employment and improving livelihoods. Other entry points are strengthening regional hydrological services for flood mitigation (including data sharing), and hydropower development and trade. The northeast part of India has approximately 1,800 km of potential waterways and navigation, which unfortunately has been much ignored. With the current government's investment on inland waterways, the Brahmaputra National Waterway 2 would act as a critical economic corridor with direct access to Chittagong Port in Bangladesh and the Haldia Port in West Bengal, and boost trade with Southeast Asian countries.

Bangladesh has over 24,000 km of rivers, rivulets and canals, of which one-fourth are navigable during the monsoon and one-sixth during the dry periods. The India–Bangladesh Protocol on Inland Water Transit and Trade (PIWTT) signed in 2015 allows for inland vessels of one country to transit through specified routes of the other with each of them providing facilities of 'port of call'. This remains a stable framework to expand transit trade through Bangladesh and realign its long-term strategy with India.

There are other ways to pursue positive interactions on the Brahmaputra, exclusive of China. An important element of India's hydro-diplomacy would be to initiate a lower-riparian partnership stretching from the Ganga–Meghna–Brahmaputra to the Thanlwin/Salween and Mekong basins. India's hydro-diplomacy has to ensure that the partnership is not seen as a counterforce or even as a pressure group to China, but rather, as a concerned alignment, seeking to open channels of communication and transparency with Beijing on upstream usage based on the principles of 'equity' and 'no-harm'.[44]

The subregional groupings, like the Bay of Bengal Initiative for Multi-Sectoral Technical and Economic Cooperation (BIMSTEC) and Bangladesh–Bhutan–India–Nepal (BBIN), can act as a catalyst. Whether it is tourism, culture, transport or communication, rivers can be a force multiplier. More than knee-jerk counter-responses, India needs to think of cohesive engagement. The Mekong Ganga Cooperation (MGC) and the government's recent initiatives to expand the areas of cooperation among the member countries that include Thailand, Myanmar, Cambodia, Laos and Vietnam are vital to the sustainability of India's Act East policy.

At the politico-diplomatic front, India needs to bring the transboundary rivers with China as a core issue in bilateral discussions. This space is important to provide the political push for the two countries to think of mitigating risks and sharing benefits on the Yarlung Tsangbo/Brahmaputra and Sutlej. India's downstream position increases its vulnerability to China, particularly in flood season. There are also huge concerns of natural disasters, like the glacial lake outburst flood that happened on the Pareechu river in 2005 that lead to enormous damage downstream in Himachal Pradesh.

China has always been reluctant to discuss water issues, but the onus is on India to frame the water agenda beyond the volumetric and bring in larger environmental conventions, like climate change, wetland protection and biodiversity, to the table. This will help in adding a fresh perspective to the existing MoUs that India has with China. Mechanisms for water cooperation have already been established and, for the time, being it is unrealistic to expect a treaty from Beijing.

It is also critical for India to articulate its middle-riparian position—first, to change the perception in the neighbourhood that India is a 'water hegemon', as is often expressed by Pakistan and Bangladesh, in spite of the robustness of the water treaties with these two countries, and second, to draw China into the South Asian water equation through a multilateral-basin approach, thereby sensitizing China to downstream concerns and upstream responsibilities. Hydro-diplomacy has to be well nuanced and not always framed in legalistic terms—but rather, with a view to managing China.

This has significant political value when dealing with China over Tibetan water resources. By raising the question, however contested it might be, that one country alone cannot be the stakeholder to the waters in Tibet, India creates the opportunity to articulate an ecological perspective and principles of resource conservation. By continuously emphasizing on water resources in Tibet as a humanitarian issue, India draws international concerns and could possibly prompt China into a water dialogue with the downstream countries on ways to preserve and share the benefits of the Tibetan waters.[45]

Conclusion

China's water needs and India's concerns will remain a recurring theme in the two countries' relations. Rivers are deeply subjective in terms of where, what and how they are used. With no legally binding treaty, apart from the norms and principles as expressed in the 1966 Helsinki Rules and the 1997 UN Convention on the

Law of the Non-Navigational Uses of International Watercourses, rivers between the two countries remain largely without formal arrangements of distribution, except for the sharing of hydrological information. It is essential for India, as a downstream riparian with China, to bring water issues into the core of bilateral discussions, which allows for lower riparian apprehensions and fears to be recognized and discussed.

India's strategic and policy initiatives on the Brahmaputra have to be carefully balanced between pursuing a 'water dialogue' with China and an emphasis on a 'basin approach' with Bangladesh and Bhutan. India must treat water as a strategic resource, and clearly outline the desired end goal and strategic outcomes. Equally important will be the need for India to carefully study the projections of future trends in water availability, flow patterns, and changes in climatic variables.

Notes

1. 'India-China Cooperation', Ministry of Jal Shakti, Government of India, http://jalshakti-dowr.gov.in/international-cooperation/bilateral-cooperation-with-neighbouring-countries/india-china-cooperation, accessed 6 June 2022.
2. Ibid.
3. Ibid
4. Ibid.
5. Information under RTI, 'Implementation Plan: Provision of Hydrological Information of the Yarlung Zangbu/Brahmaputra River in Flood Season by China to India', https://www.mea.gov.in/Images/pdf/JHarsha.pdf, accessed 6 June 2022.
6. Ibid.
7. Antonio Gramsci, *Selections from the Prison Notebooks of Antonio Gramsci*, Quintin Hoare and Geoffrey Nowell-Smith, eds and trans, New York: International Publishers, 1971, p. 170.
8. Maha Siddiqui, 'China Refuses to Share Hydrological Data as India Battles Floods', News18, 18 August 2017, https://www.news18.com/

news/india/china-refuses-to-share-hydrological-data-as-india-battles-floods-1495443.html
9. Mark Zeitoun and Jeroen Warner, 'Hydro-hegemony—a framework for analysis of trans-boundary water conflicts', *Water Policy*, vol. 8, 2008, pp. 435–460; Uttam Kumar Sinha, 'Examining China's Hydro-Behaviour: Peaceful or Assertive?', *Strategic Analysis*, vol. 36, no. 1, 2012, pp.41–56.
10. Cited in *Transboundary River Basins: Status and Trends*, vol. 3, Transboundary Waters Assessment Programme (TWAP), UNEP, 2016, www.geftwap.org/publications/river-basins-spm, accessed 7 June 2022.
11. Ibid.
12. Centre for Naval Analysis, 'Water Resource Competition in the Brahmaputra River Basin', www.cna.org/archive/CNA_Files/pdf/cna-brahmaputra-study-2016.pdf, accessed 7 June 2022.
13. 'International Cooperation on Transboundary Rivers between China and its Neighbouring Countries', Ministry of Water Resources, People's Republic of China, April 2015, p. 2, http://www.mwr.gov.cn/english/mainsubjects/201604/P020160406513798903048.pdf, accessed 6 June 2022. Also see, the National Bureau of Statistics of the People's Republic of China, http://www.stats.gov.cn/, accessed 6 June 2022.
14. 'International Cooperation on Transboundary Rivers between China and its Neighbouring Countries', Ministry of Water Resources, People's Republic of China, April 2015, p. 2, http://www.mwr.gov.cn/english/mainsubjects/201604/P020160406513798903048.pdf, accessed 7 June 2022.
15. Ibid.
16. 'Per Capita Availability of Water', Ministry of Water Resources, Government of India, http://pib.nic.in/newsite/PrintRelease.aspx?relid=119797, accessed 7 June 2022.
17. Sabita Kushal, 'What Does Being "Water Stressed" Mean for India and Her Neighbours?', India Water Portal, 10 September 2015, http://www.indiawaterportal.org/articles/what-does-being-water-stressed-mean-india-and-her-neighbours, accessed 7 June 2022.
18. Thayer Watkins, *The Control of the Huai River System in China*, cited in Uttam Kumar Sinha, 'India–China Relations: Of Reality and Rationality', *USI Journal*, vol. 148, no. 682, April–June 2018, p. 202.

19. Karl Wittfogel, *Oriental Despotism: A Comparative Study of Power*, New Haven: Yale University Press, 1957 (reprint 1981), p. 127.
20. Carole McGranahan, 'Mao in Tibet Disguise: History, Ethnography, and Excess', *Journal of Ethnographic Theory*, vol. 2, no. 1, 2012, p. 214.
21. Cited in James Nickum, 'The Status of the South to North Water Transfer Plans in China', United Nations Development Programme, http://hdr.undp:org/en/reports/global/hdr2006/papers/james_nickum_china_water_transfer.pdf, accessed 5 June, 2022.
22. Brahma Chellaney, *Water: Asia's New Battleground*, Washington, DC: Georgetown University Press, 2011, p.182.
23. 'Tibet Since 1951: Liberation, Development and Prosperity', State Council Information Office of the People's Republic of China, p. 3, http://english.www.gov.cn/archive/whitepaper/202105/21/content_WS60a724e7c6d0df57f98d9da2.html, accessed 5 June 2022.
24. Ibid., p. 6.
25. Ibid., p. 34.
26. Ibid., p. 35.
27. 'The Himalayan Climate and Water Atlas', ICIMOD, CICERO and GRID Publication, 2015, p. 21.
28. Zamlha Tempa Gyaltsen, 'China's Sixty Years of Environmental Destruction in Tibet', Central Tibetan Authority, 4 April 2019, https://tibet.net/chinas-60-years-of-environmental-destruction-in-tibet/ accessed 7 June 2022.
29. Article 28 of Regional National Autonomy by the People's Republic of China. The law was adopted at the second session of the Sixth National People's Congress in May 1984 and amended at the 20th Meeting of the Standing Committee of the Ninth National People's Congress in February 2001, https://www.ilo.org/dyn/natlex/docs/ELECTRONIC/35194/124676/F2146249224/CHN35194%20ChnEng.pdf, accessed 7 June 2022.
30. Full text of Xi Jinping's speech at opening ceremony of Boao Forum, Xinhua, 10 April 2013, http://www.china.org.cn/business/Boao_Forum_2013/2013-04/10/content_28501562.htm, accessed 7 June 2022.

31. Li Jing, 'Ban Lifted on Controversial Nu River Dam Projects', *South China Morning Post*, 25 January 2013, http://www.scmp.com/news/china/article/1135463/ban-lifted-controversial-nu-river-dam-projects, accessed 7 June 2022.
32. See text of the 14th Five-Year Plan of the People's Republic of China: Fostering High-Quality Development, p.12, www.adb.org/sites/default/files/publication/705886/14th-five-year-plan-high-quality-development-prc.pdf, accessed 21 June 2022.
33. Ibid., p. 21.
34. Ibid., pp. 21–22.
35. 'South-to-North Water Diversion Project', Water Technology, https://www.water-technology.net/projects/south_north/, accessed on 10 June 2022.
36. Xinhua, 'Xi Focus: Xi Convenes Symposium on Follow-Up Development of China's Mega Water Diversion Project', XinhuaNet, 14 May 2021, http://www.xinhuanet.com/english/2021-05/14/c_139946207.htm, accessed 10 June 2022.
37. Ibid.
38. Ananth Krishnan, 'China Hydropower Company Plans First Downstream Dam on Brahmaputra', *The Hindu*, 29 November 2020, https://www.thehindu.com/news/international/china-hydropower-company-plans-first-downstream-dam-on-brahmaputra/article33206687.ece, accessed 13 June 2022.
39. Himanshu Thakkar, 'Chinese Checkers', *Hindustan Times*, 12 February 2013, https://www.hindustantimes.com/india/chinese-checkers/story-ofjMvqQbSP3V4smToM3ZcP.html, accessed 13 June 2022.
40. Zhou Wei, 'Divided Waters in India', *China Dialogue*, 20 September 2011, http://www.chinadialogue.net/article/show/single/en/4539-Divided-waters-in-China, accessed 16 June 2022.
41. Standing Committee on Water Resources (2009-2010), Fourth Report, August 2010, p. 43, http://wwfenvis.nic.in/files/Water%20Resources/Working%20of%20Brahmaputra%20Board.pdf, accessed on 14 June 2022.
42. 'Parched Tiger to Thirsty Dragon: No Concerns about Dams on Brahmaputra', Water Politics, 8 February 2011, http://www.

waterpolitics.com/2011/02/08/parched-tiger-to-thirsty-dragon-no-concerns-about-dams-on-brahmaputra/, accessed 14 June 2022.

43. Jayanta Bandyopadhyay, Nilanjan Ghosh and Chandan Mahanta, 'IRBM for Brahmaputra Sub-basin', https://www.orfonline.org/wp-content/uploads/2016/10/Monograph_IRBM-for-Brahmaputra_Z-Final.pdf, Observer Research Foundation, pp. 8–9, accessed 7 June 2022.

44. The community of co-riparian states is an important principle in the waters of an international river. According to Salman M.A. Salman, 'The basis ... is that the entire river basin is an economic unit, and the rights over the waters of the entire river are vested in the collective body of the riparian states or divided among them either by agreement or on the basis of proportionality. Clearly, this is an ideal principle that overlooks sovereignty and nationalism.' See, Salman M.A. Salman, 'Helsinki Rules, the UN Watercourses Convention and the Berlin Rules: Perspective on International Water Law', *Water Resources Development*, vol. 23, no.4, December 2007, p. 627.

45. Uttam Kumar Sinha, 'Tibet's Watershed Challenge', *The Washington Post*, 14 July 2010.

CHAPTER 10

The Sky Above and the Air Around

New Domains of Contention: In Cyber and Outer Space

KIRAN KARNIK

Described as 'the last frontier', outer space has, over the last few decades, become increasingly important from the viewpoints of technology, national prestige, economic benefits and—in ever-greater measure—military advantage. Beginning in the heyday of the Cold War, and the US shock at the Soviet lead (evidenced by the launch of the first-ever satellite in 1957[1]), the space race has only continued heating up. Now, it isn't just two countries that have the capabilities to send vehicles into space and vie with each other; more players have entered the arena—all acutely aware of the potential benefits and, therefore, of the need to invest in this field. In the last few years, corporate entities have begun to take on a big and comprehensive role in this field too, with many implications. As a country with capabilities, needs and ambitions in this area, India has much at stake.

Another 'new' field is cyberspace. Its origin can be traced back to almost a century ago, and the phenomenal progress in electronics—driving more recent progress in artificial intelligence (AI) and software—has opened altogether new avenues in many fields. The military use of cyber capabilities has created a 'revolution in military affairs'. National security—both direct (i.e., militarily) and indirect (through economic, health and food security, for example)—could be threatened by cyberattacks. Individual well-being too is at risk, through cybercrime. Cyberspace has, therefore, become another domain of great importance.

These areas—cyberspace and outer space—have immense strategic significance, and are already critical to India's security. This chapter covers both areas, but is not intended as a comprehensive look, particularly as some aspects have been covered in other chapters. It does not trace the history nor predict the future trajectory of key technologies involved. In what follows, the focus is limited mainly to the major threats and opportunities in the two domains, and possible strategic and policy responses.

Before we discuss these newer areas, though, it is worthwhile to briefly recount how the conventional domains of contestation between nations—land, sea and air—have been evolving. This would not only place them in context, but also point to how they aid, amplify and synergize with the historical domains of importance.

In ancient times, land was a coveted asset, and empires were defined by their geographical size and physical boundaries. Armies were raised to protect or capture land, and wars were fought to do so. Alexander the Great, the Romans and Genghis Khan all used armies to conquer more land and expand their empires. This has continued in the centuries since, and the importance of land and occupation has not quite gone away, even in modern times.

However, the growth of trade through sea routes made the maritime realm grow in importance. Pirates (non-state armed groups, in today's parlance) were the earlier interdictors, against whom traders—and, in due course, the state—had to ensure protection, but soon, it was countries that were fighting each other on the high seas to dominate and control trade routes through which commerce flowed. British and European rivalry in the seas was sealed by the victory of the British Royal Navy over the combined naval might of France and Spain in the Battle of Trafalgar (1805), putting paid to Napoleon's ambitions of invading Britain. It established British supremacy over the seas for more than a century. Long before this, Kalinga and the rulers in the southern India had prospered through overseas (literally) trade, facilitated by their maritime abilities. Thus, Indian influence extended from the Arab countries and the Gulf in the west to Southeast Asia and Indonesia in the east. Later, the Maratha empire under Shivaji was amongst the pioneers in the creation and use of naval forces, through Kanhoji Angre (1669–1729). Since then, navies have evolved and become an essential part of military might. The British Empire's rapid expansion was based as much on its naval power as its duplicitous shrewdness. The exploits of the Indian Navy in the 1971 war with Pakistan are well known, as is India's firm stand in the face of attempted US gun-boat diplomacy through the despatch of a US Navy task force led by an aircraft carrier (USS Enterprise) into the Bay of Bengal from its war-time station in the Gulf of Tonkin (Vietnam).

Airspace and its control became possible only in the twentieth century, but it very quickly became extremely important. Its beginning can be traced to the use of aircraft during Spain's civil war (1936–1939), immortalized through a painting (Pablo Picasso's *Guernica*[2]) depicting the horror of an air attack by fascist forces on the village of Guernica.[3] Air power was particularly evident in the latter part of the Second World War, when the role of the air force—fighter and bomber aircraft, as well as those that ferried and dropped troops and material—became vital to winning battles. Air cover supported and facilitated the role of ground forces, even as bombers destroyed strategic targets and aimed to demoralize the enemy's civilian population—one terrible example being the dropping of atomic bombs in Hiroshima and Nagasaki in 1945. Air power played a role in a different way in 1948-49, when West Berlin was under siege by Soviet forces, which blocked all land access. The US and its allies flew sorties day and night in a record airlift of supplies (food, water and medicine) for almost a year for the two million residents in the city. This was ironical for, at the height of the Second World War, the Soviets were at the receiving end of a siege: the famous '900-day siege' of Leningrad by German and Finnish troops. It was withstood only by the bravery and fortitude of the population (at horrendous cost—an estimated 6,50,000 died in 1942 alone).[4] At the time, airlift of supplies to the beleaguered city was not possible, and only very limited supplies of food and fuel could reach the people.

Air power has made enormous strides since, in terms of technology (and so, war doctrines). Aircraft have reached new levels of technological and performance heights. Amongst newer developments are unmanned aerial vehicles (UAV), which are now used on an extensive scale and with phenomenal scope: from 'swarms' of drones (e.g., the drone and missile attack—apparently by Iran-backed Houthis from Yemen—on Saudi oil facilities in 2019), to the large UAVs that carry precision (smart) bombs used so extensively in Afghanistan. Yet, superior air power no longer seems to be a war winner. US dominance of the skies—whether in Vietnam (in the 1960s) or in Afghanistan (2001–2021)—had little impact, with the Americans practically losing the war in both instances. The same is true, even if in a less visible way, in Iraq and Syria.

Missiles, as another form of air power, just began to come into play towards the end of the Second World War (the German V-2 being an example). They are now an essential part of a nation's armoury. Combining elements of space technology with traditional aeronautics, they provide a reach ranging from tens of kilometres to tens of thousands of kilometres, and have a wider scope: from carriers of conventional explosives to nuclear-armed missiles; from ground launch to air or sea launch.

Underwater has become an additional 'sea' domain, with submarines—extensively used for the first time during the Second World War—being a potent platform: first for attacks on ships, and now, as platforms for the launch of missiles. Nuclear-powered submarines can stay underwater and operate for extended periods of time, expanding the reach of naval forces. Earlier, aircraft carriers were developed as platforms that served, in effect, as airbases in distant locations and enabled domination of a wide swathe of the sea.

Cyber Threat Scenarios

This long summary of the traditional domains (land, air, sea and—more recently—underwater) is a necessary segue into the new domains of space and cyber, because both of these are linked to the traditional ones, and most often serve to supplement and enhance their capabilities.

Unlike outer space, cyberspace is not all that recent, with computers predating large-scale space efforts and going back to the middle of the last century. However, the major gamechangers (extensive, high-bandwidth communication links and the Internet, in particular, besides the phenomenal capabilities of new computers) are more recent. Aided by revolutions in electronics, materials and demand-inducing new products and applications, computers have become relatively inexpensive, portable and versatile, making them ubiquitous. Today, hand-held devices like cell phones, with over seven billion users worldwide,[5] have more computing power than what a large computer in an office had but a couple of decades ago. These developments have made possible the widespread use of computers and cell phones in almost every field of human activity. This has increased efficiency and transparency, but also poses serious challenges and threats. One good way of understanding and examining this is through plausible events.

As one example, imagine this scenario. Deep within the military establishment in Pakistan, a computer buzzes a warning. However, this time it is not one more alert about drone-spotted Indian troop movement along the troubled LoC in Kashmir, but about the opening of India's missile silos and the take-off of Sukhoi aircraft from two Indian airbases, as reported by computer-processed satellite imagery. These aircraft are known carriers of nuclear bombs, as are the missiles. Red lights blink everywhere as the information is instantly shared up the command chain in Rawalpindi and Islamabad. Confirmation is sought by other means and through a hotline to Indian military commanders, but anticipating that an air and missile strike may be imminent in a few minutes, Pakistan's forces are put on full war alert and things set in motion for a missile counterstrike.

India's intelligence apparatus—including surveillance satellites and signals intelligence—detect this, and an instant alert is put out. Confirmation is immediately available, including from US intel satellites. India scrambles its aircraft and prepares for missile launches. This information makes its way to Pakistan, as being verified by on-ground agents. The initial Indian denial (over the hotline) is assumed to be subterfuge. Both sides are convinced that the other is about to launch a first strike, and prepare to pre-empt it or to counterstrike.

Mutual distrust and a ticking clock—which warns of only minutes from a missile launch to a hit—make discussions near impossible. By the time humans from each side talk to each other, machines are making their own judgements. Snap decisions, based on intuition and computer data, will have to be made. Yet, how authentic was the first piece of information, the starting point of a possible nuclear war? Might it be a cyber hacker who has successfully breached firewalls and maliciously fed wrong information into the Pakistani computers? Any interested state, or even a non-state player (including terrorist groups), with sufficient technical capability could be the hacker who plants wrong information into the system. Such a possible tragedy of errors is not only conceivable, but plausible, despite the many safeguards in place.

Scenarios involving independent groups of hackers are now the staple of many a fictional movie. In *Live Free or Die Hard*[6] (the fourth instalment in the *Die Hard* franchise), for example, a group of hackers creates mayhem first in New York's traffic system and then, by attempting to use a gas pipeline to create a massive explosion in a power plant, as part of a 'fire sale'.[7] In a movie from the popular James Bond franchise (*Tomorrow Never Dies*),[8] a media baron uses a cyberterrorist hacker to manipulate the GPS coordinates of a British frigate in the South China Sea, steering it into China's territorial waters. When a Chinese aircraft goes to investigate, the hacker group shoots it down and also blows up the British frigate—with Chinese ammunition. The aim: to provoke a war between the UK and China. All this is done just to be the first to publish the 'breaking news'!

In other movies, hacker groups are seen as wanting to control governments. In a spoof (*Johnny English Strikes Again*),[9] a computer expert hacks into the UK systems and exposes British secret agents. Other systems too are hacked into, creating chaos. A 'saviour' from Silicon Valley (the real culprit behind the hacking) offers to set right the systems, and is handed over control of cyber assets to do so. He leverages this to seek global power by threatening a nuclear strike from a British submarine which he controls through his hacking.

In a more recent television series (*Salvation*),[10] a tech company is the only one with the technology to save the world from an imminent asteroid strike which could devastate Earth. The US government is forced to work with them to save the country and humanity. Meanwhile, a hacker group effectively takes charge of the world by hacking into the US and Russian military systems, enabling them to threaten a nuclear strike against any country which does not fall in line.

Though they are fictional, these stories are important because each of them (like all good science fiction) is already technologically feasible or will soon be. They tell us what hackers could do, and hence, about the immense threats from cyberspace. Also noteworthy is that these storylines are built around independent hacker groups and powerful private tech companies—facets of reality that we are already facing. How long before fiction becomes fact?

Most fictional stories typically portray independent groups as the antagonists because this is a distinct possibility in reality too; however, hackers could well be state-sponsored or even the state itself. Locating the origin of such actions is well-nigh impossible, if a smart hacker wants to cover their tracks, making plausible deniability easy. This makes deterrence and retaliation difficult. Unlike other threats (chemical, biological, nuclear or conventional), there is no physical material required, and so no supply line that can lead to the source of the threat, or which can be traced and interdicted. Delivery is generally through communication/data channels; thus, again, eliminating the possibility of checks to stop the actions. Blocking data channels is not a feasible alternative because the hacking/malware could originate from anywhere (even in-country) and—thanks to the interconnectedness of the Internet—be routed through any link. Even data channels may not be required, as is seen from the following real-life example.

According to hacking folklore, the greatly successful destruction of a large number of centrifuges at Iran's Natanz facility (used for enriching uranium, presumably to weapons-grade)[11] was done without a data link, as the computers there were 'air-gapped' (i.e., not linked) to the Internet. The malware, Stuxnet, called the 'world's first digital weapon', is said to have been loaded into USBs, and a large number of these were then strewn in various places (apparently toilets being an important location!) to be picked up by employees of the plant. When these were hooked on to their computers (who would not be curious about the contents of a randomly found USB?), the malware got loaded into the system. An alternative explanation is that the USB flash drives were used to first infect the computers of outside companies that had access to the systems in Natanz. Stuxnet worked by infecting a Siemens-supplied logic controller, instructing the motor to speed up the centrifuges and not let them stop. Going beyond the stipulated limits, they just burnt up. Simple, elegant and phenomenally successful (according to reports, this very considerably set back the enrichment programme), but extremely dangerous, as an explosion could have been set off, releasing radioactive gases across the whole area. Earlier, what must have been 'test' attacks led to failures of some centrifuges, and neither the Iranians nor the International Atomic Energy Agency (IAEA) inspectors could fathom why. Difficulty in tracing the origin of any cyberattack made it impossible to pinpoint the source in this case too. Despite suspicions and conjecture (with fingers pointing at the obvious originator: Israel), there is no concrete evidence to identify the attacker.

In another real-life case, the network in an entire country was hacked, as early as 2007: a series of coordinated cyberattacks targeted websites of Estonian organizations.[12] Over a three-week period, government and parliamentary portals, ministries, news outlets, internet service providers, major banks and small businesses were all targeted, predominantly by a Distributed Denial of Service (DDoS). The cyberattacks were accompanied by hostile political rhetoric by Russian officials and economic measures, following a dispute over the relocation of a statue in Tallinn. This, and circumstantial evidence, pointed to the attack originating from and being sponsored by Russia, but no conclusive evidence was available.

Similar cyberattacks occurred in Lithuania, Georgia and Kyrgyzstan in 2008-09, apparently integrated and synchronized with a wide spectrum of other measures, such as economic or diplomatic pressure, resulting in increasing strategic effects.[13] This establishes a new form of coercive battle, without arms, and necessitates new strategic thinking and responses.

In October 2020, part of India's power system was brought down for a brief period, apparently by hackers.[14] According to a report, the Maharashtra cyber department confirmed that a malware attack was behind the blackout, with 'Trojans' installed in the Maharashtra State Electricity Board (MSEB) system by unverified sources. Another organization (Recorded Future) said that Chinese cybercriminals, dubbed RedEcho, were targeting India's power grid with background Trojans called ShadowPad. Apparently, this was a show of force, or research for bigger future attacks. Again, concrete proof of the origin is not possible.

There are other challenges in handling cyberattacks. In most (non-cyber) threat areas, finances are critical. However, mounting a cyberattack does not necessarily require large funding; hence, following a money trail or choking financial resources may not be the solution. Also, there is no supply chain to interdict. The crucial requirement is only human resources—though of the highest calibre. Depending on the kind of hacking, computer capability too is required. But this is a trivial problem today, with even laptops having phenomenal capability.

Cyberthreats are not limited to a direct attack by an enemy country, but could take other forms: State-sponsored (and yet deniable) groups, global terrorist organizations, in-country militant groups, or bounty-hunters looking for 'ransom' money ('pay us, or else we will bring down your air-traffic control system at airports'). Though far-fetched, it could also be a private corporation doing this for power, money or favourable decisions. In each case, the scope and magnitude of the threat may be different—from catastrophic to nuisance-value.

These factors, and the asymmetric nature of the threat, pose huge challenges to every country. Firewalls, pre-emptive action (using ethical hackers to find vulnerabilities, for example), early detection, threat mitigation and other protective actions are essential. However, while these would help and may take care of a huge number of threats, one needs to recognize that this is a continuously evolving, fast-changing threat scenario.

The protective measures are also vital to minimize a far commoner threat: that of cybercrime. This takes on a variety of forms, all aimed at stealing money or data from individuals and organizations. It may also attempt to interfere with the computer system, either for disrupting systems (as a goal in itself) or to seek a ransom. Such crimes have become increasingly common and use evermore sophisticated technology. One recent study[15] indicates that as many as 74 per cent of small and medium businesses (SMBs) in India witnessed a cyber incident in the last twelve months, with 85 per cent of them losing customer information to malicious actors and creating a tangible impact on their business.

With the emphasis on digitalization, and the very rapid growth of online financial transactions (further accelerated by the COVID-19-induced lockdowns constraining physical movement), the scope for stealing and misusing data (bank account details, IDs, passwords, etc.) has vastly increased. The JAM trinity (combining the Jan Dhan bank account of hundreds of millions of individuals, their Aadhar and mobile numbers) has led to direct benefits transfer (of money) from the government to the account of each of these millions of persons. Since the transfers amount to thousands of crores of rupees, hacking into the system could mean unimaginable losses.

In the last few years, as part of the overall process of digitalization, India has created public platforms like Aadhar and Unified Payments

Interface (UPI). Soon, there will be one that stores a health ID and the health records of each individual. These platforms store vast amounts of personal and sensitive data, and are honeypots for hackers. While data theft is dealt with under a number of other laws, there is yet no law specific to data protection in India, unlike in many other countries. Further, more and more of our systems—power, telecom, air-traffic control, financial systems, etc.—are now based on computers. While the benefits are obvious and substantial, so too is the potential risk that comes with it. However, we will not dwell here on cybercrime per se, but will keep the focus on strategic aspects. From this point of view, one needs to note the dangers to the nationwide, large-scale systems from organized crime, as much as from cyber attackers, whose aim may be beyond money. For example, a disruption in payments systems could throw the whole financial system out of gear and cause a major problem for the economy. Similarly, theft of sensitive health information of an important individual could possibly lead to problems beyond extortion of money.

Technology aims at lowering vulnerability to cyberattacks. Encryption has always been one way of protecting the confidentiality or secrecy of messages. Amongst the early and famous instances is Enigma,[16] used by the Germans in the Second World War. The British put in an enormous effort to break the code, and finally succeeded. Some claim that this changed the course of the war. Encryption has since moved on to greater sophistication, with coding and decoding being locked in a continuous upward spiral. Now, quantum computing is touted to be the ultimate codebreaker, which can unravel any encryption. Not surprisingly, at the same time, there are claims that quantum encryption will be unbreakable!

Depending on the extent of sophistication, tracing of cyberattacks and their source is difficult, facilitating plausible deniability. Therefore, deterrence may not be as effective as in the case of more conventional (even nuclear) threats. Mutual assured destruction (MAD) as a military doctrine may have had its uses in an earlier era of direct warfare. Today, with proxy wars, there are serious threats to the economy, financial systems, health, power and other utilities from an enemy who is often faceless, nameless and with no 'address'. Dealing with this threat is going to be a major strategic issue in the years to come.

One approach to such threats is to build strong defensive capabilities, to try and ensure that hackers cannot get through and attack critical computer networks. However, the problem—as with any defensive strategy against a terrorist action—is that the defender has to succeed 100 per cent of the time, whereas the attacker has to succeed only once. Yet, defence is critical and there is need to develop very strong protection. This includes continuous anticipation, understanding, tracking, detecting and intercepting of all kinds of malware and threats, the 'hardening', protection and resilience of computer systems, apart from mitigation and recovery protocols. Education and awareness-building amongst users is essential since the starting point of vulnerabilities is most often the carelessness of users themselves. Also, code writers and software programmers need to ensure secure and robust programmes. One way of doing so is to ensure that cybersecurity is part of their core curriculum in educational institutions.

Another possible strategic response may be to counterattack the *likely* source (organization/country) based on circumstantial evidence. Such a strategy turns the difficulty in pinpointing the origin of a cyberattack into an advantage: the counterattack too cannot be attributable, and plausible deniability can be fully used. For this to work, it requires strong offensive cyber capability, so that the counterattack can be effective and damaging enough to act as a deterrent. But if the source is uncertain, there is a risk that the target of the counterattack may be the wrong organization/country. This may lead to retaliation and escalating attacks from both sides. Does the country's strategic posture allow for such risks? This is a question that policymakers need to answer, after weighing the pros and cons.

Yet, in the reality of global geopolitics, India has little alternative. Some countries are known to have immense cyber-offensive capabilities. China's 'hacker army' is reported to number 50,000 to 1,00,000,[17] and some feel this estimate is on the lower side. Its formal structure includes an innocuously named Strategic Support Force, an equivalent to the US Cyber Command. Israeli capabilities too are well known, even if the magnitude is not. Other countries also are known to have capabilities. In addition, there are non-state groups (some, as noted earlier, supported by the state).

In this situation, given the real and growing threat of serious cyberattacks, and the likelihood of these becoming a major weapon in the armoury of terrorist groups (whether truly independent or state-sponsored), the development of large, high-capability defensive as well as offensive groups is an urgent necessity for India. Such capability is as essential—and must have the same priority and funding—as physical weaponry like planes, submarines, tanks or guns.

Cyberattacks aimed at interfering with or disabling computer systems, and other direct forms of cyber action, are being supplemented by more subtle and insidious attacks. Akin to soft power, these 'soft cyber threats' are a form of psychological warfare that target the minds of people rather than hardware. They use the reach and power of social media to plant and circulate views and news (often fake) using popular platforms like WhatsApp, Instagram or Facebook. The aim is to influence people to think or act in certain ways—for instance, to affect voting patterns in an election, or to sully/build reputations. While such efforts by domestic groups have become a part of the political process, there have also been accusations of one country seeking to influence events (for instance, an election) in another. For instance, serious allegations were made of Russian interference in the 2020 US presidential election.

The war in Ukraine has demonstrated again the power and use of 'soft power', combined with cyberattacks. President Zelenskyy of Ukraine has been on TV practically every day, with carefully formulated messages and equally well-crafted couture and backgrounds. A former actor, he has become a media superstar. Social media activists around the world have vigorously provided support as have almost all Western media. To quote one observer: 'Western governments' information agencies are also assertively responding to Russia. The United States Agency for Global Media (USAGM) has undertaken a massive effort to create an information "ring around Russia" that delivers programming designed not only for Russians, but is also directed to the public in countries such as Belarus, Moldova, Kazakhstan and other neighbours of Russia. Since the February invasion began, the agency has also introduced a new Ukrainian—and Russian-language—satellite channel that reaches all of Ukraine and parts of Russia.'[18] These and other efforts have clearly tilted the 'soft war' very substantially in Ukraine's favour. This is not unimportant at a time when global public opinion matters a great deal.

Social media is also being used to build sympathy for terrorist groups, to mobilize support and even for recruitment. The reach—enabling wide circulation—of messages and of video clips (often doctored or fake) on social media aids these groups.

Such threats are difficult to deal with, particularly if one is mindful of not compromising basic rights like freedom of information and privacy. In this case, unlike cyberattacks, the origin of a particular message/post is traceable, but would require the platform's cooperation. The platform company will not generally be of assistance, without a full legal process. Their own guidelines require them to take down certain posts and even block accounts of repeat offenders. The debate on whether to do so at the behest of governments—which may want to stifle critical or dissenting opinions—is still on.[19] Governments justify 'take downs', or origin-tracing, as necessary for national security or to maintain law and order, whereas human rights organizations argue that freedom of information should be guaranteed. It is true that all governments would like to minimize dissent, and one needs to guard against this, especially since it is not easy to draw a clear line between mobilizing people for a democratic protest and assembling a mob to trigger a riot. However, it is also a fact that enemies (terrorist groups or countries) are now increasingly using subtle and sophisticated methods, through social media, to attack countries.

In this scenario, it is important to recognize that private players wield enormous power because of their massive customer base and the consequent data that they collect. Facebook, for example, has 2.85 billion users. It is known that they use this in ways that increase their commercial revenue (through data analytics and other means, leveraging their user data); tomorrow, an ambitious CEO could use this to gain even greater power. Further, one does not know to what extent these MNCs share information with governments (either of their country of origin or with others). The influence and power of these large social media and tech companies are now causing global concern. Some have revenues that far exceed the GDP of most countries; a few have data on more individuals than the population of the biggest country in the world, China. Data is seen as a most important resource, raw material from which great value can be extracted: these treasure troves can be analysed using machine learning and artificial intelligence to build predictive models that could, with increasing accuracy, forecast not only when and what an individual may buy next, but even their behaviour. This, combined with their financial clout and the ability to subtly shape online conversations, gives these companies tremendous power.

Some of them are registered—for tax and other reasons—in various offshore locations (i.e., outside their 'home' country); they have complicated, multicountry legal structures and operate in a large number of countries. These factors often put them out of reach of the legal jurisdiction of any one country. In effect, they operate autonomously, almost like an independent nation. As a result, and in light of the extent of power of these megacorporations, this is a strategic issue; one that will grow in importance in the years to come.

Another aspect that requires strategic thinking is the deep web and, within it, the dark web. The former has content on the Internet that, for various technical reasons, is not indexed by search engines. The dark web is that part of the deep web which is intentionally hidden and is inaccessible through standard browsers.[20] The anonymity that it makes possible is an advantage for many dissenters in a totalitarian state; but it also facilitates the work of criminals: as a contact point for those who launder money or sell illicit drugs; it can even allegedly be used to hire assassins. Terror organizations too are said to make extensive use of the dark web.

Another threat comes from companies that create surveillance mechanisms through hardware or software ('spyware'). The former could be inbuilt in the chips or other components that go into a computer or any device that is part of the system. Backdoors can be incorporated at the time of manufacture, or spyware implanted into a packaged or bespoke programme. Since all such devices—from the smallest sensor to the ubiquitous cell phone to large computers—depend on a global supply chain with electronic elements and software emanating from many countries, the danger of an implanted surveillance element is high. Also, detection of this through testing is not easy. India, being preponderantly an importer of electronic parts and components, is definitely vulnerable. The dream of being self-sufficient in electronics hardware has long been pursued, but is neither viable nor feasible. A fab plant (a facility for producing electronic chips) has been on the to-do list for decades now, but is not on the horizon yet. Strategically, we desperately need to quickly produce more—and critical—components domestically, but the need to import will never completely go away.

The much-publicized issue of Pegasus, involving the surveillance of some individuals, has brought into the limelight the extent and capability of such spyware.[21] Apparently, it self-installs through an innocuous WhatsApp call. Created by a company based in Israel, the software not only taps into conversations and data exchange, but also has full access to all the stored data in the cell phone. It is capable of tracking you through your phone's GPS and, more scarily, taking control of the camera and microphone function—turning them on at will. In effect, it uses your own cell phone to spy on you. It is mind-boggling to imagine what could result from such access to conversations, data and individual cell phones. This could well be a weapon that rivals the latest piece of military hardware. While the company says it sells this software only to select governments, there is no way of knowing which governments, which agencies or even which private entities may be its customers. Also a matter of concern is who really controls the company today, and who may buy it or take control of it tomorrow.

New Delhi needs to formulate strategic options of dealing with the new phenomenon of commercial non-state players who could affect its security. The present security framework—even strategic thinking—is probably limited to states, non-state terrorist groups and domestic militant organizations. It now needs to add private corporations in the threat matrix. India's large market makes it attractive to these companies, as does its talent base. The country needs to see how it can leverage these to its strategic advantage.

Overall, the strategic and policy response must include the following key elements (not in order of priority or chronology):

1. Create a strong manufacturing base for electronics hardware and components, particularly critical ones. Incentives like the production-linked incentive (PLI) scheme may not suffice; direct investment—through a public sector undertaking (PSU) or equity investment in a private company—may be required. Indian ownership of appropriate manufacturing facilities abroad is another option. These could be used for chip manufacturing, based on designs created within the country (an area where our capability is high).
2. Put in place mechanisms to immediately (and mandatorily) share information on any cyberattack with a designated government agency, which can disseminate warnings and recommended countermeasures to other organizations in that sector.
3. Develop powerful and offensive cyberattack capabilities, with enough professional staff and generous funding. Safeguards may be required to ensure a Frankenstein's monster isn't created, through staff who become rogue hackers—or even the agency itself turning rogue.
4. Strengthen and ensure adequate funding and staff to organizations like Indian Computer Emergency Response Team (CERT-In), which are responsible for safeguarding and defending systems. Mandate regular penetration and vulnerability testing in all identified organizations; and it is essential to have an annual (or more frequent, for select organizations) cybersecurity audit. It is imperative that organizations that can do this are developed.
5. Ensure stringent data protection, through both law and technology. Work proactively on creating global frameworks for the protection, sharing and transborder flow of data.

6. Upgrade India's cyber capability in the long term, through intensive programmes on cybersecurity in the country's educational and research institutions. This can be done immediately, by substantial addition of professionals to India's cybersecurity organizations.
7. Fully leverage the capabilities within India's IT industry. Use their knowledge and connections to find high-capability cybersecurity companies abroad which can be bought, using a special fund set up for this purpose exclusively.
8. Develop and stay abreast of critical emerging technologies (quantum computing is one example)—apart from existing fields like artificial intelligence, data analytics, cyber-physical systems, the internet of things, augmented and virtual reality, etc., with the goal of being in the top five at least within five years. This will require both funding and facilitation, as also the setting up of new institutions: for example, an organization that does for quantum (computing, but also communication other quantum-related fields), what the Tata Institute of Fundamental Research (TIFR) did for nuclear technology, or what the Indian Institute of Science (IISc) and the Physical Research Laboratory (PRL) did for space.
9. Formulate a strategy and a framework of appropriate policies to deal with possible threats (and leverage opportunities) that may emerge from the growing power of mega-private companies in this space.
10. Explore bilateral/multilateral partnerships or global laws and rules to strengthen cybersecurity, so as to curb or control the power of private tech and media corporations.

On the global plane, India must ensure that it plays the role of a rule-maker. In parallel, it must safeguard its own interests, through both global and domestic action. In doing so, it must keep in mind that this is one case where its capabilities, especially in software, put it amongst the top few countries. In many respects, it may be closer to Europe, rather than the US (which houses a majority of the private megacompanies in the cyber/tech space) or developing countries, most of whom have minimal cyber capabilities. A moot point is whether we should seek to actively promote Indian companies which can compete with global giants.

The new cyber domain is going to be of vital importance in the years to come. India must formulate a clear and forward-looking, future-proof strategy to capitalize on the many opportunities and tackle the numerous threats that will emerge in this space.

Outer Space: A Domain of Endless Possibilities

Space has always fascinated humankind. The life-giving sun, the ever-changing kaleidoscope of stars, and the waxing and waning moon have been sources of wonder, myth and curiosity. In one sense, then, space—in the form of astronomy—is amongst the most ancient of sciences. In this, India was an early pioneer. In the era of modern space technology too, the country did not lag behind. Its scientists—especially from IISc, PRL and TIFR—did world-class work in space sciences from the middle of the last century. Their interest in cosmic rays led to the desire to position instruments above the atmosphere. Given the limitations of balloon flights (which were also used), rocket-borne payloads were seen as essential. The launch of these—first, imported rockets, and later, indigenous ones—from the early 1960s marked the start of the Indian space programme.

With the advent of satellites, as technologists in advanced countries began to experiment with communication and remote sensing, India's space effort moved beyond space science to include such applications. Recognizing their potential impact, and with a philosophy that the programme must be geared to deliver concrete benefits, technology development focused on hardware necessary for space applications. It included payloads for science and applications, satellites, rockets, ground systems to receive signals, track and send commands to satellites and rockets, test facilities and capabilities to analyse data (e.g., remote-sensing imagery). Each of these involved a large number of different elements and subsystems, requiring expertise in a wide range of fields.

Uniquely, India's space efforts began with—and focused on—civilian use, unlike the programmes of other major space powers that had their origin in military use (e.g., missiles for weapons delivery that were converted to carry scientific instruments or to launch satellites). Given this fungibility of use, and especially of the underlying technology, the few space-capable countries began putting in place systems of technology denial for anything that was deemed as 'dual-use technology' (later formalized in the Missile Technology Control Regime, a *non-treaty* agreement amongst nations—including Russia—that do not wish others to gain access to technologies that have missile applications). This extended all the way down the chain: For example, not only maraging steel (needed for rockets), but the technology to make it was placed under this. Undaunted by these odds—or possibly spurred on by them—India steadily developed its own technological capability.

At the same time, the Indian Space Research Organization (ISRO) did collaborate actively with other countries: US (NASA), France (CNES), European (ESA), and Soviet (later Russian) space agencies, amongst others. The most technologically advanced collaboration was the agreement with Russia for not only the supply, but also the technology for cryogenic engines. This was scuttled (in the 1990s) by the US; ultimately, India did get some engines, however it didn't get any technology. Indigenous development meant setting the programme back by many years. Yet, the approach of collaborating where desirable/possible and being self-reliant where necessary has been helpful.

Extraordinary leadership—especially in the crucial early decades—with a clear vision, and the creation of a high-motivation organization with efficient execution capabilities, are key elements in the development of India's space programme. Equally important was political support received from the highest level. The ethos of ISRO ensured cost-effectiveness and problem-solving through innovation. Examples abound, and together they contributed to both, success and frugality.

Chandrayaan and Mangalyaan (the moon and Mars missions) captured public imagination in a way not seen in any country since the US's 'man on the moon' days. The fact that these were carried out on shoestring budgets, compared to similar efforts by other countries, garnered international publicity and acclaim. Yet, the biggest achievements of ISRO are probably in the field of space applications: in remote sensing, weather forecasting, telecommunication and broadcasting, position location, etc. Of course, these ongoing programmes lack the glamour of one-time events (like a mission to a planet), with their arresting visuals and nail-biting final moments.

What is important, though, from a strategic point of view is that, taken together, all these efforts have led to a tremendous amount of technology development in a very wide range of crucial fields. Most of them are dual-use technologies—capable of military use as much as civilian applications. Mastery over solid, liquid and cryogenic rocket engines, navigation and guidance systems, imaging from space and analysis of the images, communication from, to and in space, re-entry systems (from outer space into the atmosphere), linking of orbiting elements are all just some examples of dual-use applications. India's capabilities in these fields place it in the top few countries in any overall (civil and military) ranking. Even so, there is little room for comfort.

China, a possible adversary of the country, has made tremendous progress in the field of outer space. It has a wide-ranging civilian programme which includes satellites, putting humans in space, an earth-orbiting space station, lunar missions with landers and rovers, plans for an outpost on the moon (in collaboration with Russia) and missions to Mars. Details of its military programme are not widely known, but anti-satellite tests have demonstrated (probably by intention) its capability, as did its hypersonic glide vehicle (missile) launched from space—the rapid development and demonstration of which took even the US by surprise.

Not only is China's space programme substantially ahead of India's, but, by all accounts, the gap is only widening. This asymmetry, in a vital domain of growing importance, has serious strategic implications. One long-term response is for India to rapidly step up its rate of technology development, with the aim of being at least closer to leaders in the field over the next ten years. In this, it has the advantage of a strong talent base, with an innovative mindset. It is only in recent years that we see this coming into its own outside ISRO, through entrepreneurial ventures.

Meanwhile, some of the large conglomerates, with well-established engineering capabilities, are seeing new opportunities in space, and are willing to invest effort and money to tap into it. ISRO has long involved the industry in its programmes, and has slowly increased what is sourced. However, these companies' dependence on ISRO orders, and the lack of bulk and continuing orders has meant that this is not lucrative, nor conducive to long-term dedication of staff and facilities. This must be corrected through an assured long-term procurement programme, so that the companies are encouraged to develop dedicated 'space divisions'.

Recent policy changes[22] have opened up space for the private sector, enabling them to take their own initiatives—this has also given a fillip to the nascent start-ups in this sector. This policy could unleash innovations and rapid progress, even as it may free up ISRO's own staff to do more R&D instead of being tied up in the manufacture of already developed hardware. Taking these two parallel—and mutually reinforcing—streams forward must be a part of the strategy to 'race with the winners' in a decade. It would require a big increase in R&D spend by New Delhi, which will include outlays not only for ISRO, but also for academia and the private sector. A separate fund for space start-ups is also required, to stimulate entrepreneurship and innovation.

A short- to medium-term response (which could, of course, be ongoing) is to forge partnerships that would provide access to critical services (launch, imagery/data, position location/navigation, etc.), if not technology, to Indian industry. As noted, the country has a history of collaborating with other space nations, though access to technology has been limited. The proposed agreement with the US for Space Situational Awareness (for tracking objects in space) may point the way forward. Though we were not a collaborator in the International Space Station, we now have to decide whether to sign the Artemis Accords, an agreement initiated by the US to guide activities on the moon. This is part of the major US 'back to the moon' programme, which will include landing humans on the satellite, a moon-orbiting space station and, from all indications, mining. New launchers and a major technological thrust will be part of the effort. Some countries have already signed the accords, and India too will have to do so if it wants to be a part of the initiative. An alternative is coming up, in the form of the Russia–China International Lunar Research Station (ILRS). Its aims are not dissimilar to that of the Artemis programme.

These plans are claimed to be within the guidelines of the outer space treaty (negotiated in the United Nations and signed by over 100 countries) and the moon treaty;[23] however, careful examination will be required, especially with regard to mining and sovereignty. The treaty states that 'the exploration and use of outer space, including the Moon and other celestial bodies, shall be carried out for the benefit ... of all countries',[24] and that 'they are not subject to national appropriation'. It adds that 'exploration and use of the Moon shall be the province of all mankind and shall be carried out for the benefit and in the interests of all countries'. The treaty also bans orbiting nuclear weapons in outer space and their installation on celestial bodies, or stationing weapons in outer space.

In the context of these rival moves (Artemis and ILRS), India will need to ponder on its options, keeping in mind long-term strategic interests, of which a key element must be the rapid build-up of our own autonomous technological capabilities. Will we lose by staying out of both? Can we afford to go it alone, in terms of the resources and time required? If not, which one is the better alternative? There are no easy answers, and what we decide needs to be part of an overall strategic framework.

In technology development, it may be wise to pick a few key areas and focus sharply on them. Given the growing dependence on space assets—for communication, weather forecasting, surveillance, position location, etc.—we need to ensure their full protection. In many ways, this is analogous to the need to protect our digital/cyber infrastructure discussed earlier. As in that field, here too 'protection' has to include offensive capability as a deterrent. Anti-satellite weapons—ground or space based, kinetic or electromagnetic—are, therefore, crucial. India has conducted a successful test of an anti-satellite weapon, but continuous technological upgradation is essential. All-weather, high-resolution surveillance from space (through synthetic aperture radars, for example), radiation-hardened components that can survive an electromagnetic attack, and quick-launch capability (for replacing a failed/destroyed satellite) are other key capabilities. In looking at these priorities, we may wonder where our human spaceflight programme fits in. It is a high-resource and high-risk programme, which is already far behind those of countries like the US, China and Russia. How much does it contribute to our essential technological imperatives, or is it a prestige/vanity programme with possible soft-power spin-offs? Should it be left to the private sector as a space tourism initiative, to be carried out with (foreign) collaboration? These difficult questions need to be asked and the answers must be evaluated within an overall strategic framework.

The war in Ukraine has highlighted the importance of satellites and space technology in warfare. Beginning with the disruption of communication links in Ukraine on 24 February, just as Russian troops invaded the country, the attack is said to have disrupted tens of thousands of modems across Europe (the extent can be gauged from the fact that as many as 30,000 replacement modems had to be shipped).[25] The attack caused a major loss in communications in Ukraine in the early hours of the Russian invasion, according to a Ukrainian official. Viasat, the owner of the satellite which provided the communication links (customers included the Ukrainian government and military), said: 'We believe the purpose of the attack was to interrupt service.' As noted earlier, pinpointing the source of the cyberattack is difficult, but—for obvious reasons—Russian hackers are suspected. It is known that both Ukrainian and Russian hackers are both active, as the war progressed. This shows the importance of satellites for vital communication links, including for military operations, and also their vulnerability. Satellites are also being extensively used for intelligence gathering. Reports indicate that the precise position of the Russian warship Moskva, Russia's flagship Black Sea missile cruiser, may have been provided by US agencies to Ukraine, helping Ukrainian forces to destroy it.[26]

More on inter-state military confrontations and the space technology capabilities of other major powers is covered elsewhere in this book and is not addressed further here. However, it is noteworthy that the military importance of space technology has been growing. Surveillance, intelligence gathering, precision targeting, control and command have been well-established uses of space technology. Now, battlefield uses—including at the level of individual infantrymen—are growing, as ground equipment becomes more portable and lighter. Hypersonic missiles and new anti-satellite (ASAT) laser weapons are being developed and deployed, though the US has pledged to stop conducting destructive direct-ascent anti-satellite (DA-ASAT) tests, presumably to avoid the dangers of the space debris that these may generate. India needs to be wary about this following the path of the discriminatory Nuclear Proliferation Treaty (NPT) and its fall-out in terms of signatories (excluding the few 'privileged' countries) being barred from testing. Before this happens, we need to ascertain and decide whether a ban on ASAT tests at this stage is in national interest. In any case, India must accelerate development of its capabilities in these and all related space technologies. These developments highlight the importance of space technology at both the overall strategic level and the operational level, including in actual warfare. India will need to look at how best to develop the necessary technologies and possibly speed up its acquisition of capabilities through collaboration and cooperation. In this context, India's decision to have separate agencies for defence and civil/peaceful purposes (unlike in nuclear technology) was wise, and provides us considerable leeway in collaborations. This needs to continue, with appropriate points of information exchange. One important point of convergence is industry, and this will grow in importance as more space work is assigned to them, and they take on their own initiatives. This could be the third pillar (apart from civil and defence agencies), and may mean a conscious policy of promoting and supporting a few Indian companies to become serious global contenders in space.

Space capabilities are now being increasingly integrated with those in the more conventional domains for a variety of uses. Apart from the battlefield, they are also being used in covert operations. As in other spheres, this is a growing menace, more likely than a direct confrontation. A recent example of covert operations is the murder of Mohsen Fakhrizadeh, a key figure in Iran's nuclear programme, in 2020. According to various reports,[27] he was killed by bullets fired on his car from a pick-up truck parked at the roadside on his known route. The investigative report provides further details: The weapon used, a robot-controlled machine gun weighing a ton, was smuggled into the country in pieces by the Mossad, the Israeli intelligence agency. A skilled sniper, helped by computers, artificial intelligence, and with inputs from multiple cameras, was located thousands of kilometres away, and operated via satellite. The truck too was blown up (to minimize any evidence). In addition to a command function (to fire the gun, and then to explode the truck), all camera feeds to track and identify Dr Fakhrizadeh also used a satellite connection. The precision of the operation ensured that while the target was shot, his wife (with him in the car) was unhurt.

This is one instance of how space resources can be used in situations where one cannot (or does not want to) use aircraft, drones or other such means. A response to such 'unattributable' covert operations, as in the case of cybercrime (and also for anti-satellite weapons), will have to be through offensive capabilities of our own. Much as this is distasteful, is there an alternative in the world of realpolitik?

A new factor in space is the entry of private companies as full-fledged and independent players. This poses altogether a different set of challenges from a strategic viewpoint. Earlier, private involvement in space was mainly in the form of contractors for specific systems or subsystems, and for services, working up to the point of delivering a product or system—a launch vehicle, or a satellite, for example—to the concerned civilian or military agency, and working under their supervision. Now, thanks to new technologies and innovations that have vastly reduced the costs for satellites and their launch into space, there are companies which have taken up what government agencies would do: from designing and making/buying a launch vehicle to delivering a payload in space and operating it.

Ventures set up by Jeff Bezos, Elon Musk and Richard Branson have already flown passengers into space, on their own launchers. Space tourism, as a commercial venture, is here. Companies like Kuiper (owned by Amazon), OneWeb (partly owned by Bharti Airtel) and Starlink/SpaceX are setting up constellations—comprising many hundreds (thousands, in some cases) of low-earth-orbit satellites—to provide fast broadband connectivity with low latency (important for near real-time communication needs). This is re-energizing the satellite communication market in a big way. In the area of imaging, there are already quite a few companies who operate their own satellites (including new-generation small satellites, or cubesats), and sell the images and data collected. Clearly, private players are into space activities in a big way, and have placed large bets on the sector.

Elon Musk, of Starlink/SpaceX, in one step further, has announced plans for habitations on Mars. He and others are also looking at mining minerals in space. It may not be long before private players begin to go beyond the civil–commercial and look at the military–commercial potential. Secure, encrypted communication systems or navigation/guidance or surveillance/imaging are already on the cards. These could be for peacetime monitoring, strategic purposes or tactical, battlefield applications. In all likelihood, these would initially be for their host (own) country, and may be sold to others with the permission of their government. However, sea-based launches (already proven) and global manufacturing will make them less dependent on any one country, thus removing many constraints and giving companies greater autonomy in choosing clients. In times to come—and this is not too far away—one can conceive of a scenario where this and the size of these companies enables them to make their own decisions, independent of governments.

Given their technological prowess (buttressed by drawing talent globally), private companies could develop anti-satellite (weapons) capability, from land/sea bases on Earth, or from space. The power that this confers on them—either as mercenaries willing to sell to any high bidder or for their own purposes—and their enormous resources, could make them quasi-countries. More imaginatively, just as many global companies are registered today in tax/regulatory havens, tomorrow, they could be located not offshore, but off-Earth (in space, or on the moon)!

Highlighting these dangers is a recent incident: a note from China to the United Nations, sent in December 2021, revealed that on two occasions (in July and October 2021), a satellite of the Starlink constellation (owned by Space X/Elon Musk) had a near encounter with China's manned space station, putting it in danger.[28] It had to manoeuvre to avoid a collision. While there has so far been no response from the company or the US government (which, by space law, would be the party responsible), apparently the satellites were moved for technical reasons. However, conspiracy theorists speculate that this was an anti-satellite test carried out by Space X (either on its own or at the behest of Washington), which also tested the capability of the Chinese space station to detect a possible collision and take evasive action. It is noteworthy that Starlink plans to have thousands of satellites in orbit soon. Fears of collisions—accidental or otherwise—with other space vehicles is, therefore, justified.

The strategic challenges that could emerge from the growing privatization of outer space are somewhat analogous to those posed in cyberspace. Crafting an appropriate response to these will require a very different framework. While this is many years in the future, we need to begin thinking and planning from now, because—as has often been seen—the future comes sooner than you expect.

There are a whole host of other aspects related to outer space which deserve our attention from a strategic viewpoint. These are not addressed here as many have been covered in other chapters. One needs to, though, re-emphasize the broader point that this domain (like cyberspace) requires fresh thinking and a relook at traditional security strategies.

Conclusion: Strategic Dimensions

In studying the issues related to the two new domains, it is necessary to keep in mind the unique characteristics that define them and which, therefore, call for thinking—particularly strategies and policies—that may be different from the conventional. The key characteristics include:

1. The inherently global nature of cyber and outer space, and limitations of national sovereignty over them.
2. These are high-tech, high-skill, high-risk, high-investment areas. Risks and investments are particularly high in the arena of space, where failures are not uncommon. Though software work in cyberspace can be done without high investment, full and independent capability requires the manufacture of electronic components, necessitating large capital outlays. Also, these are fast-changing, high-obsolescence fields, requiring a constant input of large R&D funding.
3. The increasing dependence on these domains for the nation's economy, security and well-being means that disruptions have a huge multiplier effect and serious consequences.
4. The difficulty in tracing the point of origin, and the consequent ease with which attribution for an attack can be avoided in the case of cyberspace. Plausible deniability is also possible for attacks on orbiting assets, but it isn't as easy as it is in the case of cyberattacks.
5. The growing role and importance of private players, some of whom have technological capabilities and even the

financial resources to put them at par with countries. This has implications for both the economy and security.
6. In the cyberspace, private players include organized hacker groups which are not corporatized or registered, and which may be completely independent or state-sponsored. Some may be criminals, out to make money by stealing data, identity or by directly transferring funds. A few may be mercenaries, on hire to anyone who pays. Others may be driven by ideology—with the aim of harming an enemy country, rather than making money.
7. The force-multiplier effect of cyber and space, especially when integrated with conventional forces. A similar effect-multiplier or benefit-multiplier results from their integration into the social and economic spheres (e.g., finance, health, education, manufacturing, logistics, etc.).

Each—and in sum, all—of these dimensions of cyber and outer space call for a strategic response which addresses concerns, meets challenges and exploits the opportunities. It is clear from the discussion above that, in both cases, it would be wise to develop a well-honed and substantial offensive capability, even as a purely defensive/deterrent strategy. In the case of cyber, this should include 'independent' groups with no directly traceable state connections.

Substantial outlays on R&D, with a focus on attaining leadership in a few select areas, are essential. So is a programme of human resource development, especially at the top end. Attracting talent from abroad must be an ongoing and large-scale effort. Getting technology (possibly by acquiring companies) must be another quick-win strategy.

Partnerships with other countries would provide a good way of participating in important (civilian) programmes, especially in space, and a possible means of accelerating technology acquisition. On the global plane, India must be an active player and aim at being a rule-maker, so as to protect our national interests.

While these are specific suggestions, at the broader level, it is necessary to understand the possible ramifications and impact of the new domains, identify options and develop a strategy that needs to be dynamic in these rapidly evolving fields.

Note: Apart from references specifically mentioned, the author has also drawn from personal knowledge and conversations with experts.

Notes

1. The first artificial Earth satellite was Sputnik 1, launched by the USSR into an elliptical low Earth orbit on 4 October 1957 from the Baikonur cosmodrome in Kazakhstan. It orbited for three weeks before its batteries died and then orbited silently for two months before it fell back into the atmosphere on 4 January 1958. In many ways, this marked the start of the space age. The satellite's unanticipated launch took the US by surprise, and triggered the Space Race, part of the Cold War. See 'Sputnik', Encyclopaedia Britannica, https://www.britannica.com/technology/Sputnik; 'Sputnik and the Dawn of the Space Age', NASA History Division, https://history.nasa.gov/sputnik.html; 'Sputnik Launched', History Channel.
2. This painting by the legendary Pablo Picasso, was done by him in 1937, as his immediate reaction to the bombing of Guernica.
3. Guernica—a town in the province of Biscay, Basque region of Northern Spain—was bombed by Nazi and fascist forces at the behest of Spanish nationalists on 26 April 1937, resulting in the wounding or killing of an estimated 1,600 civilians. This was a 'punishment' for their loyalty to the left-wing government.
4. The siege of Leningrad actually lasted for 872 days, from September 1941 to January 1944. Sparse food and fuel supplies reached the city by barge in the summer and by truck and ice-borne sled in winter across Lake Ladoga. These supplies kept the city's arms factories operating

and its two million inhabitants barely alive in 1942, while one million more of its children, sick, and elderly were being evacuated. From 1943, vegetables from new gardens in all open spaces provided some succour. Sourced from Encyclopaedia Britannica, available at: Siege of Leningrad | Soviet history | Britannica.
5. Forecast number of mobile users worldwide 2020–2025 | Statista.
6. *Die Hard 4*, released in 2007, is fourth in the series of eponymous films which have grossed a combined USD 1.4 billion worldwide. It is produced by 20th Century Studios (The Walt Disney Company).
7. A Fire Sale is an all-out cyberwarfare attack that performs a three-stage systematic attack on a nation's computer infrastructure. Hackers called it Fire Sale because 'Everything must go'. *Stage 1:* Shutting down all transportation systems, such as traffic lights, railroad lines, subway system and airport systems. *Stage 2:* Disable the financial systems; including stock markets, banks and financial records. *Stage 3:* Turning off public utility systems, such as electricity, gas lines, telecommunication and satellite systems.
8. *Tomorrow Never Dies* is a 1997 spy film and the eighteenth in the ever-popular James Bond series, and is produced by Eon Productions/United Artists.
9. *Johnny English Strikes Again* is the third a series of spy-action comedy films parodying the James Bond secret agent genre. It was distributed by Universal Pictures and released in 2018.
10. *Salvation*, produced by CBS Television Studios, is an American suspense drama television series, that premiered on 12 July 2017. In India, it is being streamed on Netflix.
11. A number of reports covered various details. These include 'An Unprecedented Look at Stuxnet, the World's First Digital Weapon' | WIRED and Here's 'How Israel Hacked Iran's Nuclear Facility', TRT World, trtworld.com.
12. Damien McGuinness, 'How a Cyber-Attack Transformed Estonia', BBC News, 27 April 2017, https://www.bbc.com/news/39655415; Hannes Grassegger and Mikael Krogerus, 'Fake News And Botnets: How Russia Weaponised the Web', *The Guardian*, 2 December 2017, https://www.theguardian.com/technology/2017/dec/02/fake-news-botnets-how-russia-weaponised-the-web-cyber-attack-estonia, accessed 10 June 2022.

13. James Pamment, Vladimir Sazonov, Francesca Granelli et al., 'Hybrid Threats: 2007 Cyber-Attacks on Estonia', NATO Strategic Communications Centre of Excellence, 6 June 2021, NATO Strategic Communications Centre of Excellence, https://stratcomcoe.org/publications/hybrid-threats-2007-cyber-attacks-on-estonia/86, accessed 10 June 2022.
14. 'Maharashtra Cyber Cell Submits Report on Mumbai Power Outage, Confirms Malware Attack Hit Power Grid', *India Today*, 1 March 2021, https://www.indiatoday.in/india/story/maharashtra-cyber-cell-mumbai-power-outrage-1774522-2021-03-01. Also covered in 'China's cyberattack on Maharashtra Power Grid was to Improve PLA's Bargaining Position', The Print, 12 March 2021, https://theprint.in/opinion/chinas-cyberattack-on-maharashtra-power-grid-was-to-improve-plas-bargaining-position/620274/, accessed 10 June 2022.
15. 'Cybersecurity for SMBs: Asia Pacific Businesses Prepare for Digital Defense', Cisco report, September 2021, https://www.cisco.com/c/en_sg/products/security/cybersecurity-for-smbs-in-asia-pacific/index.html, accessed 10 June 2022.
16. The Enigma machine was invented by the German engineer Arthur Scherbius at the end of World War I. His firm, Scherbius & Ritter, patented ideas for a cipher machine in 1918 and began marketing the finished product under the brand name Enigma in 1923, initially targeted at commercial markets. It was used extensively by the German military during World War II. The security of the system depends on a set of machine settings that were generally changed daily during the war, based on secret key lists distributed in advance, and on other settings that were changed for each message. This made decryption extremely difficult. Sourced from: History of the Enigma, The Crypto Museum, https://www.cryptomuseum.com/crypto/enigma/hist.htm; '7 Spy gadgets that Will Blow Your Mind', *The Times of India*, https://timesofindia.indiatimes.com/7-spy-gadgets-that-will-blow-your-mind/photostory/51039996.cms; 'The Enigma Machine Is Introduced', History of Information.
17. Mara Hvistendahl, 'China's Hacker Army', *Foreign Policy*, 3 March 2010, https://foreignpolicy.com/2010/03/03/chinas-hacker-army/, accessed 10 June 2022.

18. Philip Seib, 'Why Russia Is Losing the Information War', Centre on Public Diplomacy, University of Southern California, 9 May 2022, https://uscpublicdiplomacy.org/blog/why-russia-losing-information-war, accessed 10 June 2022.
19. A compliance report from Facebook notes that it took action against 32 million posts in India for content violations and that WhatsApp (a part of the same company) took down 2.07 million accounts in August 2021. (As reported in *The Times of India*, 3 October 2021, 'FB Acted against 3cr Posts in Aug, WhatsApp Shut Down 20.7L Accounts' https://timesofindia.indiatimes.com/business/india-business/fb-acted-against-3cr-posts-in-aug-whatsapp-shut-20-7l-accounts/articleshow/86719927.cms). Google's compliance report for August 2021 says it received 35,191 complaints from users and removed 93,550 pieces of content based on those complaints. In addition to reports from users, Google also removed 651,933 pieces of content in August as a result of automated detection ('Google Removes 93,550 Content Pieces in August in India, Shows Compliance Report', *Business World*, 4 October 2021, ttps://www.businessworld.in/article/Google-Removes-93-550-Content-Pieces-In-August-In-India-Shows-Compliance-Report/04-10-2021-407095/, accessed 10 June 2022.).
20. Michael Chertoff and Toby Simon, 'The Impact of the Dark Web on Internet Governance and Cyber Security', (Global Commission on Internet Governance), February 2015.
21. Pegasus is a spyware developed by Israeli company NSO Group (named after the initials of the three founders) based in Herzliya, near Tel Aviv. It is said to be a subsidiary of Q Cyber Technologies group of companies. Sourced from: 'The NSO Group behind Pegasus List & Its Murky Past—From Mexico to Jamal Khashoggi to India', The Print, 22 July 2021, https://theprint.in/theprint-essential/the-nso-group-behind-pegasus-list-its-murky-past-from-mexico-to-jamal-khashoggi-to-india/700425/ NSO Group, company description on Cybersecurity Intelligence, https://www.cybersecurityintelligence.com/nso-group-5113.html, accessed 10 June 2022.
22. 'How India's Space Sector Is Opening Up Its Skies', *India Today*, 14 October 2021, https://www.indiatoday.in/india-today-insight/story/how-india-s-space-sector-is-opening-up-its-skies-1864871-2021-10-14, accessed 10 June 2022.

23. Treaty on Principles Governing the Activities of States in the Exploration and Use of Outer Space, including the Moon and Other Celestial Bodies, finalized in the United Nations (1967), commonly known as the Outer Space Treaty; Agreement Governing the Activities of States on the Moon and Other Celestial Bodies (United Nations, 1979), generally known as the Moon Treaty.
24. Ibid.
25. 'Satellite Modems Nexus of Worst Cyberattack of Ukraine War', ETSatcom, 31 March 2022, https://telecom.economictimes.indiatimes.com/news/satellite-modems-nexus-of-worst-cyberattack-of-ukraine-war/90567036, accessed 11 June 2022.
26. 'Moskva Sinking: US Gave Intelligence that Helped Ukraine Sink Russian Cruiser—reports', BBC News, https://www.bbc.com/news/world-us-canada-61343044, accessed 11 June 2022.
27. This was covered in various reports. Details here are drawn from these, but especially from *The New York Times*, reproduced in part in *The Times of India*, 19 September 2021 ('The Scientist and the AI-Assisted, Remote-Control Killing Machine', https://timesofindia.indiatimes.com/world/middle-east/the-scientist-and-the-ai-assisted-remote-control-killing-machine/articleshow/86333523.cm, accessed 11 June 2022).
28. Note verbale dated 3 December 2021 from the Permanent Mission of China to the United Nations (Vienna) addressed to the Secretary-General, retrieved from AAC105_1262E.pdf (unoosa.org) on 10 June 2022.

About the Contributors

Vijay Keshav Gokhale studied at the University of Delhi before joining the Indian Foreign Service in 1981. He served as head of mission in Malaysia, Germany and China. He was foreign secretary of India from January 2018 until January 2020. Since retirement he teaches at Symbiosis International, Pune. He is also Senior Non-resident Fellow at Carnegie India and has authored two books on China, *Tiananmen Square: The Making of a Protest* and *The Long Game: How the Chinese Negotiate with India*. Vijay Gokhale has also published in foreign and India media. He lives in Pune, India.

Jayadeva Ranade is the editor of this volume. For more information about him, see 'About the Editor' on page 307.

Vikram Sood was a career intelligence officer and served in the Research and Analysis Wing (R&AW), India's external intelligence agency till his retirement in March 2003 after heading the organization. He has been regularly writing on various strategic, security and intelligence strategic issues in journals and newspapers since 2004 including chapters in books on these subjects.

He is the author of *The Unending Game: A Former R&AW Chief's Insights into Espionage*, published in August 2018. His second book, *The Ultimate Goal: A Former R&AW Chief Deconstructs How Nations Construct Narratives*, was published by HarperCollins India in October 2020.

Arun K. Singh was India's ambassador to the US (2015–16), France (2013–15) and Israel (2005–08); and a member of India's National Security Advisory Board (2021–22). He was involved in the formulation and implementation of India's policies on Pakistan, Afghanistan and Iran for nearly ten years. He is visiting professor at Ashoka University, GSI Fellow at Emory University (Atlanta) and distinguished non-resident senior fellow at German Marshall Fund of US. In 2017, he taught courses on US Foreign Policy in South Asia and Current Global Trends and Challenges at American University and at the School of Advanced International Studies, Johns Hopkins University, Washington DC.

P.S. Raghavan was a career diplomat, who has been India's ambassador to the Czech Republic, Ireland and Russia, and has held other diplomatic assignments in the then USSR, Poland, the United Kingdom, Vietnam and South Africa. He served in the office of Prime Minister Atal Bihari Vajpayee from 2000 to 2004, dealing with foreign affairs, defence, national security and nuclear energy.

Ambassador Raghavan was chairman of India's National Security Advisory Board from 2016 to 2020. He is a distinguished fellow at the Vivekananda International Foundation, New Delhi.

Lt Gen. (Dr) Rakesh Sharma (Retd) had a career in the Indian Army spanning forty years. General Sharma commanded the Fire and Fury Corps in Ladakh, facing both Pakistan and China. Later, he was the adjutant general of the Indian Army. A PhD in defence studies, he was research fellow at the Institute for Defence Studies and Analyses (IDSA). He is a regular participant in seminars, lectures in various institutions, and contributes to newspapers, military journals and edited books. He is on the executive council of IDSA and Global Counter Terrorism Council (GCTC) and distinguished fellow with Vivekananda International Foundation (VIF) and Centre for Land Warfare Studies (CLAWS).

Air Marshal Raghunath Nambiar (Retd), PVSM, AVSM, VM & BAR is an experimental test pilot and was commissioned as a fighter pilot in the IAF. He has been the Commander-in-Chief of both the Western Air Command and Eastern Air Command as well as the Deputy Chief of the Air Staff.

He flew the Mirage 2000 during the Kargil conflict. For his bravery, and his decisive role during the conflict, he was awarded the Vayu Sena Medal (Gallantry). He was one of the first test pilots for the indigenous 'Tejas' aircraft.

The Air Marshal is married to Luxmi. His son, Ashwin, is a commercial pilot.

Vice Admiral Shekhar Sinha retired from the Indian Navy after four decades of naval service. A naval aviator who has flown from all three aircraft carriers, he has commanded three naval warships and a Coast Guard ship, two fighter squadrons and an air station, and was flag officer, naval aviation. Later he commanded the Western Fleet. The Vice Admiral was the chief of integrated defence staff reporting to the defence minister. He retired as Commander-in-Chief of Western Naval Command. Post retirement he has been active strategic analyst.

He is a highly decorated sailor with two gallantry awards. He is a trustee of India Foundation, and is on the governing bodies of MP-IDSA, ICWA, USI, Policy Perspective Foundation and CENJOWS.

Prof. Prabhat Ranjan is a nuclear fusion scientist, a futurist, an educator, an innovator and a science communicator. He is the vice chancellor of DY Patil International University, Akurdi, Pune. He obtained his PhD from University of California, Berkeley. He studied at IIT Kharagpur and the University of Delhi, after his schooling from Netarhat School near Ranchi.

After working in national laboratories, he served as professor at DA-IICT, Gandhinagar, for eleven years. His remarkable innovative contributions include India's Moon mission, wildlife, assistive technology and brain–computer interface. From 2013 to 2018, he headed India's technology think tank, TIFAC, Delhi.

Uttam Kumar Sinha is a leading commentator on transboundary water issues, climate change, and the Arctic region. He leads the non-traditional security centre at the Manohar Parrikar-IDSA, and is the managing editor of the Routledge-published *Strategic Analysis*.

He is a recipient of many fellowships including senior fellow at the Nehru Memorial Museum and Library (2018–20); academic visitor at the Harvard Kennedy School (2015); Chevening 'Gurukul' leadership at the LSE.

He is the author of several books including *Indus Basin Interrupted: A History of Territory and Politics from Alexander to Nehru* (published in 2021), and regularly writes for the *Hindustan Times*.

Kiran Karnik is a public policy and strategy analyst, columnist, and author. His latest book is *Decisive Decade: India 2030, Gazelle or Hippo* (published in 2021).

He has worked in India's atomic energy and space programmes (1968–91). He also worked in the United Nations—in New York and Vienna—and for UNESCO in Afghanistan. Later, he was founder-director of CEC (1991–95), which oversaw UGC's countrywide classroom TV programmes, and CEO of Discovery Channel India (1995–2001).

He was president, NASSCOM, from 2001 to 2008, and later helped to put fraud-hit Satyam Computers back on track as chairperson of its government-appointed board. Karnik has been conferred many awards, including the Padma Shri.

About the Editor

Jayadeva Ranade, a former additional secretary, Research and Analysis Wing, is a security and intelligence expert. He is a seasoned China analyst with over forty-five years of experience in the field and has studied Chinese at the Jawaharlal Nehru University, New Delhi, and Hong Kong University.

His foreign assignments have included Hong Kong and Beijing, and his last foreign posting, prior to retirement in late 2008, was as minister in the Indian Embassy in Washington. Ranade was a member of the National Security Advisory Board and is presently president of the Centre for China Analysis and Strategy and a distinguished fellow with the Centre for Air Power Studies. He frequently contributes articles on China to many national newspapers, magazines and publications.